D0923283

# AN ADVANCED
# ENGLISH GRAMMAR

## WITH EXERCISES

BY

### GEORGE LYMAN KITTREDGE

GURNEY PROFESSOR OF ENGLISH LITERATURE IN
HARVARD UNIVERSITY

AND

### FRANK EDGAR FARLEY

PROFESSOR OF ENGLISH LITERATURE IN
WESLEYAN UNIVERSITY

## GINN AND COMPANY
BOSTON · NEW YORK · CHICAGO · LONDON
ATLANTA · DALLAS · COLUMBUS · SAN FRANCISCO

# PREFACE

This grammar is intended for students who have already received instruction in the rudiments. Still, every such text-book must begin at the beginning. Part One, therefore, which occupies pp. 1–24, gives a succinct treatment of the Parts of Speech in the Sentence and of their substitutes, the Phrase and the Clause, concluding with a Summary of Definitions. Thus it clears the way for what follows, and may be utilized as a review, if the student needs to refresh his memory.

Part Two deals specifically and fully with Inflections and Syntax (pp. 25–182). It includes also a chapter on the use of subordinate clauses as nouns, adjectives, and adverbs (pp. 157–162), as well as a chapter in which such clauses are logically classified in accordance with their particular offices in the expression of thought (pp. 163–182).

Part Three (pp. 183–226) develops the subject of Analysis in its natural order, first explaining how sentences are put together, and then illustrating the process by which they may be resolved into their constituent parts. Modifiers and Complements are classified, and the so-called Independent Elements are discussed. There is added a special chapter on Combinations of Clauses, in which the grammatical and logical relations of coördination and subordination are set forth, and their functions in the effective use of language are considered. This portion of the book, it is hoped, will be especially useful to students of English composition.

The Appendix furnishes lists of verbs, tables of conjugation, rules for capitals and marks of punctuation, a summary of important rules of syntax, and a brief history of the English language.

The Exercises (pp. 227–290) are collected at the end of the text, so as not to break continuity. References prefixed to each, as well as page-numbers in the Table of Contents, enable the teacher to attach them, at will, to the topics which they concern. The passages for parsing, analysis, etc., have been carefully selected from a wide range of eminent British and American writers. The name of the author is often appended to the quotation, when the passage is particularly noteworthy either for its contents or its form. In most cases, however, this has not been done; but the student may always feel confident that he is occupying himself with specimens of English as actually composed by distinguished authors. The constructive exercises call particular attention to those matters in which error is especially prevalent.

An advanced grammar must aim to be serviceable in two ways. It should afford the means for continuous and systematic study of the subject or of any part of it; and it should also be useful for reference in connection with the study of composition and of literature. With this latter end in view, many notes and observations have been included, in smaller type, to show the nature and development of the various forms and constructions, and to point out differences between the usage of to-day and that which the student observes in Shakspere and other English classics. The fulness of the index makes it easy to find anything that the volume contains.

In accordance with the desire of many teachers, certain topics of importance have been treated with unusual thoroughness. Among these may be mentioned the uses of *shall* and *will*, *should* and *would*, the infinitive and the infinitive clause, conditional sentences, indirect discourse, and the combination of clauses in sentences of different kinds.

The authors are indebted to several teachers for suggestions and criticism. Particular acknowledgment is due to Mr. Theodore C. Mitchill, of the Jamaica High School, New York, and Mr. C. L. Hooper, of the Chicago Normal School.

# CONTENTS

# CONTENTS

vii

## CHAPTER VI — VERBS

# CONTENTS

## CHAPTER VIII — ELLIPTICAL SENTENCES

## EXERCISES

## APPENDIX

# INTRODUCTION

## LANGUAGE AND GRAMMAR

### I. THE NATURE OF LANGUAGE

Language is the expression of thought by means of spoken or written words.

The English word *language* comes (through the French *langue*) from the Latin *lingua*, "the tongue." But the tongue is not the only organ used in speaking. The lips, the teeth, the roof of the mouth, the soft palate (or uvula), the nose, and the vocal chords all help to produce the sounds of which language consists. These various organs make up one delicate and complicated piece of mechanism upon which the breath of the speaker acts like that of a musician upon a clarinet or other wind instrument.

Spoken language, then, is composed of a great **variety** of sounds made with the vocal organs. A word may consist of one sound (as *Ah!* or *O* or *I*), but most words consist of two or more different sounds (as *go, see, try, finish*). Long or short, however, a word is merely a sign made to express thought.

Thought may be imperfectly expressed by signs made with the head, the hands, etc. Thus, if I grasp a person's arm and point to a dog, he may understand me to ask, "Do you see that dog?" And his nod in reply may stand for "Yes, I see him." But any dialogue carried on in this way must be both **fragmentary** and uncertain. To express our thoughts fully, freely, and accurately, we must use words, — that is, signs made with the voice. Such voice-signs have had meanings associated with them by custom or tradition, so that their sense is at once understood by all. Their advantage is twofold: they are far more numerous and varied than other signs; and the meanings attached to them are much more definite than those of nods and gestures.

Written words are signs made with the pen to represent and recall to the mind the spoken words (or voice-signs). Written language (that is, composition) must, of necessity, be somewhat fuller than spoken language, as well as more formal and exact. For the reader's understanding is not assisted by the tones of the voice, the changing expressions of the face, and the lively gestures, which help to make spoken language intelligible.

Most words are the signs of definite ideas. Thus, *Charles, captain, cat, mouse, bread, stone, cup, ink*, call up images or pictures of persons or things; *strike, dive, climb, dismount*, express particular kinds of action; *green, blue, careless, rocky, triangular, muscular*, enable us to describe objects with accuracy. Even general terms like *goodness, truth, courage, cowardice, generosity*, have sufficiently precise meanings, for they name qualities, or traits of character, with which everybody is familiar.

By the use of such words, even when not combined in groups, we can express our thoughts much more satisfactorily than by mere gestures. The utterance of the single word "Charles!" may signify: "Hullo, Charles! are you here? I am surprised to see you." "Bread!" may suggest to the hearer: "Give me bread! I am very hungry." "Courage!" may be almost equivalent to, "Don't be down-hearted! Your troubles will soon be over."

Language, however, is not confined to the utterance of single words. To express our thoughts we must put words together, — we must combine them into groups; and such groups have settled meanings (just as words have), established (like the meanings of single words) by the customs or habits of the particular language that we are speaking or writing. Further, these groups are not thrown together haphazard. We must construct them in accordance with certain fixed rules. Otherwise we shall fail to express ourselves clearly and acceptably, and we may even succeed in saying the opposite of what we mean.

In constructing these groups (which we call **phrases, clauses, and sentences**) we have the aid of a large number of short words like *and, if, by, to, in, is, was,* which are very different from the definite and picturesque words that we have just examined. They do not call up distinct images in the mind, and we should find it hard to define any of them. Yet their importance in the expression of thought is clear; for they serve to join other words together, and to show their relation to each other in those groups which make up connected speech.

Thus, "box heavy" conveys some meaning; but " *The* box *is* heavy" is a clear and definite statement. *The* shows that some particular box is meant, and *is* enables us to make an assertion about it. *And,* in " Charles and John are my brothers," indicates that Charles and John are closely connected in my thought, and that what I say of one applies also to the other. *If,* in " If Charles comes, I shall be glad to see him," connects two statements, and shows that one of them is a mere supposition (for Charles may or may not come).

In grouping words, our language has three different ways of indicating their relations : (1) the forms of the words themselves ; (2) their order ; (3) the use of little words like *and, if, is,* etc.

I. **Change of form.** Words may change their form. Thus the word *boy* becomes *boys* when more than one is meant ; *kill* becomes *killed* when past time is referred to ; *was* becomes *were* when we are speaking of two or more persons or things ; *fast* becomes *faster* when a higher degree of speed is indicated. Such change of form is called **inflection,** and the word is said to be **inflected.**

Inflection is an important means of showing the relations of words in connected speech. In " Henry's racket weighs fourteen ounces," the form *Henry's* shows at once the relation between Henry and the racket, — namely, that Henry owns or possesses it. The word *Henry*, then, may change its form to *Henry's* to indicate ownership or possession.

**II. Order of words.** In "John struck Charles," the way in which the words are arranged shows who it was that struck, and who received the blow. Change the order of words to "Charles struck John," and the meaning is reversed. It is, then, the **order** that shows the relation of *John* to *struck*, and of *struck* to *Charles*.

**III. Use of other words.** Compare the two sentences:

> The train *from* Boston has just arrived.
> The train *for* Boston has just arrived.

Here *from* and *for* show the relation between the *train* and *Boston*. "The Boston train" might mean either the train *from* Boston or the train *for* Boston. By using *from* or *for* we make the sense unmistakable.

Two matters, then, are of vital importance in language,— the forms of words, and the relations of words. The science which treats of these two matters is called **grammar**.

**Inflection is a change in the form of a word indicating some change in its meaning.**

**The relation in which a word stands to other words in the sentence is called its construction.**

**Grammar is the science which treats of the forms and the constructions of words.**

**Syntax is that department of grammar which treats of the constructions of words.**

Grammar, then, may be said to concern itself with two main subjects, — inflection and syntax.

English belongs to a family of languages—the Indo-European Family [1] — which is rich in forms of inflection. This richness may be seen in other members of the family, — such as Greek or Latin. The Latin word *homo*, "man," for example, has

---

[1] For a brief history of the English language, see p. 316.

subject (*gold*) in such a way that *a metal* serves as a description or definition of *gold*.

In sentences 4–7, *becomes*, *seemed*, *proved*, and *grows* are similarly used.

In such sentences *is* and other verbs that are used for the same purpose are called **copulative** (that is, "joining") **verbs**.

*Is* in this use is often called the **copula**, that is, the "joiner" or "link."

The forms of the verb *is* are very irregular. Among the commonest are: *am, is, are, was, were,* and the verb-phrases *has been, have been, had been, shall be, will be.*[1]

## V. ADVERBS

**18. An adverb is a word which modifies a verb, an adjective, or another adverb.**

To **modify** a word is to change or affect its meaning in some way. Thus in "The river fell *rapidly*," the adverb *rapidly* modifies the verb *fell* by showing *how* the falling took place. In "I am *never* late," "This is *absolutely* true," "That is *too* bad," the italicized words are adverbs modifying adjectives; in "He came *very* often," "He spoke *almost* hopefully," "The river fell *too* rapidly," they are adverbs modifying other adverbs.

Most adverbs answer the question "How?" "When?" "Where?" or "To what degree or extent?"

**19.** Observe that adverbs modify verbs in much the same way in which adjectives modify nouns.

| ADJECTIVES | ADVERBS |
|---|---|
| A *bright* fire burned. | The fire burned *brightly*. |
| A *fierce* wind blew. | The wind blew *fiercely*. |

**A word or group of words that changes or modifies the meaning of another word is called a modifier.**

Adjectives and adverbs, then, are both **modifiers**. Adjectives modify substantives; adverbs modify verbs, adjectives, or other adverbs.

[1] For full inflection see pp. 300–301.

## VI. PREPOSITIONS

**20.** A preposition is a word placed before a substantive to show its relation to some other word in the sentence.

The substantive which follows a preposition is called its object.

A preposition is said to **govern** its object.

In "The surface *of* the water glistened," *of* makes it clear that *surface* belongs with *water*. In "Philip is *on* the river," *on* shows Philip's position with respect to the river. *In*, or *near*, or *beyond* would have indicated a different relation. *Water* is the object of the preposition *of*, and *river* is the object of the preposition *on*.

**21.** A preposition often has more than one object.

> Over *hill* and *dale* he ran.
> He was filled with *shame* and *despair*.

## VII. CONJUNCTIONS

**22.** A conjunction connects words or groups of words.

A conjunction differs from a preposition in having no object, and in indicating a less definite relation between the words which it connects.

In "Time *and* tide wait for no man," "The parcel was small *but* heavy," "He wore a kind of doublet *or* jacket," the conjunctions *and*, *but*, *or*, connect single words, — *time* with *tide*, *small* with *heavy*, *doublet* with *jacket*. In "Do not go *if* you are afraid," "I came *because* you sent for me," "Take my key, *but* do not lose it," "Sweep the floor *and* dust the furniture," each conjunction connects the entire group of words preceding it with the entire group following it.

## VIII. INTERJECTIONS

**23.** An interjection is a cry or other exclamatory sound expressing surprise, anger, pleasure, or some other emotion or feeling.

Interjections usually have no grammatical connection with the groups of words in which they stand; hence their name, which means "thrown in."

EXAMPLES: *Oh!* I forgot. *Ah*, how I miss you! *Bravo! Alas!*

## THE SAME WORD AS DIFFERENT PARTS OF SPEECH

**24.** The meaning of a word in the sentence determines to what part of speech it belongs.

The same word may be sometimes one part of speech, sometimes another.

Words of entirely separate origin, meaning, and use sometimes look and sound alike: as in "The minstrel sang a plaintive *lay*," and "He *lay* on the ground." But the following examples (§ 25) show that the same word may have more than one kind of grammatical office (or function). It is the **meaning** which we give to a word **in the sentence** that determines its classification as a part of speech.

**25.** The chief classes of words thus variously used are (1) nouns and adjectives, (2) nouns and verbs, (3) adjectives and adverbs, (4) adjectives and pronouns, (5) adverbs and prepositions.

### I. Nouns and Adjectives

| Nouns | Adjectives |
|---|---|
| *Rubber* comes from South America. | This wheel has a *rubber* tire. |
| That *brick* is yellow. | Here is a *brick* house. |
| The *rich* have a grave responsibility. | A *rich* merchant lives here. |

The first two examples show how words that are commonly nouns may be used as adjectives; the third shows how words that are commonly adjectives may be used as nouns.

### II. Nouns and Verbs

| Nouns | Verbs |
|---|---|
| Hear the *wash* of the tide. | *Wash* those windows. |
| Give me a *stamp*. | *Stamp* this envelope. |
| It is the *call* of the sea. | Ye *call* me chief. |

Other examples are: act, address, ally, answer, boast, care, cause, close, defeat, doubt, drop, heap, hope, mark, offer, pile, place, rest, rule, sail, shape, sleep, spur, test, watch, wound.

### III. ADJECTIVES AND ADVERBS

| ADJECTIVES | ADVERBS |
|---|---|
| That is a *fast* boat. | The snow is melting *fast.* |
| Draw a *straight* line. | The arrow flew *straight.* |
| *Early* comers get good seats. | Tom awoke *early*. |

For an explanation of the form of these adverbs, see § 191.

### IV. ADJECTIVES AND PRONOUNS

| ADJECTIVES | PRONOUNS |
|---|---|
| *This* man looks unhappy. | *This* is the sergeant. |
| *That* book is a dictionary. | *That* is a kangaroo. |
| *Each* day brings its opportunity. | I received a dollar from *each*. |

For further study of this class of words, see pp. 62–65.

### V. ADVERBS AND PREPOSITIONS

| ADVERBS | PREPOSITIONS |
|---|---|
| Jill came tumbling *after*. | He returned *after* the accident. |
| We went *below*. | *Below* us lay the valley. |
| The weeds sprang *up*. | We walked *up* the hill. |

Other examples are: aboard, before, beyond, down, inside, underneath.

Miscellaneous examples of variation are the following : —

| NOUN. | The *calm* lasted for three days. |
|---|---|
| ADJECTIVE. | *Calm* words show quiet minds. |
| VERB. | *Calm* your angry friend. |

Other examples are : iron, stone, paper, sugar, salt, bark, quiet, black, light, head, wet, round, square, winter, spring.

| NOUN. | *Wrong* seldom prospers. |
|---|---|
| ADJECTIVE. | You have taken the *wrong* road. |
| ADVERB. | Edward often spells words *wrong*. |
| VERB. | You *wrong* me by your suspicions. |

| NOUN. | The *outside* of the castle is gloomy. |
|---|---|
| ADJECTIVE. | We have an *outside* stateroom. |
| ADVERB. | The messenger is waiting *outside*. |
| PREPOSITION. | I shall ride *outside* the coach. |

eight different inflectional forms, — *homo*, " a man"; *hominis*, " of a man"; *homini*, "to a man," and so on. Thus, in Latin, the grammatical construction of a word is, in general, shown by that particular inflectional ending (or termination) which it has in any particular sentence. In the Anglo-Saxon period,[1] English was likewise well furnished with such inflectional endings, though not so abundantly as Latin. Many of these, however, had disappeared by Chaucer's time (1340–1400), and still others have since been lost, so that modern English is one of the least inflected of languages. Such losses are not to be lamented. By due attention to the order of words, and by using *of, to, for, from, in*, and the like, we can express all the relations denoted by the ancient inflections. The gain in simplicity is enormous.

## II. GRAMMAR AND USAGE

Since language is the expression of thought, the rules of grammar agree, in the main, with the laws of thought. In other words, grammar is usually logical, — that is, its rules accord, in general, with the principles of logic, which is the science of exact reasoning.

The rules of grammar, however, do not derive their authority from logic, but from good usage, — that is, from the customs or habits followed by educated speakers and writers. These customs, of course, differ among different nations, and every language has therefore its own stock of peculiar constructions or turns of expression. Such peculiarities are called **idioms**.

Thus, in English we say, " It is I "; but in French the idiom is " C'est moi," which corresponds to " It is me." Many careless speakers of English follow the French idiom in this particular, but their practice has not yet come to be the accepted usage. Hence, though " C'est moi" is correct in French, we must still regard " It is me " as ungrammatical in English. It

[1] Compare pp. 316–317.

would, however, become correct if it should ever be adopted by the great majority of educated persons.

Grammar does not enact laws for the conduct of speech. Its business is to ascertain and set forth those customs of language which have the sanction of good usage. If good usage changes, the rules of grammar must change. If two forms or constructions are in good use, the grammarian must admit them both. Occasionally, also, there is room for difference of opinion. These facts, however, do not lessen the authority of grammar in the case of any cultivated language. For in such a language usage is so well settled in almost every particular as to enable the grammarian to say positively what is right and what is wrong. Even in matters of divided usage, it is seldom difficult to determine which of two forms or constructions is preferred by careful writers.

Every language has two standards of usage, — the colloquial and the literary. By "colloquial language," we mean the language of conversation ; by "literary language," that employed in literary composition. Everyday colloquial English admits many words, forms, phrases, and constructions that would be out of place in a dignified essay. On the other hand, it is an error in taste to be always "talking like a book." Unpractised speakers and writers should, however, be conservative. They should avoid, even in informal talk, any word or expression that is of doubtful propriety. Only those who know what they are about, can venture to take liberties. It is quite possible to be correct without being stilted or affected.[1]

Every living language is constantly changing. Words, forms, and constructions become **obsolete** (that is, go out of use) and others take their places. Consequently, one often notes in the older English classics, methods of expression which, though formerly correct, are ungrammatical now. Here a twofold

---

[1] In this book, well-established colloquial idioms or constructions are mentioned from time to time, but always with a note as to their actual status in the language.

caution is necessary. On the one hand, we must not criticise Shakspere or Chaucer for using the English of his own time; but, on the other hand, we must not try to defend our own errors by appealing to ancient usage.

Examples of constructions once in good use, but no longer admissible, are: "the best of the two" (for "the better of the two"); "the most unkindest cut of all"; "There's two or three of us" (for *there are*); "I have forgot the map" (for *forgotten*); "Every one of these letters are in my name" (for *is*); "I think it be" (for *is*).

The language of poetry admits many old words, forms, and constructions that are no longer used in ordinary prose. These are called **archaisms** (that is, ancient expressions). Among the commonest archaisms are *thou, ye, hath, thinkest, doth.* Such forms are also common in prose, in what is known as the **solemn style,** which is modelled, in great part, on the language of the Bible.[1]

In general, it should be remembered that the style which one uses should be appropriate, — that is, it should fit the occasion. A short story and a scientific exposition will differ in style; a familiar letter will naturally shun the formalities of business or legal correspondence. Good style is not a necessary result of grammatical correctness, but without such correctness it is, of course, impossible.

## SUMMARY OF GENERAL PRINCIPLES

1. Language is the expression of thought by means of spoken or written words.

2. Words are the signs of ideas.

Spoken words are signs made with the vocal organs; written words are signs made with the pen to represent the spoken words.

[1] In this book, several old forms and constructions which the student is constantly encountering in the English classics are treated in their proper places, — always with an indication of their difference from the modern standard

The meanings of these signs are settled by custom or tradition in each language.

**3.** Most words are the signs of definite ideas: as, — *Charles, captain, cat, strike, dive, climb, triangular, careless.*

Other words, of less definite meaning, serve to connect the more definite words and to show their relations to each other in connected speech.

**4.** In the expression of thought, words are combined into groups called phrases, clauses, and sentences.

**5.** The relation in which a word stands to other words in the sentence is called its construction.

The construction of English words is shown in three ways: (1) by their form; (2) by their order; (3) by the use of other words like *to, from, is,* etc.

**6.** Inflection is a change in the form of a word indicating some change in its meaning: as, — *boy, boy's; man, men; drink, drank.*

**7.** Grammar is the science which treats of the forms and the constructions of words.

Syntax is that department of grammar which treats of the constructions of words.

**8.** The rules of grammar derive their authority from good usage, — that is, from the customs or habits followed by educated speakers and writers.

# ENGLISH GRAMMAR

## PART ONE

## THE PARTS OF SPEECH IN
## THE SENTENCE

**Summary.** The Sentence: Subject and Predicate; Kinds of Sentences. — Use of words in the Sentence: the Eight Parts of Speech; Infinitives and Participles. — Comparative Importance of the Parts of Speech in the Sentence: the Subject Noun (or Simple Subject); the Predicate Verb (or Simple Predicate); Compound Subject and Predicate. — Substitutes for the Parts of Speech: Phrases; Clauses; Compound and Complex Sentences.

### THE SENTENCE

**1. A sentence is a group of words which expresses a complete thought.**

> Fire burns.
> Wolves howl.
> Rain is falling.
> Charles is courageous.
> Patient effort removes mountains.
> London is the largest city in the world.
> A man who respects himself should never condescend
> to use slovenly language.

Some of these sentences are short, expressing a very simple thought; others are comparatively long, because the thought is more complicated and therefore requires more words for its expression. But every one of them, whether short or long, is complete in itself. It comes to a definite end, and is followed by a full pause.

1

**2.** Every sentence, whether short or long, consists of two parts, — a **subject** and a **predicate**.

**The subject of a sentence designates the person, place, or thing that is spoken of; the predicate is that which is said of the subject.**

Thus, in the first example in § 1, the subject is *fire* and the predicate is *burns*. In the third, the subject is *rain;* the predicate, *is falling*. In the last, the subject is *a man who respects himself;* the predicate, *should never condescend to use slovenly language.*

Either the subject or the predicate may consist of a single word or of a number of words. But neither the subject by itself nor the predicate by itself, however extended, is a sentence. The mere mention of a thing (*fire*) does not express a complete thought. Neither does a mere assertion (*burns*), if we neglect to mention the person or thing about which the assertion is made. Thus it appears that both a subject and a predicate are necessary to make a sentence.

**3.** Sentences may be declarative, interrogative, imperative, or exclamatory.

     **1.** A declarative sentence declares or asserts something as a fact.

> Dickens wrote " David Copperfield."
> The army approached the city.

     **2.** An interrogative sentence asks a question.

> Who is that officer ?
> Does Arthur Moore live here ?

     **3.** An imperative sentence expresses a command or a request.

> Open the window.
> Pronounce the vowels more distinctly.

     **4.** An exclamatory sentence expresses surprise, grief, or some other emotion in the form of an exclamation or cry.

> How calm the sea is !
> What a noise the engine makes !

A declarative, an interrogative, or an imperative sentence is also **exclamatory**, if it is uttered in an intense or excited tone of voice.

**4.** In imperative sentences, the subject (*thou* or *you*) is almost always omitted, because it is **understood** by both speaker and hearer without being expressed.

Such omitted words, which are present (*in idea*) to the minds of both speaker and hearer, are said to be "understood." Thus, in "Open the window," the subject is "*you* (understood)." If expressed, the subject would be emphatic : as, — "*You* open the window."

**5.** The subject of a sentence commonly precedes the predicate, but sometimes the predicate precedes.

> Here comes Tom.
> Next came Edward.
> Over went the carriage.

A sentence in which the predicate precedes the subject is said to be in the **inverted order**. This order is especially common in interrogative sentences.

> Where is your boat ?
> When was your last birthday ?
> Whither wander you ? — SHAKSPERE.

## THE PARTS OF SPEECH

**6.** If we examine the words in any sentence, we observe that they have different tasks or duties to perform in the expression of thought.

Savage beasts roamed through the forest.

In this sentence, *beasts* and *forest* are the **names** of objects ; *roamed* **asserts action,** telling us what the beasts *did ; savage* **describes** the beasts ; *through* shows the **relation** in thought between *forest* and *roamed ; the* **limits** the meaning of *forest,* showing that one particular forest is meant. Thus each of these words has its **special office** (or **function**) **in the sentence.**

**7.** In accordance with their use in the sentence, words are divided into eight classes called parts of speech, — namely, nouns, pronouns, adjectives, verbs, adverbs, prepositions, conjunctions, and interjections.

## I. NOUNS

**8.** A noun is the name of a person, place, or thing.

EXAMPLES : Lincoln, William, Elizabeth, sister, engineer, Chicago, island, shelf, star, window, happiness, anger, sidewalk, courage, loss, song.

## II. PRONOUNS

**9.** A pronoun is a word used instead of a noun. It designates a person, place, or thing without naming it.

In "*I* am ready," the pronoun *I* is a convenient substitute for the speaker's name. In "*You* have forgotten *your* umbrella," the pronouns *you* and *your* designate the person to whom one is speaking.

Other pronouns are : *he, his, him ; she, hers, her ; it, its ; this, that ; who, whose, whom, which ; myself, yourself, himself, themselves.*

Since pronouns stand for nouns, they enable us to talk about a person, place, or thing without constantly repeating the name.

**10.** Nouns and pronouns are called substantives.

Nouns and pronouns are very similar in their use. The difference between them is merely that the noun designates a person, place, or thing by **naming** it, and that the pronoun **designates,** but does not **name.** Hence it is convenient to have a general term (**substantive**) to include both these parts of speech.

**11.** The substantive to which a pronoun refers is called its antecedent.

*Frank* introduced the boys to *his* father. [*Frank* is the antecedent of the pronoun *his*.]

*Eleanor* is visiting *her* aunt.

The *book* has lost *its* cover.

The *trappers* sat round *their* camp fire.

*Washington* and *Franklin* served *their* country in different ways. [*Their* has two antecedents, connected by *and*.]

### III. ADJECTIVES

**12.** An adjective is a word which describes or limits a substantive.[1]

This it usually does by indicating some quality.

An adjective is said to belong to the substantive which it describes or limits.

**13.** An adjective limits a substantive by restricting the range of its meaning.

The noun *box*, for example, includes a great variety of objects. If we say *wooden* box, we exclude boxes of metal, of paper, etc. If we use a second adjective (*small*) and a third (*square*), we limit the size and the shape of the box.

Most adjectives (like *wooden*, *square*, and *small*) describe as well as limit. Such words are called descriptive adjectives.

We may, however, limit the noun *box* to a single specimen by means of the adjective *this* or *that* or *the*, which does not describe, but simply points out, or designates. Such words are called definitive adjectives.[2]

### IV. VERBS

**14.** A verb is a word which can assert something (usually an action) concerning a person, place, or thing.[3]

| | |
|---|---|
| The wind *blows*. | Her jewels *sparkled*. |
| The horses *ran*. | Tom *climbed* a tree. |
| The fire *blazed*. | The dynamite *exploded*. |

Some verbs express state or condition rather than action.

The treaty still *exists*.
The book *lies* on the table.
Near the church *stood* an elm.
My aunt *suffers* much from headache.

[1] In the technical language of grammar an adjective is said to *describe* a substantive when it describes the object which the substantive denotes.

[2] Definitive adjectives are often called limiting adjectives. All adjectives, however, *limit*, even those that also *describe*.

[3] The usual brief definition of a verb is, "A verb is a word which asserts." But this definition in strictness applies only to verbs in declarative sentences.

**15.** A group of words may be needed, instead of a **single** verb, to make an assertion.

**A group of words that is used as a verb is called a verb-phrase.**

> You *will see.*
> The tree *has fallen.*
> We *might have invited* her.
> Our driver *has been discharged.*

**16.** Certain verbs, when used to make verb-phrases, are called **auxiliary** (that is, "aiding") **verbs,** because they help other verbs to express action or state of some particular kind.

Thus, in "You *will see,*" the auxiliary verb *will* helps *see* to express **future** action ; in "We *might have invited* her," the auxiliaries *might* and *have* help *invited* to express action that was **possible** in past time.

The auxiliary verbs are *is* (*are, was, were,* etc.), *may, can, must, might, shall, will, could, would, should, have, had, do, did.* Their forms and uses will be studied in connection with the inflection of verbs.

The auxiliary verb regularly comes first in a verb-phrase, and may be separated from the rest of it by some other word or words.

> Where *was* Washington *born ?*
> The boat *was* slowly but steadily *approaching.*

**17.** *Is* (in its various forms) and several other verbs may be used to frame sentences in which some word or words in the predicate describe or define the subject.

> 1. Gold *is* a metal.
> 2. Charles *is* my friend's name.
> 3. The colors of this butterfly *are* brilliant.
> 4. Iron *becomes* red in the fire.
> 5. Our condition *seemed* desperate.
> 6. Bertram *proved* a good friend in this emergency.
> 7. My soul *grows* sad with troubles. — SHAKSPERE.

In the first sentence, the verb *is* not only **makes an assertion,** but it also **connects** the rest of the predicate (*a metal*) with the

| ADJECTIVE. | *That* boat is a sloop. |
| PRONOUN. | *That* is my uncle. |
| CONJUNCTION. | You said *that* you would help **me**. |

| ADJECTIVE. | *Neither* road leads to Utica. |
| PRONOUN. | *Neither* of us arrived in time. |
| CONJUNCTION. | *Neither* Tom nor I was late. |

| PREPOSITION. | I am waiting *for* the train. |
| CONJUNCTION. | You have plenty of time, *for* the train is late. |

| INTERJECTION. | *Hurrah!* the battle is won. |
| NOUN. | I heard a loud *hurrah*. |
| VERB. | The enemy flees. Our men *hurrah*. |

## INFINITIVES AND PARTICIPLES

**26.** Two classes of verb-forms illustrate in a striking way the fact that the same word may belong to different parts of speech; for they really belong to two different parts of speech at one and the same time. These are the **infinitive** (which is both **verb** and **noun**) and the **participle** (which is both **verb** and **adjective**).

**27.** Examples of the **infinitive** may be seen in the following sentences :

> *To struggle* was useless.
> *To escape* is impossible.
> *To exercise* regularly preserves the health.

*To struggle* is clearly a **noun,** for (1) it is the subject of the sentence, and (2) the noun *effort* or *exertion* might be put in the place of *to struggle.* Similarly, the noun *escape* might be substituted for *to escape ;* and, in the third sentence, *regular exercise* (a noun modified by an adjective) might be substituted for *to exercise regularly.*

But these three forms (*to struggle, to escape,* and *to exercise*) are also **verbs,** for they express action, and one of them (*to exercise*) is modified by an adverb (*regularly*). Such forms, therefore, are noun-forms of the verb. They are classed with verbs, and are called **infinitives.**

**28.** The infinitive is a verb-form which partakes of the nature of **a** noun. It is commonly preceded by the preposition *to*, which is called **the** sign of the infinitive.

**29.** The infinitive without *to* is used in a great variety of verb-phrases.

| | |
|---|---|
| I *shall go*. | Mary *may recite*. |
| John *will win*. | Jack *can swim*. |

Such phrases will be studied in connection with the inflection of verbs.

NOTE. That *go, win, recite,* and *swim* are infinitives may be seen by comparing the following sentences: — "I intend *to go*," "John is sure *to win*," "Mary is permitted *to recite*," "Jack is able *to swim*."

**30.** The following sentence contains two **participles** : —

*Shattered* and slowly *sinking*, the frigate drifted out to sea.

In this sentence, we recognize *shattered* as a form of the **verb** *shatter*, and *sinking* as a form of the **verb** *sink*. They both express action, and *sinking* is modified by the adverb *slowly*. But *shattered* and *sinking* have also the nature of **adjectives,** for they are used to describe the noun *frigate*. Such words, then, are adjective forms of the verb. They are classed as verbs, and are called **participles,** because they share (or participate in) the nature of adjectives.

**31.** The participle is a verb-form which has no subject, but which partakes of the nature of an adjective and expresses action or state in such a way as to describe or limit a substantive.

A participle is said to **belong** to the substantive which it describes or limits.

**32.** The chief classes of participles are **present participles** and **past participles,** so called from the time which they denote.

All present participles end in *ing*. Past participles have several different endings, which will be studied in connection with the inflection of verbs (§ 334).

**33.** Participles are used in a variety of verb-phrases.

| | |
|---|---|
| Tom *is coming*. | Your book *is found*. |
| Our boat *was wrecked*. | They *have sold* their horses. |
| I *have sent* the money. | You *have broken* your watch. |
| He *has brought* me a letter. | The ship *had struck* on the reef. |

Such phrases will be studied in connection with the inflection of verbs.

NOTE. The double nature of the infinitive (as both verb and noun) and the participle (as both verb and adjective) almost justifies one in classifying each as a distinct part of speech (so as to make ten parts of speech instead of eight). But it is more convenient to include them under the head of verbs, in accordance with the usual practice.

## SIMPLE AND COMPLETE SUBJECT AND PREDICATE

**34.** Our survey of the eight parts of speech has shown, (1) that these have very different offices or functions in the sentence, and (2) that their functions are not of equal importance.

Clearly, the most important parts of speech are **substantives** (nouns and pronouns) and **verbs**.

Substantives enable us to **name or designate** persons, places, or things, and verbs enable us to **make statements** about them. Both substantives and verbs, then, are absolutely necessary in framing sentences. Without a substantive, there can be no **subject**; without a verb, there can be no **predicate**: and both a subject and a predicate, as we have seen, are needed to make a sentence.

**Adjectives** and **adverbs** are less important than substantives and verbs. Their function is to **modify** other parts of speech, that is, to change their meaning in some way. Thus adjectives modify substantives (by describing or limiting), and adverbs usually modify verbs (by indicating *how*, *when*, or *where* the action took place). Without substantives, there would be no use for adjectives; without verbs, there would be little use for adverbs.

**Prepositions** and **conjunctions** are also less important than substantives and verbs. Their office is to connect and to show relation. Of course, there would be no place for connectives if there were nothing to connect.

**Interjections** are the least important of all. They add liveliness to language, but they are not actual necessities. We could express all the thoughts that enter our minds without ever using an interjection.

**35.** A sentence may consist of but two words,— a noun or pronoun (the subject) and a verb (the predicate). Thus, —

Charles | swims.

Commonly, however, either the subject or the predicate, or both, will contain more than one word. Thus, —

Young Charles | swims slowly.

Here the **complete subject** (*young Charles*) consists of a noun (*Charles*) and an adjective (*young*), which describes *Charles*. The **complete predicate** consists of a verb (*swims*) and an adverb (*slowly*), which modifies *swim* by indicating *how* the action is performed. The subject noun (*Charles*) and the predicate verb (*swims*) are the chief words in the sentence, for neither could be omitted without destroying it. They form, so to speak, the frame or skeleton of the whole. Either of the two modifiers, the adjective or the adverb, or both, might be omitted, without destroying the sentence; for this would still exist as the expression of a thought (*Charles swims*), though the thought would be less definite and exact than it is when the modifiers are included.

**36.** The simple subject of a sentence is a noun or pronoun.

The simple predicate of a sentence is a verb or verb-phrase.

The simple subject, with such words as explain or complete its meaning, forms the complete subject.

The simple predicate, with such words as explain or complete its meaning, forms the complete predicate.

In each of the following sentences the **complete subject** and the **complete predicate** are separated by a vertical line, and the **simple subject** and the **simple predicate** are printed in italics : —

The *spider* | *spreads* her web.

The fiery *smoke* | *rose* upward in billowing volumes.

A nameless *unrest* | *urged* me forward.

Our frantic *horses* | *swept* round an angle of the road.

The *infirmities* of age | *came* early upon him.

The general *feeling* among the English in Bengal | *was* strongly in favor of the Governor General.

*Salutes* | *were fired* from the batteries.

The *Clives* | *had been settled* ever since the twelfth century on an estate of no great value near Market Drayton in Shropshire.

*I* | *have written* repeatedly to Mr. Hobhouse.

**37.** Two or more simple subjects may be joined to make one **compound subject,** and two or more simple predicates to make one **compound predicate.**

1. *Charles* and *Henry* | play tennis well.
2. *Moore* and *I* | passed some merry days together.
3. *Frances* and *she* | are friends.
4. *Hats, caps, boots,* and *gloves* | were piled together in confusion.
5. The watch | *sank* and *was lost.*
6. The balloon | *rose* higher and higher and finally *disappeared.*
7. He | neither *smiled* nor *frowned.*
8. *Snow* and *ice* | *covered* the ground and *made* our progress difficult.

**38.** A compound subject or predicate consists of two or more simple subjects or predicates, joined, when necessary, by conjunctions.

Either the subject or the predicate, or both, may be compound.

In the first example in § 37, two simple subjects (*Charles* and *Henry*) are joined by the conjunction *and* to make a compound subject. In the fourth, four substantives (*hats, caps, boots, gloves*) form a series in which the last two are joined by *and.* In the fifth, sixth, and seventh, the predicates are compound; in the eighth, both the subject and the predicate.

**39.** The following conjunctions may be used to join the members of a compound subject or predicate: *and* (*both . . . and*), *or* (*either . . . or ; whether . . . or*), *nor* (*neither . . . nor*).

SUBSTITUTES FOR PARTS OF SPEECH

### PHRASES

**40.** A group of words may take the place of a part of speech

> *The Father of Waters* is the Mississippi.
> A girl *with blue eyes* stood *at the window*.
> You *are looking* well.

*The Father of Waters* is used as a noun, since it names something.

*With blue eyes* takes the place of an adjective (*blue-eyed*), and modifies *girl*.

*At the window* indicates, as an adverb might, where the girl stood, and modifies *stood*.

*Are looking* could be replaced by the verb *look*.

**41.** A group of connected words, not containing a subject and a predicate, is called a **phrase.**

A phrase is often equivalent to a part of speech.

1. A phrase used as a noun is called a **noun-phrase.**
2. A phrase used as a verb is called a **verb-phrase.**
3. A phrase used as an adjective is called an **adjective phrase.**
4. A phrase used as an adverb is called an **adverbial phrase.**

In the examples in § 40, *The Father of Waters* is a noun-phrase; *with blue eyes*, an adjective phrase; *at the window*, an adverbial phrase; *are looking*, a verb-phrase.

**42.** Many adjective and adverbial phrases consist of a **preposition and its object,** with or without other words.

> Your umbrella is *in the corner*.
> He has a heart *of oak*.
> A cup *with a broken handle* stood *on the shelf*.
> My house *of cards* fell *to the floor in a heap*.

Adjective or adverbial phrases consisting of a preposition and its object, with or without other words, may be called **prepositional phrases.**

### CLAUSES — COMPOUND AND COMPLEX SENTENCES

**43.** Phrases must be carefully distinguished from **clauses.** The difference is that a clause contains a subject and a predicate and a phrase does not.

**44.** A clause is a group of words that forms part of a sentence and that contains a subject and a predicate.

> The lightning flashed | and | the thunder roared.
> The train started | when the bell rang.

Each of these sentences contains two clauses; but the relation between the clauses in the first sentence is very different from that between the clauses in the second.

In the first example, each of the two clauses makes a separate and distinct statement, and might stand by itself as a simple sentence, — that is, as a sentence having but one subject and one predicate. These clauses are joined by the conjunction *and*, which is not a part of either. No doubt the speaker feels that there is some relation in thought between the two statements, or he would not have put them together as clauses in the same sentence. But there is nothing in the form of expression to show what that relation is. In other words, the two clauses are grammatically **independent**, for neither of them modifies (or affects the meaning of) the other. The clauses are therefore said to be **coördinate**, — that is, of the same " order " or rank, and the sentence is called **compound**.

In the second example, on the contrary, the relation between the two clauses is indicated with precision. One clause (*the train started*) makes the main statement, — it expresses the chief fact. Hence it is called the **main** (or **principal**) **clause**. The other clause (*when the bell rang*) is added because the speaker wishes to **modify** the main verb (*started*) by defining the time of the action. This clause, then, is used as a **part of speech.** Its function is the same as that of an adverb (*promptly*) or an adverbial phrase (*on the stroke of the bell*). For this purpose alone it exists, and not as an independent statement. Hence it is called a **dependent** (or **subordinate**) **clause**, because it **depends** (that is, " hangs ") upon the main clause, and so occupies a lower or " subordinate " rank in the sentence. When thus constructed, a sentence is said to be **complex.**

**45.** An ordinary **compound sentence** (as we have seen in § 44) is made by joining two or more simple sentences, each of which thus becomes an **independent coördinate clause.**

In the same way we may join two or more **complex sentences,** using them as clauses to make one compound sentence: —

The train started when the bell rang, | and | Tom watched until the last car disappeared.

This sentence is manifestly **compound,** for it consists of two **coördinate clauses** (*the train started when the bell rang; Tom watched until the last car disappeared*) joined by *and*. Each of these two clauses is itself **complex,** for each could stand by itself as a complex sentence.

Similarly, a **complex** and a **simple** sentence may be joined as coördinate clauses to make a compound sentence.

The train started when the bell rang, | and | Tom gazed after it in despair.

Such a sentence, which is **compound in its structure,** but in which one or more of the coördinate clauses are **complex,** is called a **compound complex sentence.**[1]

**46.** A clause is a group of words that forms part of a sentence and that contains a subject and a predicate.

A clause used as a part of speech is called a subordinate clause. All other clauses are said to be independent.

Clauses of the same order or rank are said to be coördinate.

Sentences may be simple, compound, or complex.

1. A simple sentence has but one subject and one predicate, either or both of which may be compound.

2. A compound sentence consists of two or more independent coördinate clauses, which may or may not be joined by conjunctions.

3. A complex sentence consists of two or more clauses, one of which is independent and the rest subordinate.

A compound sentence in which one or more of the coördinate clauses are complex is called a compound complex sentence.

---

[1] Compound complex sentences are also called complex compound sentences For further treatment of such sentences, see pp. 187, 190, 215–216.

## I. Simple Sentences

Iron rusts.

George V is king.

Dogs, foxes, and hares are quadrupeds. [Compound subject.]

The defendant rose and addressed the court. [Compound predicate.]

Merton and his men crossed the bridge and scaled the wall. [Both subject and predicate are compound.]

## II. Compound Sentences

Shakspere was born in 1564; he died in 1616. [Two coördinate clauses; no conjunction.]

A rifle cracked, and the wolf fell dead. [Two clauses joined by the conjunction *and*.]

You must hurry, or we shall lose the train. [Two clauses joined by *or*.]

James Watt did not invent the steam engine, but he greatly improved it. [Two clauses joined by *but*.]

Either you have neglected to write or your letter has failed to reach me. [Two clauses joined by *either . . . or*.]

The following conjunctions may be used to join coördinate clauses: *and* (*both . . . and*), *or* (*either . . . or*), *nor* (*neither . . . nor*), *but*, *for*.

## III. Complex Sentences

Examples will be found in §§ 48–50.

### Clauses as Parts of Speech

**47.** Subordinate clauses, like phrases, are used as **parts of speech.** They serve as substitutes for **nouns,** for **adjectives,** or for **adverbs.**

1. A subordinate clause that is used as a noun is called a noun (or substantive) clause.

2. A subordinate clause that modifies a substantive is called an adjective clause.

3. A subordinate clause that serves as an adverbial modifier is called an adverbial clause.

**48.** I. Noun (or Substantive) Clauses.

> *Success*
> *That we should succeed in this plan* } is improbable.

The thought in these two sentences is the same, but in the second it is more fully expressed. In the first sentence, the subject is the noun *success ;* in the second, the subject is the noun clause, *that we should succeed in this plan.* This clause is introduced by the conjunction *that ;* the simple subject of the clause is the pronoun *we,* and the simple predicate is the verb-phrase *should succeed.* The first sentence is **simple ;** the second is **complex.**

Substantive clauses are often introduced by the conjunction *that.*

**49.** II. Adjective Clauses. The following sentences illustrate the use of (1) an **adjective,** (2) an **adjective phrase,** (3) an **adjective clause,** as a modifier of the subject noun.

> An *honorable* man
> A man *of honor* } will not lie.
> A man *who values his honor*

> A *seasonable* word
> A word *in season* } may save a soul.
> A word *that is spoken at the right moment*

> My *native* land
> The land *of my birth* } lies far across the sea.
> The land *where I was born*

The first two sentences in each group are **simple,** the third is **complex.**

**50.** III. Adverbial Clauses. The following sentences illustrate the use of (1) an **adverb,** (2) an **adverbial phrase,** (3) an **adverbial clause,** as a modifier of the predicate verb (or verb-phrase).

> The lightning struck { *here.*
>                        *on this spot.*
>                        *where we stand.*

> Mr. Andrews lives { *near.*
>                     *in this neighborhood.*
>                     *where you see that elm.*

The game began $\begin{cases} \textit{punctually.} \\ \textit{on the stroke of one.} \\ \textit{when the clock struck.} \end{cases}$

The banker will make the loan $\begin{cases} \textit{conditionally.} \\ \textit{on one condition.} \\ \textit{if you endorse my note.} \end{cases}$

The first two sentences in each group are **simple,** the third is **complex.**

**51.** Adjective clauses may be introduced (1) by the pronouns *who, which,* and *that,* or (2) by adverbs like *where, whence, whither, when.*

Adverbial clauses may be introduced (1) by the adverbs *where, whither, whence, when, while, before, after, until, how, as,* or (2) by the conjunctions *because, though, although, if, that (in order that, so that), lest,* etc.

NOTE. The use of **phrases and clauses** as parts of speech increases enormously the richness and power of language. Though English has a huge stock of words, it cannot provide a separate noun or adjective or adverb for every idea. By grouping words, however, in phrases and clauses we, in effect, make a great variety of new nouns, adjectives, and adverbs, each precisely fitted to the needs of the moment in the expression of thought.

## SUMMARY OF DEFINITIONS

### THE SENTENCE

**1.** Language is thought expressed in words.

**2.** To express thought words are combined into sentences.

**3.** A sentence is a group of words which expresses a complete thought.

**4.** Sentences may be declarative, interrogative, imperative, or exclamatory.

(1) A declarative sentence declares or asserts something as a fact.

(2) An interrogative sentence asks a question.

(3) An imperative sentence expresses a command or a request.

(4) An exclamatory sentence expresses surprise, grief, or some other emotion in the form of an exclamation or cry.

A declarative, an interrogative, or an imperative sentence may also be exclamatory.

## SUBJECT AND PREDICATE

**5.** Every sentence consists of a subject and a predicate.

The subject of a sentence designates the person, place, or thing that is spoken of; the predicate is that which is said of the subject.

**6.** The simple subject of a sentence is a noun or pronoun.

The simple predicate of a sentence is a verb or verb-phrase.

**7.** The simple subject, with such words as explain or complete its meaning, forms the complete subject.

The simple predicate, with such words as explain or complete its meaning, forms the complete predicate.

**8.** A compound subject or predicate consists of two or more simple subjects or predicates, joined, when necessary, by conjunctions.

Either the subject or the predicate, or both, may be compound.

## THE PARTS OF SPEECH

**9.** In accordance with their use in the sentence, words are divided into eight classes called parts of speech, — namely, nouns, pronouns, adjectives, verbs, adverbs, prepositions, conjunctions, and interjections.

(1) A noun is the name of a person, place, or thing.

(2) A pronoun is a word used instead of a noun. It designates a person, place, or thing without naming it.

Nouns and pronouns are called substantives.

The substantive to which a pronoun refers is called its antecedent.

(3) An adjective is a word which describes or limits a substantive. This it usually does by indicating some quality.

An adjective is said to belong to the substantive which it describes or limits.

An adjective which describes is called a descriptive adjective; one which points out or designates is called a definitive adjective.

(4) A verb is a word which can assert something (usually an action) concerning a person, place, or thing.

Some verbs express state or condition rather than action.

A group of words that is used as a verb is called a verb-phrase.

Certain verbs, when used to make verb-phrases, are called auxiliary (that is, "aiding") verbs, because they help other verbs to express action or state of some particular kind.

*Is* (in its various forms) and several other verbs may be used to frame sentences in which some word or words in the predicate describe or define the subject. In such sentences, *is* and other verbs that are used for the same purpose are called copulative (that is, "joining") verbs.

(5) An adverb is a word which modifies a verb, an adjective, or another adverb.

A word or group of words that changes or modifies the meaning of another word is called a modifier.

Adjectives and adverbs are both modifiers.

(6) A preposition is a word placed before a substantive to show its relation to some other word in the sentence.

The substantive which follows a preposition is called its object.

(7) A conjunction connects words or groups of words.

(8) An interjection is a cry or other exclamatory sound expressing surprise, anger, pleasure, or some other emotion or feeling.

10. The meaning of a word in the sentence determines to what part of speech it belongs.

The same word may be sometimes one part of speech, sometimes another.

11. The infinitive is a verb-form which partakes of the nature of a noun. It is commonly preceded by the preposition *to*, which is called the sign of the infinitive.

12. The participle is a verb-form which has no subject, but which partakes of the nature of an adjective and expresses action or state in such a way as to describe or limit a substantive.

A participle is said to belong to the substantive which it describes or limits.

The chief classes of participles are present participles and past participles, so called from the time which they denote.

## Substitutes for the Parts of Speech

### Phrases

13. A group of connected words, not containing a subject and a predicate, is called a phrase.

A phrase is often equivalent to a part of speech.

(1) A phrase used as a noun is called a noun-phrase.

(2) A phrase used as a verb is called a verb-phrase.

(3) A phrase used as an adjective is called an adjective phrase.

(4) A phrase used as an adverb is called an adverbial phrase.

**14.** Adjective or adverbial phrases consisting of a preposition and its object, with or without other words, may be called prepositional phrases.

### CLAUSES

**15.** A clause is a group of words that forms part of a sentence and that contains a subject and a predicate.

**16.** A clause used as a part of speech is called a subordinate clause. All other clauses are said to be independent.

**17.** Clauses of the same order or rank are said to be coördinate.

**18.** Sentences may be simple, compound, or complex.

(1) A simple sentence has but one subject and one predicate, either or both of which may be compound.

(2) A compound sentence consists of two or more independent coördinate clauses, which may or may not be joined by conjunctions.

(3) A complex sentence consists of two or more clauses, one of which is independent and the rest subordinate.

A compound sentence in which one or more of the coördinate clauses are complex is called a compound complex sentence.

**19.** Subordinate clauses, like phrases, are used as parts of speech. They serve as substitutes for nouns, for adjectives, or for adverbs.

(1) A subordinate clause that is used as a noun is called a noun (or substantive) clause.

(2) A subordinate clause that modifies a substantive is called an adjective clause.

(3) A subordinate clause that serves as an adverbial modifier is called an adverbial clause.

# PART TWO

## INFLECTION AND SYNTAX

### CHAPTER I

#### INFLECTION

**52.** Inflection is a change of form in a word indicating some change in its meaning. A word thus changed in form is said to be inflected.

Thus the nouns *man, wife, dog,* may change their form to *man's, wife's, dog's,* to express possession ; or to *men, wives, dogs,* to show that two or more are meant.

The pronouns *I, she,* may change their form to *our, her.*

The adjectives *large, happy, good,* may change their form to *larger, happier, better,* to denote a higher degree of the quality ; or to *largest, happiest, best,* to denote the highest degree.

The verbs *look, see, sing,* may change their form to *looked, saw, sang,* to denote past time.

The examples show that a word may be inflected (1) by the addition of a final letter or syllable (*dog, dogs ; look, looked*), (2) by the substitution of one letter for another (*man, men*), or (3) by a complete change of form (*good, better, best*).

**53.** The inflection of a substantive is called its **declension;** that of an adjective or an adverb, its **comparison;** that of a verb, its **conjugation.**

NOTE. Some forms which we regard as due to inflection are really distinct words. Thus *we* is regarded as a form of the pronoun *I,* but it is in fact an altogether different word. Such irregularities, however, are not numerous, and are properly enough included under the head of inflection.

The table below gives a summary view of inflection, and **may** be used for reference with the following chapters.

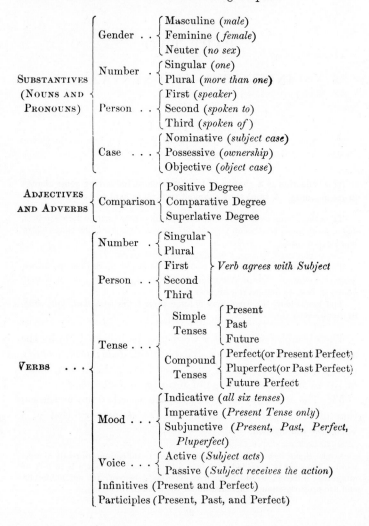

**SUBSTANTIVES (NOUNS AND PRONOUNS)**

Gender
- Masculine (*male*)
- Feminine (*female*)
- Neuter (*no sex*)

Number
- Singular (*one*)
- Plural (*more than one*)

Person
- First (*speaker*)
- Second (*spoken to*)
- Third (*spoken of*)

Case
- Nominative (*subject case*)
- Possessive (*ownership*)
- Objective (*object case*)

**ADJECTIVES AND ADVERBS**

Comparison
- Positive Degree
- Comparative Degree
- Superlative Degree

**VERBS**

Number
- Singular
- Plural

Person
- First
- Second
- Third

*Verb agrees with Subject*

Tense
- Simple Tenses
  - Present
  - Past
  - Future
- Compound Tenses
  - Perfect (or Present Perfect)
  - Pluperfect (or Past Perfect)
  - Future Perfect

Mood
- Indicative (*all six tenses*)
- Imperative (*Present Tense only*)
- Subjunctive (*Present, Past, Perfect, Pluperfect*)

Voice
- Active (*Subject acts*)
- Passive (*Subject receives the action*)

Infinitives (Present and Perfect)

Participles (Present, Past, and Perfect)

# CHAPTER II

## NOUNS

### CLASSIFICATION — COMMON NOUNS AND PROPER NOUNS

**54.** A noun is the name of a person, place, or thing.

**55.** Nouns are divided into two classes — proper nouns and common nouns.

1. A proper noun is the name of a particular person, place, or thing.

EXAMPLES: Lincoln, Napoleon, Ruth, Gladstone, America, Denver, Jove, Ohio, Monday, December, Yale, Christmas, Britannia, Niagara, Merrimac, Elmwood, Louvre, Richardson, Huron, Falstaff.

2. A common noun is a name which may be applied to any one of a class of persons, places, or things.

EXAMPLES: general, emperor, president, clerk, street, town, desk, tree, cloud, chimney, childhood, idea, thought, letter, dynamo, cruiser, dictionary, railroad.

Proper nouns begin with a capital letter; common nouns usually begin with a small letter.

NOTE. Although a proper noun is the name of a particular person, place, or thing, that name may be given to more than one individual. More than one man is named *James;* but when we say *James,* we think of one particular person, whom we are calling by his own name. When we say *man,* on the contrary, we are not calling any single person by name: we are using a noun which applies, in common, to all the members of a large class of persons.

Any word, when mentioned merely **as a word,** is a noun. Thus, —

> *And* is a conjunction.

**56.** A common noun becomes a proper noun when used as the particular name of a ship, a newspaper, an animal, etc.

> Nelson's flagship was the *Victory.*
> Give me this evening's *Herald.*
> My dog is named *Rover.*
> The *Limited Express* is drawn by the *Pioneer.*

**57.** A proper noun often consists of a group of words, some of which are perhaps ordinarily used as other parts of speech.

EXAMPLES : James Russell Lowell, Washington Elm, Eiffel Tower, Firth of Clyde, North Lexington Junction, Stony Brook, Westminster Abbey, Measure for Measure, White House, Brooklyn Bridge, Atlantic Railroad, Sherman Act, The Return of the Native, Flatiron Building.

NOTE. These are (strictly speaking) noun-phrases (§ 41); but, since all are particular names, they may be regarded as proper nouns.

**58.** A proper noun becomes a common noun when used as a name that may be applied to any one of a class of objects.

> The museum owns two *Rembrandts* and a *Titian.*
> I exchanged my old motor car for a new *Halstead.*
> My fountain pen is a *Blake.*
> Lend me your *Webster.*
> He was a *Napoleon* of finance.
> I am going to buy a *Kazak.*

**59.** Certain proper nouns have become common nouns when used in a special sense. These generally begin with a small letter.

EXAMPLES : macadam (crushed stone for roads, so called from Macadam, the inventor), mackintosh (a waterproof garment), napoleon (a coin), guinea (twenty-one shillings), mentor (a wise counsellor), derringer (a kind of pistol).

**60.** A lifeless object, one of the lower animals, or any human quality or emotion is sometimes regarded as a person.

This usage is called **personification,** and the object, animal, or quality is said to be **personified.**

> Each old poetic *Mountain*
> Inspiration breathed around. — GRAY.

> Who'll toll the bell ?
> "I," said the *Bull,*
> "Because I can pull."

> His name was *Patience.* — SPENSER.

> Smiles on past *Misfortune's* brow
> Soft *Reflection's* hand can trace ;
> And o'er the cheek of *Sorrow* throw
> A melancholy grace. — GRAY.

> *Love* is and was my lord and king,
> And in his presence I attend. — TENNYSON.

> *Time* gently shakes his wings. — DRYDEN.

The name of anything personified is regarded as a proper noun and is usually written with a capital letter.

NOTE. The rule for capitals is not absolute. When the personification is kept up for only a sentence or two (as frequently in Shakspere), the noun often begins with a small letter.

## SPECIAL CLASSES OF NOUNS

**61.** An abstract noun is the name of a quality or general idea.

EXAMPLES : blackness, freshness, smoothness, weight, height, length, depth, strength, health, honesty, beauty, liberty, eternity, satisfaction, precision, splendor, terror, disappointment, elegance, existence, grace, peace.

Many abstract nouns are derived from adjectives.

EXAMPLES : greenness (from *green*), depth (from *deep*), freedom (from *free*), wisdom (from *wise*), rotundity (from *rotund*), falsity or falseness (from *false*), bravery (from *brave*).

**62.** A collective noun is the name of a group, class, or multitude, and not of a single person, place, or thing.

EXAMPLES : crowd, group, legislature, squadron, sheaf, battalion, squad, Associated Press, Mediterranean Steamship Company, Senior Class, School Board.

The same noun may be **abstract** in one of its meanings. **collective** in another.

> They believe in *fraternity*. [Abstract.]
> The student joined a *fraternity*. [Collective.]

**63.** Abstract nouns are usually common, but become proper when the quality or idea is personified (§ 60).

Collective nouns may be either proper or common.

**64.** A noun consisting of two or more words united is called a compound noun.

EXAMPLES : (1) common nouns, — tablecloth, sidewalk, lampshade, bedclothes, steamboat, fireman, washerwoman, jackknife, hatband, headache, flatiron, innkeeper, knife-edge, steeple-climber, brother-in-law, commander-in-chief, window curtain, insurance company; (2) proper nouns, — Johnson, Williamson, Cooperstown, Louisville, Holywood, Elkhorn, Auburndale, Stratford-on-Avon, Lowell Junction.

As the examples show, the parts of a compound noun may be joined (with or without a hyphen) or written separately. In some words usage is fixed, in others it varies. The hyphen, however, is less used than formerly.

NOTE. The first part of a compound noun usually limits the second after the manner of an adjective. Indeed, many expressions may be regarded either (1) as compounds or (2) as phrases containing an adjective and a noun. Thus *railway conductor* may be taken as a compound noun, or as a noun (*conductor*) limited by an adjective (*railway*).

### INFLECTION OF NOUNS

**65.** In studying the inflection of nouns and pronouns we have to consider **gender, number, person,** and **case.**

**1. Gender** is distinction according to sex.

**2. Number** is that property of substantives which shows whether they indicate one person or thing or more than one.

**3. Person** is that property of substantives which shows whether they designate (1) the speaker, (2) the person spoken to, or (3) the person or thing spoken of.

**4. Substantives** have inflections of case to indicate their grammatical relations to verbs, to prepositions, or to other substantives.

These four properties of substantives are included under inflection for convenience. In strictness, however, nouns are inflected for number and case only. Gender is shown in various ways, — usually by the meaning of the noun or by the use of some pronoun. Person is indicated by the sense, by the pronouns used, and by the form of the verb.

### I. GENDER

**66.** Gender is distinction according to sex.

Nouns and pronouns may be of the masculine, the feminine, or the neuter gender.

**1.** A noun or pronoun denoting a male being is of the masculine gender.

EXAMPLES : Joseph, boy, cockerel, buck, footman, butler, brother, father, uncle, he.

**2.** A noun or pronoun denoting a female being is of the feminine gender.

EXAMPLES : girl, Julia, hen, waitress, maid, doe, spinster, matron, aunt, squaw, she.

**3.** A noun or pronoun denoting a thing without animal life is of the neuter gender.

EXAMPLES : pencil, light, water, star, book, dust, leaf, it.

A noun or pronoun which is sometimes masculine and sometimes feminine is often said to be of **common gender**.

EXAMPLES : bird, speaker, artist, animal, cat, European, musician, operator, they.

**67.** A pronoun must be in the same gender as the noun for which it stands or to which it refers.

Each of the following pronouns is limited to a single gender :

> MASCULINE : *he, his, him.*
> FEMININE : *she, her, hers.*
> NEUTER : *it, its.*

All other pronouns vary in gender.

> *Robert* greeted *his* employer.  [Masculine.]
> A *mother* passed with *her* child.  [Feminine.]
> This *tree* has lost *its* foliage.  [Neuter.]
> *Who* laughed ?  [Masculine or feminine.]
> How do *you* do ?  [Masculine or feminine.]
> *They* have disappeared.  [Masculine, feminine, or neuter.]
> I do not care for *either*.  [Masculine, feminine, or neuter.]

**68.** A neuter noun may become masculine or feminine **by personification** (§ 60).

> Thou who didst waken from his summer **dreams**
> The blue Mediterranean. — SHELLEY.

> Stern daughter of the Voice of God!
> O Duty! — WORDSWORTH.

> Nature from her seat
> Sighing through all her works, gave signs of woe. — MILTON.

**69.** In speaking of certain objects, such as a ship and the moon, it is customary to use *she* and *her*. In like manner, *he* is used in speaking of the sun and of most animals, without reference to sex, although *it* often designates an insect or other small creature, and even a very young child.

*Who* and *which* are both used in referring to the **lower animals**. *Which* is the commoner, but *who* is not infrequent, especially if the animal is thought of as an intelligent being.

Thus one would say, "The dog *which* is for sale is in that kennel," even if one added, "*He* is a collie." But *which* would never be used in such a sentence as, "I have a dog *who* loves children."

**70.** The **gender** of masculine and of feminine nouns may be shown in various ways.

**1.** The male and the female of many kinds or classes of living beings are denoted by different words.

| MASCULINE | FEMININE | MASCULINE | FEMININE |
|---|---|---|---|
| father | mother | gander | goose |
| husband | wife | drake | duck |
| uncle | aunt | cock | hen |
| king | queen | ram | ewe |
| monk | nun | bull | cow |
| wizard | witch | hart | hind |
| lord | lady | buck | doe |
| horse | mare | fox | vixen [1] |

[1] *Vixen* is really formed from *fox* (compare the German *Füchsin* from *Fuchs*).

**2.** Some masculine nouns become feminine by the addition of an ending.

| MASCULINE | FEMININE | MASCULINE | FEMININE |
|-----------|----------|-----------|----------|
| heir | heiress | executor | executrix |
| baron | baroness | administrator | administratrix |
| lion | lioness | hero | heroine |
| prince | princess | Joseph | Josephine |
| emperor | empress | sultan | sultana |
| tiger | tigress | Philip | Philippa |

NOTE. The feminine gender is often indicated by the ending *ess*. Frequently the corresponding masculine form ends in *or* or *er*: as, — actor, actress; governor, governess; waiter, waitress. The ending *ess* is not so common as formerly. Usage favors *proprietor, author, editor*, etc., even for the feminine (rather than the harsher forms *proprietress, authoress, editress*), whenever there is no special reason for emphasizing the difference of sex.

**3.** A few feminine words become masculine by the addition of an ending. Thus, — *widow, widower; bride, bridegroom.*

**4.** Gender is sometimes indicated by the ending *man, woman, maid, boy,* or *girl.*

EXAMPLES : salesman, saleswoman ; foreman, forewoman ; laundryman ; milkmaid ; cash boy, cash girl.

**5.** A noun or a pronoun is sometimes prefixed to a noun to indicate gender.

EXAMPLES : manservant, maidservant ; mother bird ; cock sparrow, hen sparrow ; boy friend, girl friend ; he-wolf, she-wolf.

**6.** The gender of a noun may be indicated by some accompanying part of speech, usually by a pronoun.

My *cat* is always washing *his* face.
The *intruder* shook *her* head.
I was confronted by a pitiful *creature*, haggard and *unshaven*.

NOTE. The variations in form studied under 2 and 3 (above) are often regarded as inflections. In reality, however, the masculine and the feminine are different words. Thus, *baroness* is not an inflectional form of *baron*, but a distinct noun, made from *baron* by adding the ending *ess*, precisely as *barony* and *baronage* are made from *baron* by adding the endings *y* and *age*. The process is rather that of derivation or noun-formation than that of inflection.

## II. NUMBER

**71.** Number is that property of substantives which shows whether they indicate one person, place, or thing or more than one.

There are two numbers, — the singular and the plural.

The singular number denotes but one person, place, or thing. The plural number denotes more than one person, place, or thing.

**72.** Most nouns form the plural number by adding *s* or *es* to the singular.

Examples: mat, mats; wave, waves; problem, problems; bough, boughs; John, Johns; nurse, nurses; tense, tenses; bench, benches; dish, dishes; class, classes; fox, foxes.

### Special Rules

**1.** If the singular ends in *s*, *x*, *z*, *ch*, or *sh*, the plural ending is *es*.

Examples: loss, losses; box, boxes; buzz, buzzes; match, matches; rush, rushes.

**2.** Many nouns ending in *o* preceded by a consonant also take the ending *es* in the plural.

Examples: hero, heroes; cargo, cargoes; potato, potatoes; motto, mottoes; buffalo, buffaloes; mosquito, mosquitoes.

**3.** Nouns ending in *o* preceded by a vowel form their plural in *s*: as, — *cameo, cameos; folio, folios.*

**4.** The following nouns ending in *o* preceded by a consonant also form their plural in *s*: —

| | | | | | |
|---|---|---|---|---|---|
| banjo | casino | dynamo | memento[1] | quarto | torso |
| bravo | chromo | halo[1] | octavo | solo | tyro |
| burro | contralto | junto | piano | soprano | zero[1] |
| canto | duodecimo | lasso | proviso | stiletto | |

**73.** In some nouns the addition of the plural ending alters the spelling and even the sound of the singular form.

---

[1] *Halo, memento, zero* also form a plural in *es* (*haloes*, etc.).

**1.** Nouns ending in *y* preceded by a consonant change *y* to *i* and add *es* in the plural.

EXAMPLES : sky, skies ; fly, flies ; country, countries ; berry, berries. (Contrast : valley, valleys ; chimney, chimneys ; monkey, monkeys ; boy, boys ; day, days.)

Most proper names ending in *y*, however, take the plural in *s*.

EXAMPLES : Mary, Marys ; Murphy, Murphys ; Daly, Dalys ; Rowley, Rowleys ; May, Mays.

**2.** Some nouns ending in *f* or *fe*, change the *f* to *v* and add *es* or *s*.

EXAMPLES : wharf, wharves ; wife, wives ; shelf, shelves ; wolf, wolves ; thief, thieves ; knife, knives ; half, halves ; calf, calves ; life, lives ; self, selves ; sheaf, sheaves ; loaf, loaves ; leaf, leaves ; elf, elves ; beef, beeves.

**74.** A few nouns form their plural in *en*.

These are : ox, oxen ; brother, brethren (*or* brothers) ; child, children.

NOTE. Ancient or poetical plurals belonging to this class are : *eyne* (for *eyen*, from *eye*), *kine* (cows), *shoon* (shoes), *hosen* (hose).

**75.** A few nouns form their plural by a **change of vowel.**

These are : man, men ; woman, women ; merman, mermen ; foot, feet ; tooth, teeth ; goose, geese ; mouse, mice ; louse, lice. Also compound words ending in *man* or *woman*, such as fireman, firemen ; saleswoman, saleswomen ; Dutchman, Dutchmen.

NOTE. *German, Mussulman, Ottoman, dragoman, firman,* and *talisman,* which are not compounds of *man*, form their plurals regularly : as, — *Germans, Mussulmans. Norman* also forms its plural in *s*.

**76.** A few nouns have the same form in both singular and plural.

EXAMPLES : deer, sheep, heathen, Japanese, Portuguese, Iroquois.

NOTE. This class was larger in older English than at present. It included, for example, *year*, which in Shakspere has two plurals : — " six thousand *years*," " twelve *year* since."

**77.** A few nouns have two plurals, but usually with some difference in meaning.

| SINGULAR | PLURAL |
|---|---|
| brother | { brothers (relatives) <br> { brethren (members of the same society) |
| horse | { horses (animals) <br> { horse (cavalry) |
| foot | { feet (parts of the body) <br> { foot (infantry) |
| sail | { sails (on vessels) <br> { sail (vessels in a fleet) |
| head | { heads (in usual sense) <br> { head (of cattle) |
| fish | { fishes (individually) <br> { fish (collectively) |
| penny | { pennies (single coins) <br> { pence (collectively) |
| cloth | { cloths (pieces of cloth) <br> { clothes (garments) |
| die | { dies (for stamping) <br> { dice (for gaming) |

The *pennies* were arranged in neat piles.

English money is reckoned in pounds, shillings, and *pence*.

**78.** When **compound nouns** are made plural, the last part usually takes the plural form; less often the first part; rarely both parts.

EXAMPLES: spoonful, spoonfuls; bathhouse, bathhouses; forget-me-not, forget-me-nots; editor-in-chief, editors-in-chief; maid-of-honor, maids-of-honor; gentleman usher, gentlemen ushers; Knight Templar, Knights Templars; Lord Justice, Lords Justices; manservant, men-servants.

**79.** Letters of the alphabet, figures, signs used in writing, and words regarded merely as words take *'s* in the plural.

" Embarrassed " is spelled with two *r's* and two *s's*.

Your *3's* look like *8's*.

Tell the printer to change the §'s to ¶'s.

Don't interrupt me with your *but's*!

**80.** Foreign nouns in English sometimes retain their foreign plurals; but many have an English plural also.

Some of the commonest are included in the following list:[1]

| SINGULAR | PLURAL | SINGULAR | PLURAL |
|---|---|---|---|
| alumna (feminine) | alumnæ | genius | genii / geniuses |
| alumnus (masculine) | alumni | | |
| amanuensis | amanuenses | genus | genera |
| analysis | analyses | gymnasium | gymnasia / gymnasiums |
| animalculum | animalcula[2] | | |
| antithesis | antitheses | hippopotamus | hippopotami |
| appendix | appendices / appendixes | hypothesis | hypotheses |
| | | larva | larvæ |
| axis | axes | memorandum | memoranda / memorandums |
| bacillus | bacilli | | |
| bacterium | bacteria | nebula | nebulæ |
| bandit | banditti / bandits | oasis | oases |
| | | parenthesis | parentheses |
| basis | bases | phenomenon | phenomena |
| beau | beaux / beaus | radius | radii |
| | | seraph | seraphim / seraphs |
| candelabrum | candelabra | | |
| cumulus | cumuli | species | species |
| cherub | cherubim / cherubs | stratum | strata |
| | | synopsis | synopses |
| crisis | crises | tableau | tableaux |
| curriculum | curricula | tempo | tempi |
| datum | data | terminus | termini |
| ellipsis | ellipses | thesis | theses |
| erratum | errata | trousseau | trousseaux |
| formula | formulæ / formulas | vertebra | vertebræ |

The two plurals sometimes differ in meaning: as, —

Michael Angelo and Raphael were *geniuses*.
Spirits are sometimes called *genii*.
This book has two *indices*.
The printer uses signs called *indexes*.

[1] This list is intended for reference.
[2] The English word *animalcule* (plural *animalcules*) is preferable. The plural *animalculæ* is erroneous.

**81.** When a **proper name** with the title *Mr.*, *Mrs.*, *Miss*, or *Master*, is put into the plural, the rules are as follows : —

1. The plural of *Mr.* is *Messrs.* (pronounced *Messers* [1]). The name remains in the singular. Thus, —

> *Mr. Jackson*, plural *Messrs.* (or the *Messrs.*) *Jackson*.

2. *Mrs.* has no plural. The name itself takes the plural form. Thus, —

> *Mrs. Jackson*, plural *the Mrs. Jacksons*.

3. In the case of *Miss*, sometimes the title is put into the plural, sometimes the name. Thus, —

> *Miss Jackson*, plural *the Misses Jackson* or *the Miss Jacksons*.

The latter expression is somewhat informal. Accordingly, it would not be used in a formal invitation or reply, or in addressing a letter.

4. The plural of *Master* is *Masters*. The name remains in the singular. Thus, —

> *Master Jackson*, plural *the Masters Jackson*.

Other titles usually remain in the singular, the name taking the plural form : as, — *the two General Follansbys*. But when two or more names follow, the title becomes plural : as, — *Generals Rolfe and Johnson*.

**82.** Some nouns, on account of their meaning, are seldom or never used in the plural.

Such are many names of qualities (as *cheerfulness*, *mirth*), of sciences (as *chemistry* [2]), of forces (as *gravitation*).

Many nouns, commonly used in the singular only, may take a plural in some special sense. Thus, —

| | |
|---|---|
| earth (the globe) | earths (kinds of soil) |
| ice (frozen water) | ices (food) |
| tin (a metal) | tins (tin dishes or cans) |
| nickel (a metal) | nickels (coins) |

---

[1] *Messrs* is an abbreviation of the French *messieurs*.

[2] When such nouns as *chemistry* refer to textbooks, they may be used in the plural : as, — " Bring your *chemistries* to-morrow."

**83.** Some nouns are used in the plural only.

Such are: annals, athletics, billiards, dregs, eaves, entrails, lees, nuptials, oats, obsequies, pincers, proceeds, riches, scissors, shears, suds, tweezers, tongs, trousers, victuals, vitals; and (in certain special senses) ashes, goods, links, scales, spectacles, stocks.

**84.** A few nouns are plural in form, but singular in meaning.

Such are: gallows, news, measles, mumps, small pox (for *small pocks*), politics, and some names of sciences (as, civics, economics, ethics, mathematics, physics, optics).

NOTE. These nouns were formerly plural in sense as well as in form. *News*, for example, originally meant "new things." Shakspere uses it both as a singular and as a plural. Thus, — "*This news* was brought to Richard" (*King John*, v. 3. 12); "But wherefore do I tell *these news* to thee?" (*1 Henry IV*, iii. 2. 121). In a few words modern usage varies. The following nouns are sometimes singular, sometimes plural: *alms, amends, bellows, means, pains* (in the sense of "effort"), *tidings*.

### III. PERSON

**85.** Person is that property of substantives which shows whether they denote (1) the speaker, (2) the person spoken to, or (3) the person spoken of.

A substantive is in the first person when it denotes the speaker, in the second person when it denotes the person spoken to, in the third person when it denotes the person or thing spoken of.

> I, the *king*, command his presence. [First person.]
> You, *Thomas*, broke the window. [Second person.]
> *Charles*, come here. [Second person.]
> He, the *fireman*, saved the train. [Third person.]
> The *diver* sinks slowly from our view. [Third person.]
> The *tower* suddenly collapsed. [Third person.]

The examples show (1) that the person of a noun has nothing to do with its form, but is indicated by the sense or connection; (2) that certain pronouns denote person with precision. Thus, *I* is always of the first person; *you* of the second; and *he* of the third. These personal pronouns will be treated in Chapter III.

### IV. CASE

**86.** Substantives have inflections of case to indicate their grammatical relations to verbs, to prepositions, or to other substantives.

There are three cases, — the **nominative**, the **possessive**, and the **objective**.

The possessive case is often called the **genitive**.

The nominative and the objective case of a noun are always alike in form. In some pronouns, however, there is a difference (as, — *I, me ; he, him*).

### DECLENSION OF NOUNS

**87.** The inflection of a substantive is called its **declension**. To **decline** a noun is to give its case-forms in order, first in the singular number and then in the plural. Thus, —

#### SINGULAR

| | | | | |
|---|---|---|---|---|
| *Nominative* | boy | horse | fly | chimney |
| *Possessive* | boy's | horse's | fly's | chimney's |
| *Objective* | boy | horse | fly | chimney |

#### PLURAL

| | | | | |
|---|---|---|---|---|
| *Nominative* | boys | horses | flies | chimneys |
| *Possessive* | boys' | horses' | flies' | chimneys' |
| *Objective* | boys | horses | flies | chimneys |

#### SINGULAR

| | | | | |
|---|---|---|---|---|
| *Nominative* | calf | lass | man | deer |
| *Possessive* | calf's | lass's | man's | deer's |
| *Objective* | calf | lass | man | deer |

#### PLURAL

| | | | | |
|---|---|---|---|---|
| *Nominative* | calves | lasses | men | deer |
| *Possessive* | calves' | lasses' | men's | deer's |
| *Objective* | calves | lasses | men | deer |

### Nominative Case

**88.** The **nominative case** is used in the following constructions: (1) the subject, (2) the predicate nominative, (3) the vocative (or nominative of direct address), (4) the exclamatory nominative, (5) appositive with a nominative, (6) the nominative absolute.

1. **The subject of a verb is in the nominative case.**

> *Water* freezes.
> *Charles* climbed the mountain.
> The boy's *face* glowed with health and exercise.
> A thousand *men* were killed in this battle.

In the third example, *face* is the simple subject; the complete subject is *the boy's face*. In the fourth, *men* is the simple subject; the complete subject is *a thousand men*. Both *face* and *men* are in the nominative case; *face* is in the singular number; *men* in the plural.

2. **A substantive standing in the predicate, but describing or defining the subject, agrees with the subject in case and is called a predicate nominative.**

A predicate nominative is also called a **subject complement** or an **attribute**.

> Lobsters are *crustaceans*.
> A good book is a faithful *friend*.
> Shakspere was a *native* of Stratford-on-Avon.
> Arnold proved a *traitor*.
> Adams was elected *president*.

The rule for the case of the predicate nominative is particularly important with respect to pronouns (§ 119).

> I am *he*.          Are you *she?*
> It is *I*.          It was *we* who did it.

The predicate nominative is commonest after the copula *is* (in its various forms). It will be further studied in connection with intransitive and passive verbs (§§ 214, 252).

**3. A substantive used for the purpose of addressing a person directly, and not connected with any verb, is called a vocative.**

A vocative is in the nominative case, and is often called a **nominative by direct address** or a **vocative nominative**.

> Come, *Ruth*, give me your hand.
> Turn to the right, *madam*.
> *Herbert*, it is your turn.
> Come with me, my *child*.

NOTE. A vocative word is sometimes said to be **independent by direct address**, because it stands by itself, unconnected with any verb. That a vocative is really in the nominative case may be seen in the use of the pronoun *thou* in this construction: as, — I will arrest thee, *thou* traitor (see § 115).

**4. A substantive used as an exclamation is called an exclamatory nominative (or nominative of exclamation).**

> *Peace*, be still.
> Fortunate *Ruth !*
> A *drum !* a *drum !* Macbeth doth come.
> Look ! a *balloon !*
> The *sun !* then we shall have a fine day.

Certain exclamatory nominatives are sometimes classed as interjections (§ 375).

**5. A substantive added to another substantive to explain it and signifying the same person or thing, is called an appositive and is said to be in apposition.**

**An appositive is in the same case as the substantive which it limits.**

Hence a substantive in apposition with a nominative is in the nominative case.

Mr. Scott, the *grocer*, is here. [Apposition with subject.]
Tom, old *fellow*, I am glad to see you. [Apposition with vocative.]
The discoverer of the Pacific was Balboa, a *Spaniard*. [Apposition with predicate nominative.]

NOTE. *Apposition* means "attachment"; *appositive* means "attached noun or pronoun." An appositive modifies the noun with which it is in apposition much as an adjective might do (compare "Balboa, a *Spaniard*" with "*Spanish* Balboa"). Hence it is classed as an adjective modifier.

## Possessive Case

**89.  The possessive case denotes ownership or possession.**

> *John's* yacht lies at her moorings.
> The *duck's* feet are webbed.
> The *mutineer's* pistol burst when he fired.

NOTE. Most uses of the possessive come under the general head of **possession** in some sense. Special varieties of meaning are **source** (as in " *hen's* eggs ") and **authorship** (as in " *Wordsworth's* sonnets ").

A possessive noun or pronoun modifies the substantive to which it is attached as an adjective might do. Hence it is classed as an adjective modifier

## Forms of the Possessive Case

**90.  The possessive case of most nouns has, in the singular number, the ending *'s*.**

EXAMPLES : the owl's feathers, Elizabeth's hat, the officer's name.

**Plural nouns ending in *s* take no further ending for the possessive. In writing, however, an apostrophe is put after the *s* to indicate the possessive case.**

EXAMPLES: the owls' feathers, the officers' names, the artists' petition, the engineers' ball.

**Plural nouns not ending in *s* take *'s* in the possessive.**

EXAMPLES : the firemen's ball, the policemen's quarters, the children's hour.

NOTE. In older English the possessive of most nouns was written as well as pronounced with the ending *-es* or *-is*. Thus, in Chaucer, the possessive of *child* is *childës* or *childis ;* that of *king* is *kingës* or *kingis ;* that of *John* is *Johnës* or *Johnis*. The use of an apostrophe in the possessive is a comparatively modern device, due to a misunderstanding. Scholars at one time thought the *s* of the possessive a fragment of the pronoun *his ;* that is, they took such a phrase as *George's book* for a contraction of *George his book*. Hence they used the apostrophe before *s* to signify the supposed omission of part of the word *his*. Similarly, in the possessive plural, there was thought to be an omission of a final *es ;* that is, such a phrase as *the horses' heads* was thought to be a contraction of the *horseses* heads. Both these errors have long been exploded.

**91.** Nouns like *sheep* and *deer*, which have the same form in both the singular and the plural, usually take *'s* in the possessive plural.

Thus, *the deer's tracks* would be written, whether one deer or more were meant.

**92.** POSSESSIVE SINGULAR OF NOUNS ENDING IN *S*.

1. Monosyllabic nouns ending in *s* or an *s*-sound usually make their possessive singular by adding *'s*.

EXAMPLES: Charles's hat, Forbes's garden, Mr. Wells's daughter, Rice's carriage, Mrs. Dix's family, a fox's brush.

NOTE. Most of these monosyllabic nouns in *s* are family names. The rule accords with the best usage; but it is not absolute, for usage varies. Hence forms like *Charles'* and *Wells'* cannot be condemned as positively wrong, though *Charles's* and *Wells's* are preferable. In speaking, the shorter form is often ambiguous, for there is no difference in sound between *Dix'* and *Dick's*, *Mr. Hills'* and *Mr. Hill's*, *Dr. Childs'* and *Dr. Child's*.

2. Nouns of two or more syllables ending in *s* or an *s*-sound, and not accented on the last syllable, may make their possessive singular by adding *'s*, or may take no ending in the possessive.

In the latter case, an apostrophe is added in writing, but in sound there is no difference between the possessive and the nominative.

EXAMPLES: Burrows's (*or* Burrows') Hotel, Æneas's (*or* Æneas') voyage, Beatrice's (*or* Beatrice') gratitude, Felix's (*or* Felix') arrival, for conscience's (*or* conscience') sake.

Most of the nouns in question are proper names. In speaking, one must often use the longer form to prevent ambiguity; for *Williams'* and *William's*, *Roberts'* and *Robert's*, *Robbins'* and *Robin's*, are indistinguishable in sound.

NOTE. Nouns of two or more syllables ending in *s* or an *s*-sound and accented on the last syllable, follow the rule for monosyllables. Thus, — *Laplace's* mathematics (not *Laplace'*); *Alphonse's* father (not *Alphonse'*).

When final *s* is silent (as in many French names), *'s* must of course be added in the possessive. Thus, — *Descartes's* philosophy (pronounced *Daycárt's*).

## Use of the Possessive Case

**93.**[1] Possession may be denoted by a phrase with *of* as well as by the possessive case. The distinction between the two forms cannot be brought under rigid rules, but the following suggestions will be of use.

I. In older English and in poetry the possessive case of nouns is freely used, but in modern prose it is rare unless the possessor is a living being. A phrase with *of* is used instead.

> The mayor *of Detroit* (NOT *Detroit's* mayor).
> The top *of the post* (NOT the *post's* top).
> The prevalence *of the epidemic* (NOT the *epidemic's* prevalence).

Contrast the poetic use : —

> *Belgium's* capital had gathered then
> Her beauty and her chivalry. — BYRON.

Other prepositions are sometimes used: as, — " the explosion in *New York* " (NOT " *New York's* explosion "), " the station *at Plymouth*."

II. When the possessor is a living being, good usage varies.

1. If there is actual ownership or possession of some material thing, the possessive case is generally used in the singular: as, — " John's hat " (not " the hat *of John* "). The possessive plural, however, is often replaced by a phrase with *of*, to avoid ambiguity or harshness : as, — " the jewels *of the ladies* " (rather than " the *ladies'* jewels ")[2], " the wings *of the geese* " (rather than " the *geese's* wings ").

2. With nouns denoting a quality, an act, or the like, either the possessive or the *of*-phrase is proper : as, — " *John's* generosity," or " the generosity *of John* " ; " *John's* condition," or " the condition *of John* " ; " the *guide's* efforts," or " the efforts *of the guide* " ; " *Cæsar's* death," or " the death *of Cæsar*."

When there is any choice, it usually depends on euphony (that is, agreeable sound), and is therefore a question of style. Sometimes, however, there is a distinction in sense. " *John's* fear," for example, indicates that John is afraid ; but " the fear *of John* " means the fear which John inspires in others.

---

[1] This section is intended chiefly for reference.
[2] Note the ambiguity to the ear though not to the eye.

III. The following phrases are established idioms with the possessive. In some of them, however, the possessive may be replaced by *of* and its object.

(1) The earth's surface, the sun's rays, the moon's reflection, the pit's mouth, a rope's end, his journey's end, at his wit's end, the ship's keel, the water's edge, the cannon's mouth, out of harm's way, at swords' points, for pity's sake, for conscience' sake ; (2) a moment's pause, a year's time, a hand's breadth, a boat's length, a month's salary, a week's notice, a night's rest, a day's work, a stone's throw, a feather's weight, an hour's delay, a dollar's worth, not a foot's difference.

In the second group of phrases ("a moment's pause," etc.), the possessive denotes not ownership, but **measure** or **extent**.

IV. The possessive case of certain pronouns (*my, our, your, his, her, its, their*) is more freely used than that of nouns in expressions that do not denote actual ownership.

I know him to *my* sorrow. [Compare : to his loss, to our detriment, to his advantage.]
The brass has lost *its* polish.
This question must be decided on *its* merits.
His arguments did not fail of *their* effect.

For the inflection of these pronouns, see § 115. For the use of *whose*, see § 152.

**94.** When a thing belongs to two or more **joint owners,** the sign of the possessive is added to the last name only.

Brown, Jones, and Richardson's factories. [Brown, Jones, and Richardson are partners.]

It is George and William's turn to take the boat. [George and William are to go in the boat together.]

On the other hand, in order to avoid ambiguity we should say, "Brown's, Jones's, and Richardson's factories," if each individual had a factory of his own ; and "George's and William's answers were correct," if each boy answered independently of the other.

**95.** In **compound nouns** the last part takes the possessive sign. So also when a phrase is used as a noun.

My *father-in-law's* home is in Easton.
We had *a quarter of an hour's* talk.

Other examples are the following : —

My brother-in-law's opinion ; the commander-in-chief's orders ; the lady-in-waiting's duties ; the coal dealer's prices ; Edward VII's reign ; the King of England's portrait ; half a year's delay ; in three or four months' time ; a cable and a half's length ; the pleasure of Major Pen-dennis and Mr. Arthur Pendennis's company (THACKERAY).

NOTE. Noun-phrases often contain two substantives, the second of which is in apposition with the first. In such phrases, *of* is generally preferable to the possessive. Thus, we may say either "Tom the blacksmith's daughter" or "the daughter of Tom the blacksmith"; but "the son of Mr. Hill the carpenter" is both neater and clearer than "Mr. Hill the carpenter's son." The use of *'s* is also avoided with a very long phrase like "the owner of the house on the other side of the street."

An objective may stand in apposition with a possessive, the latter being equivalent to *of* with an object. Thus, — "I am not yet of Percy's mind [ = of the mind of Percy], the *Hotspur* of the North" (SHAKSPERE).

**96.** The noun denoting the object possessed is often omitted when it may be readily understood, especially in the predicate.

> *Conant's* [shop] is open until noon.
> I buy my hats at *Bryant's* [shop].
> We will dine at *Pennock's* [restaurant].
> That camera is *mine*. (See § 122.)

This construction is common in such expressions as : —

> He was a relative of *John's*.
> That careless tongue of *John's* will get him into trouble.

In the first example, "a relative of John's" means "a relative of (=*from among*) John's relatives." The second example shows an extension of this construction by analogy. See § 122.

### OBJECTIVE CASE

**97.** The objective case, as its name implies, is the case of the object. Most of its uses are covered by the following rule : —

**The object of a verb or preposition is in the objective case.**

The object of a preposition has already been explained and defined (§§ 20–21).

**98.** The object of a verb may be (1) the direct object, (2) the predicate objective, (3) the indirect object, (4) the cognate object. Of these the direct object is the most important.

The objective is also used (5) adverbially (§ 109), (6) in apposition with another objective (§ 110), and (7) as the subject of an infinitive (§ 111).

### 1. Direct Object

**99.** Some verbs may be followed by a substantive denoting that which receives the action or is produced by it. These are called transitive verbs. All other verbs are called intransitive.

1. That man *struck* my *dog*.
2. The arrow *hit* the *target*.
3. Cæsar *conquered Gaul*.
4. Mr. Holland *sells flour*.
5. The farmer *raises corn*.
6. Mr. Eaton *makes stoves*.
7. My grandfather *built* that *house*.

In Nos. 1–4, the verb is followed by a noun denoting the receiver of the action. Thus, in the first sentence, the *dog* receives the blow; in the second, the *target* receives the action of hitting. In Nos. 5–7, the verb is followed by a noun denoting the product of the action. For example, the *corn* is produced by the action expressed by the verb *raises*.

In each example, the noun that follows the verb completes the sense of the verb. "That man *struck* ——." "Struck *whom?*" "He struck the *dog*." Until *dog* is added the sense of the verb *struck* is incomplete.

**100.** A substantive that completes the meaning of a transitive verb is called its direct object, and is said to be in the objective case.

Thus, in the examples above, *dog* is the direct object of the transitive verb *struck*; *target* is the direct object of *hit*, — and so on. Each of these nouns is therefore in the objective case.

The direct object is often called the object complement, or the object of the verb.

**101.** Intransitive verbs have no object.

> The lion *roared*.
> The visitor *coughed* gently.
> The log *drifted* downstream.
> We all *listened* intently.

Compare these sentences with those in § 99. We observe that the verbs (unlike those in § 99) admit no object, since their meaning is complete without the addition of any noun to denote the receiver or product of the action. " The man *struck* —— " prompts the inquiry, " Struck *whom?* " But no such question is suggested by " The lion *roared* " ; for " Roared *what?* " would be an absurdity.

**102.** The predicate nominative (§ 88, 2) must not be confused with the direct object. They resemble each other in two particulars : (1) both stand in the predicate, and (2) both complete the meaning of the verb. But they differ utterly in their relation to the subject of the sentence. For —

The predicate nominative describes or defines the subject. Hence both substantives denote the same person or thing.

Charles [SUBJECT] { is / was / became / was elected } *captain* [PREDICATE NOMINATIVE].

The direct object neither describes nor defines the subject. On the contrary, it designates that upon which the subject acts. Hence the two substantives regularly [1] denote different persons or things.

Charles [SUBJECT] { struck *James* [OBJECT]. / threw a *stone* [OBJECT]. / built a *boat* [OBJECT]. }

Both the direct object and the predicate nominative are classed as complements, because they are used to complete the sense of the predicate verb (§ 483).

---

[1] The only exception is in reflexive action, where the object is a compound personal pronoun (" Charles deceived *himself* "). See § 126.

**103.** A verb of *asking* sometimes takes **two direct objects,** one denoting the **person** and the other the **thing.**

> She asked the *boy* his *name.*
> Ask *me* no *favors.*
> I asked the *lawyer* his *opinion.*

## 2. Predicate Objective

**104.** Verbs of *choosing, calling, naming, making,* and *thinking* may take two objects referring to the same person or thing.

The first of these is the direct object, and the second, which completes the sense of the predicate, is called a predicate objective.

We chose Oscar *president.* [*Oscar* is the direct object of *chose; president* is the predicate objective.]
I call John my *friend.*
They thought the man a *coward.*
Make my house your *home.*

The **predicate objective** is often called the **complementary object** or the **objective attribute.** It is classed as a **complement.**

An adjective may serve as predicate objective.

> I call this ship *unseaworthy.*
> Your letter made your sister *anxious.*
> What makes Edwin so *careless ?*

## 3. Indirect Object and Similar Idioms

**105.** Some verbs of *giving, telling, refusing,* and the like, may take two objects, a direct object and an indirect object.

The indirect object denotes the person or thing toward whom or toward which is directed the action expressed by the rest of the predicate.

| DIRECT OBJECT ONLY | DIRECT OBJECT AND INDIRECT OBJECT |
|---|---|
| Dick sold his bicycle. | Dick sold *John* his bicycle. |
| I gave permission. | I gave this *man* permission. |
| He paid a dollar. | He paid the *gardener* a dollar. |
| She taught Latin. | She taught my *children* Latin. |

Most of the verbs that admit an indirect object are included in the following list : —

allot, allow, assign, bequeath, bring, deny, ensure, fetch, fling, forbid, forgive, give, grant, guarantee, hand, lease, leave, lend, let, owe, pardon, pass, pay, refund, refuse, remit, restore, sell, send, show, sing, spare, teach, tell, throw, toss, vouchsafe.

Pronouns are commoner as indirect objects than nouns.

> They denied *her* the necessities of life.
> I guaranteed *them* a handsome profit.
> The king vouchsafed *them* an audience.

**It is always possible to insert the preposition *to* before the indirect object without changing the sense.**

Since the indirect object is equivalent to an adverbial phrase, it is classed as a modifier of the verb.

Thus, in " Dick sold *John* his bicycle," *John* is an adverbial modifier of the predicate verb *sold*.

The indirect object is sometimes used without a direct object expressed. Thus, —

> He paid the hatter.

Here *hatter* may be recognized as an indirect object by inserting *to* before it and adding a direct object (" his *bill*," " his *money*," or the like).

**106.** The objective case sometimes expresses the person *for whom* anything is done.

> William made his *brother* a kite [ = made a kite for his brother].
> Sampson built *me* a boat [ = built a boat for me].

This construction may be called the **objective of service.**

NOTE. The objective of service is often included under the head of the indirect object. But the two constructions differ widely in sense, and should be carefully distinguished. To do an act *to* a person is not the same thing as to do an act *for* a person. Contrast " John paid the money *to* me," with " John paid the money *for* me "; " Dick sold a bicycle *to* me," with " Dick sold a bicycle *for* me."

**107.** The objective case is used after *like, unlike, near,* and *next,* which are really adjectives or adverbs, though in this construction they are often regarded as prepositions.

> She sang like a *bird*. [*Like* is an adverb.]
> The earth is like a *ball*. [*Like* is an adjective.]
> My office is near the *station*. [*Near* is an adjective.]
> That answer was unlike *Joseph*. [*Unlike* is an adjective.]
> This man walks unlike *Joseph*. [*Unlike* is an adverb.]
> A stream ran near the *hut*. [*Near* is an adverb.]

The use of the objective after these words is a peculiar idiom similar to the indirect object (§ 105). The nature of the construction may be seen (as in the indirect object) by inserting *to* or *unto* ("She sang *like unto* a bird").

NOTE. The indirect object, the objective of service, and the objective after *like, unlike,* and *near* are all survivals of old dative constructions. Besides the case of the direct object (often called **accusative**), English once had a case (called the **dative**) which meant *to* or *for* [somebody or something]. The dative case is easily distinguished in Greek, Latin, and German, but in English it has long been merged in form with the ordinary objective.

#### 4. Cognate Object

**108.** A verb that is regularly intransitive sometimes takes as object a noun whose meaning closely resembles its own.

A noun in this construction is called the **cognate object** of the verb and is in the objective case.

> He ran a *race*.
> The mayor coughed a dubious, insinuating *cough*.
> A scornful *laugh* laughed he.
> The trumpeter blew a loud *blast*.
> She sleeps the *sleep* of death.

NOTE. *Cognate* means "kindred" or "related." The cognate object repeats the idea of the verb, often with some modification, and may be classed as an adverbial modifier. Its difference from the direct object may be seen by contrasting "The blacksmith struck the *anvil*" with "The blacksmith struck a mighty *blow*" (cf. "struck *mightily*"). For the pronoun *it* as cognate object, see § 120.

### 5. Adverbial Objective

**109.** A noun, or a phrase consisting of a noun and its modifiers, may be used adverbially. Such a noun is called an adverbial objective.

> We have waited *years* for this reform.
> I am *years* older than you are.
> The river is *miles* away.
> The water rose *three feet*.
> This is *an inch* too long.
> My brother is *twenty years* old.
> I will stay *a short time*.
> Wait *a moment*.
> Come here *this instant!*
> Turn your eyes *this way*.
> This silk is *several shades* too light.

A group of words consisting of an adverbial object with its modifier or modifiers forms an **adverbial phrase** (§ 41).

### 6. Objective in Apposition

**110.** A substantive in apposition with an objective is itself in the objective case.

Yesterday I saw Williams the *expressman*. [Apposition with the direct object of *saw*.]

Tom gave his friend *John* a book. [Apposition with the indirect object *friend*.]

He lives with Andrews the *blacksmith*. [Apposition with the object of the preposition *with*.]

This rule follows from the general principle that an appositive is in the same case as the substantive to which it is attached (§ 88, 5).

### 7. Subject of an Infinitive

**111.** The subject of an infinitive is in the objective case.

This construction will be treated in connection with the uses of the infinitive (§ 325).

## Parsing

**112.** To **parse** a word is to describe its grammatical form and to give its construction.

In parsing a **noun,** we mention the class to which it belongs, give its gender, number, person, and case, and tell why it is in that case. Thus, —

1. Frank shot a wolf.

*Frank* is a proper noun of the masculine gender, in the singular number and third person. It is in the nominative case, because it is the subject of the verb *shot.*

*Wolf* is a common noun of the masculine or feminine [or common] gender, in the singular number and third person. It is in the objective case, because it is the object [or direct object] of the transitive verb *shot.*

2. Jane, come here.

*Jane* is a proper noun of the feminine gender, in the singular number and second person. It is in the nominative case, being used as a vocative (or in direct address).

3. The rope is fifteen feet long.

*Feet* is a common noun of the neuter gender, in the plural number and third person. It is in the objective case, being used as an adverbial modifier of the adjective *long.*

4. Edgar's boat is a sloop.

*Edgar's* is a proper noun of the masculine gender, in the singular number and third person. It is in the possessive case, modifying the noun *boat.*

# CHAPTER III

## PRONOUNS

**113.** A pronoun is a word used instead of a noun. It designates a person, place, or thing without naming it.

The substantive to which a pronoun refers is called its antecedent.

A pronoun must agree with its antecedent in gender, number, and person (§ 11).

Pronouns have in general the same constructions as nouns.

**114.** Pronouns may be classified as (1) **personal**, (2) **adjective**, (3) **relative**, and (4) **interrogative**.

Under adjective pronouns are included (*a*) **demonstrative pronouns** and (*b*) **indefinite pronouns**.

### PERSONAL PRONOUNS

**115.** The personal pronouns serve to distinguish (1) the speaker, (2) the person spoken to, and (3) the person, place, or thing spoken of (§ 85).

They are declined as follows : —

#### THE PRONOUN OF THE FIRST PERSON : *I*

| SINGULAR | | PLURAL | |
|---|---|---|---|
| *Nominative* | I | *Nominative* | we |
| *Possessive* | my *or* mine | *Possessive* | our *or* ours |
| *Objective* | me | *Objective* | us |

#### THE PRONOUN OF THE SECOND PERSON : *thou*

| SINGULAR | | PLURAL | |
|---|---|---|---|
| *Nominative* | thou | *Nominative* | you *or* ye |
| *Possessive* | thy *or* thine | *Possessive* | your *or* yours |
| *Objective* | thee | *Objective* | you *or* ye |

THE PRONOUN OF THE THIRD PERSON: *he, she, it*

|              | SINGULAR  |             |         | PLURAL |
|--------------|-----------|-------------|---------|--------|
|              | MASCULINE | FEMININE    | NEUTER  | MASCULINE, FEMININE, and NEUTER |
| *Nominative* | he        | she         | it      | they   |
| *Possessive* | his       | her *or* hers | its   | their *or* theirs |
| *Objective*  | him       | her         | it      | them   |

Unlike nouns, most of the personal pronouns have distinct forms for the nominative and the objective.

NOTE. The possessive case of personal pronouns never has the apostrophe. Thus, — *its, yours, theirs.*
The form *it's* is proper only as a contraction of *it is.*

### GENDER AND NUMBER

**116.** The pronouns of the first and second persons (*I* and *thou*) may be either masculine or feminine.

The pronouns of the third person have different forms for masculine, feminine, and neuter in the **singular** (*he, she, it*); but in the **plural** the form *they* serves for all three genders.

NOTE. In the oldest English *his* was both masculine and neuter. The neuter use lasted until the seventeenth century. Thus, —

> That same eye whose bend doth awe the world
> Did lose *his* lustre. — SHAKSPERE, *Julius Cæsar*, i. 2. 123.

**117.** *Thou, thy, thine, thee,* and *ye* are old forms still found in poetry and the solemn style.

In ordinary prose, *you, your,* and *yours* are the only forms used for the second person, whether singular or plural. Yet *you,* even when denoting a single person, always takes the verb-forms that go with plural subjects. Thus, —

> My friend, *you were* [NOT *was*] in error.

Hence *you* may best be regarded as always plural in form, but may be described as singular in sense when it stands for one person only.

NOTE. Members of the Society of Friends (commonly called Quakers) and of some other religious bodies use *thee* and *thy* in their ordinary conversation.

*Ye* was formerly the regular nominative plural, and *you* the objective ; but the forms were afterwards confused. *Ye* has gone out of use except in poetry and the solemn style, and *you* is now the regular form for both nominative and objective.

Where an objective form *ye* is found printed instead of *you* (as often in Shakspere, — "A southwest blow on *ye* "), it represents an indistinct pronunciation of *you* rather than the old nominative *ye*. This indistinct sound may still be heard in rapid or careless speech ("I'll tell yer the truth ").

*Ye* as an abbreviation for *the* (as in " *ye* old town ") has nothing to do with the pronoun *ye*. The *y* simply stands for the character þ (an old sign for *th*), and the abbreviation was pronounced *the*, never *ye*.

**118.** *They, you,* and *we* are often used indefinitely for " one " or " people in general."

> *They* say that Joe has gone to sea.
> To shut off the steam, *you* close both valves of the radiator.

NOTE. *We, our,* and *us* are used in editorial articles instead of *I, my,* and *me,* because the writer represents the whole editorial staff. This practice should not be followed in ordinary composition.

A sovereign ruler may use *we, our,* and *us* when speaking of himself in proclamations and other formal documents. This construction is often called "the plural of majesty." Thus, —

> Know that *we* have divided
> In three *our* kingdom. — SHAKSPERE.

The form *'em* (as in " Tell me your counsels; I will not disclose *'em,*" in *Julius Cæsar*) is not a contraction of *them,* but of *hem,* an old objective plural of *he.*

### CASE OF PERSONAL PRONOUNS

#### NOMINATIVE CASE

**119.** Nominative constructions of the personal pronouns are the same as those of nouns (§ 88).

> *I* am ready. [Subject.]
> It is *I.* [Predicate nominative.]
> Here, *you* rascal, what are you about? [Vocative, direct address.]
> Poor *you!* [Nominative of exclamation.]
> General Austin, *he* and no other, won the battle. [Apposition.]

For the nominative absolute, see § 345.

Care must be taken not to use an objective form when a predicate nominative is required.

> It is *I* [NOT *me*].
> It is *we* [NOT *us*] who did it.
> It was *he* [NOT *him*] who told us.
> It was *they* [NOT *them*] who were to blame.

**120.** *It* has several peculiar uses in the nominative.

**1.** *It* is used as the subject in many expressions like "It rains," "It snows," "It lightens," "It is cold," where no definite subject is thought of. In this use, *it* is said to be **impersonal.**

NOTE. An impersonal *it* also occurs as a cognate object (§ 108) in colloquial language: as, — "Hang it!" "Go it!" "He went it." "He farmed it for a year." Other examples of the indefinite and impersonal *it* in various constructions are: "We are roughing *it*." "Keep *it* up." "You'll catch *it*." "Let *it* all go." "He made a poor job of *it*." "He made a success of *it*."

**2.** *It* often serves as grammatical subject merely to introduce the verb *is*, the real subject of the thought standing in the predicate. In this use *it* is called an **expletive** (or "filler").

> *It* is he.
> *It* is Christmas.
> *It* was a tiresome ride.

In these examples, the subject of the thought (*he, Christmas, ride*) appears as a predicate nominative.

**3.** The antecedent of *it* is often a group of words.

> Wearing tight shoes is foolish. *It* deforms the feet.

**121.** In **imperative sentences** the subject (*you*) is commonly omitted: as, — "Shut the door."

NOTE. The subject *I* is sometimes omitted in wishes (as, "*Would* he were here!" for "I would that he were here"). So also in "Thank you," "Pray tell me" (compare *prithee* for "I pray thee").

Expressions like "Canst tell?" (for "Canst thou tell?"), "Art there?" (for "Art thou there?") are common in poetry and older English. These come from the gradual wearing away and final disappearance of the pronoun *thou* (*canst thou, canstow, canstē, canst*).

## Possessive Case

**122.** The **possessive** forms *my, thy, our, your, her,* and *their* are used when a noun follows; *mine, thine, ours, yours, hers,* and *theirs* cannot be followed by a noun, and stand commonly in the predicate. *His* may be used in either way.

| | |
|---|---|
| *My* brother has arrived. | The fault is *mine.* |
| *Our* work is done. | Those seats are *ours.* |
| I have torn *your* glove. | This pencil is *yours.* |
| *Their* turn has come. | That field is *theirs.* |
| *His* hair is black. | The book is not *his.* |

Examples of *mine, yours,* etc. not in the predicate are:

> *Mine* was a terrier; *yours* was a pointer.
> *Theirs* is a red motor car.
> *Ours* broke down last night.
> *His* leaked badly.
> His name is Martin; *hers* is Smith.

In such cases the pronoun is always emphatic. The construction is chiefly colloquial.

NOTE. In older English and in poetry *mine* and *thine* are common instead of *my* and *thy* before words beginning with a vowel or *h*: as, —

> *Mine* eyes dazzle: she died young. — JOHN WEBSTER.
> The very minute bids thee ope *thine* ear. — SHAKSPERE.

*Mine* is sometimes used after a vocative noun: as, — *brother mine.*
For expressions like "a friend of *mine,*" "that unruly tongue of *yours,*" see § 96.

**123.** When two or more separate objects are spoken of as possessed, a possessive should precede the name of each if there is danger of ambiguity.

I will send for our secretary and our treasurer. [Two persons.]
I will send for our secretary and treasurer. [One person.]
I have called for my bread and my milk. [Two things.]
I have called for my bread and milk. [A mixture.]
Have you Bacon's "Essays and Apophthegms"? [One book.]
Have you Bacon's "Essays" and his "Advancement of Learning"?
[Two books.]

### OBJECTIVE CASE

**124.** The commonest constructions in which personal pronouns take the **objective case** are the following : —

1. Object of a preposition (§ 97) : as, —

> Take it from *him*.

2. Direct object of a transitive verb (§ 99) : as, —

> I will find *you*.

3. Indirect object of a transitive verb (§ 105) : as, —

> He gave *me* a dollar.

4. Subject of an infinitive (see § 325).

NOTE. In poetry the objective *me* is sometimes used in exclamations : as, — " *Me* miserable ! " (MILTON).

In *methinks* and *meseems* (" it seems to me "), *me* is a remnant of the old dative, as in the indirect object (see § 107).

The compounds *thereof, therewith, therefrom*, etc., are equivalent to *of it, with it, from it*, etc.: as, — " Proclaim liberty throughout all the land unto all the inhabitants *thereof*" (*Leviticus* xxv. 10).

For the impersonal *it* as cognate object, see § 120.

### THE *SELF*-PRONOUNS (COMPOUND PERSONAL PRONOUNS)

**125.** The three **compound personal pronouns** are made by adding the word *self* to certain forms of the personal pronouns. Thus, —

> myself, *plural* ourselves ;
> thyself *or* yourself, *plural* yourselves ;
> himself, herself, itself, *plural* themselves.

To these may be added the indefinite *oneself*, more commonly written as two words, *one's self* (§ 139).

Observe that *yourself* is singular, and *yourselves* plural. *Hisself* and *theirselves* are incorrect forms. *Ourself* (not *ourselves*) is the compound pronoun corresponding to the royal *we* (§ 118).

> What touches us *ourself* shall be last served. — SHAKSPERE.

**126.** 1. The compound personal pronouns may be used to **emphasize** substantives.

In this use they are called intensive pronouns.

> I *myself* will go.
> King Alfred *himself* took the field.
> They did the work *themselves*.

An intensive pronoun is in apposition with the substantive to which it refers.

**2.** The compound personal pronouns may be used as the objects of transitive verbs or of prepositions when the object denotes the same person or thing as the subject.

In this use they are called reflexive pronouns.

> I have hurt *myself*.
> King Alfred interested *himself* in his subjects.
> These schemers deceived *themselves*.
> Mary was talking to *herself*.
> He gave *himself* a holiday. [Indirect object.]

These pronouns are called **reflexive** (that is, " bending back ") because they **refer back** to the subject and repeat its meaning in an object construction.

Note. A reflexive pronoun sometimes refers to a substantive in the objective case: as, — " Our captors left *us* to *ourselves*."

In older English the simple personal pronouns *me*, *thee*, etc., were often used reflexively: as, — " I held *me* [= *myself*] still "; " Yield *thee* [= *thyself*] captive"; " They built *them* [= *for themselves*] houses " (see § 106). This idiom survives in colloquial language (as, " I have hurt *me*," " I have bought *me* a rifle "), but it is avoided in writing except in a few expressions such as: " I must look about *me* "; " We gazed about *us* "; " Look behind *you*."

**127.** The adjective *own* is sometimes inserted between the first and the second part of the *self*-pronouns for emphasis.

Examples : my own self, your own self, his own self, our own selves, their own selves.

In this use, *self* is in strictness a noun limited by the possessive and by the adjective *own*, but the phrases may be regarded as compound pronouns. Other adjectives are sometimes inserted between the possessive and *self* : as, — my *very* self, his *worthless* self.

**128.** The intensive pronouns are sometimes used without a substantive. Thus, —

> It is *myself*. [*Myself = I myself*.]
> You are hardly *yourself* to-day.

In poetry and older English, the intensives are even found as subjects· as, — " *Ourself* will mingle with society " (*Macbeth*).

**129.** The intensive pronouns should not be used as simple personal pronouns.

Thus we should say : — "He was kind to Mary and *me*" (NOT *myself*) ; "They invited my wife and *me* (NOT *myself*)."

## ADJECTIVE PRONOUNS

**130.** Some words are used either as adjectives or as pronouns. Such words are called adjective pronouns.

Adjective pronouns are classified, according to their meaning, as (1) **demonstrative pronouns** and (2) **indefinite pronouns**.

### I. DEMONSTRATIVE PRONOUNS

**131.** The demonstratives are *this* (plural, *these*), *that* (plural, *those*). They point out persons or things for special attention.

The demonstratives may be used either as adjectives or as pronouns.

I. As adjectives : —

| | |
|---|---|
| *This* sailor saved my life. | *These* girls are energetic. |
| Be kind to *this* child. | I am not alarmed by *these* threats. |
| Give *this* boy a dime. | *These* cherries are sour. |
| *This* fire is too hot. | Look at *these* acorns. |
| *That* saw is dull. | *Those* trees are dying. |
| We must cross *that* stream. | Take *those* dishes away. |
| *That* train is late. | Who are *those* strangers? |
| Send *that* dog home. | Do you see *those* rocks? |
| I am tired of *that* tune. | I am sorry for *those* children. |

I. As pronouns : —

|  |  |
|---|---|
| *This* is a fine morning.[1] | *These* are cowboys. |
| *This* is my uncle. | Robert gave me *these*. |
| Can you do *this?* | I never saw *these* before. |
| *This* is the road. | Who are *these?* |
| Look at *this*. | *These* are our rackets. |
| *That* is Ellen in the canoe. | *Those* are deer. |
| *That* would please him. | *Those* are nasturtiums. |
| *That* must be he. | What are *those?* |
| What is *that?* | *Those* are kangaroos. |

If the demonstrative is followed by a noun which it limits (as in "*this* sailor"), it is an adjective. If the demonstrative points out something which it does not name (as in " *This* is a fine morning "), it takes the place of a noun and is therefore a pronoun. The simple subject of the sentence "This camera is expensive " is the noun *camera*, which is modified by the adjective *this*. The subject of the sentence " *This* is expensive " is the pronoun *this*.

NOTE. *Yon, yond,* and *yonder* are common as demonstratives in older English and in poetry. Thus, — "Nerissa, cheer *yon* stranger" (*Merchant of Venice*). "Question *yond* man " (*As You Like It*). "Is not *yond* Diomed ? " (*Troilus and Cressida*). "Call *yonder* fellow hither" (*Henry V*). "Is *yonder* the man ? " (*As You Like It*).

**132.** Demonstratives have only the inflection of number. They have the same form for all three genders. The nominative and objective cases are alike; the possessive is replaced by *of* with the objective.

| SINGULAR | | PLURAL | |
|---|---|---|---|
| *Nom. and Obj.* | this | *Nom. and Obj.* | these |
| *Possessive* | [of this] | *Possessive* | [of these] |
| *Nom. and Obj.* | that | *Nom. and Obj.* | those |
| *Possessive* | [of that] | *Possessive* | [of those] |

*Yon, yond,* and *yonder* are not inflected.

[1] The pupil should not " supply nouns " in such sentences as these. For example, it is unscientific to expand the first sentence into "This [morning] is a fine morning," and then to parse *this* as an adjective. It is even more objectionable to expand the fifth sentence by inserting *thing* or the like after *this*. The plan of " supplying " unexpressed words (as being "understood") tends to confuse real distinctions of language, and should never be resorted to when it can be avoided.

**133.** A demonstrative pronoun may be used to avoid the repetition of a noun.

My dog and *that* [ = the dog] of my friend John have been fighting.
Compare these maps with *those* [ = the maps] on the blackboard.

**134.** The singular forms *this* and *that* (not the plurals *these* and *those*) are used with the nouns *kind* and *sort*.

> I like *this* kind of grapes.
> I have met *this* sort of people before.
> *That* kind of apples grows in Idaho.

## II. INDEFINITE PRONOUNS

**135.** The indefinite pronouns point out objects less clearly or definitely than demonstratives do.

EXAMPLES : each, every, either, both, neither, some, any, such, none, other, another, each other, one another.

> *Each* has its merits.                *Either* is correct.
> *Some* are missing.                He knows *neither* of you.
> I cannot give you *any*.          I like *both*.

**136.** Most indefinites may be either **pronouns** or **adjectives**. But *none* is always a substantive in modern use, and *every* is always an adjective.

**137.** *None* may be either singular or plural. When it means distinctly *not one*, it is singular. In many instances either construction is permissible.

> *None* of us has the key.
> *None* was (*or* were) left to tell the tale.

**138.** *Each other* and *one another* are regarded as compound pronouns. They designate related persons or things.

> My neighbor and I like *each other.*
> We must bear with *one another*.

The relation indicated by these pronouns is that of reciprocity. Hence they are often called **reciprocal pronouns.**

There is no real distinction between *each other* and *one another*. The rules sometimes given for such a distinction are not supported by the best usage.

**139.** *One* (possessive *one's*) is often used as an indefinite personal pronoun. Thus, —

> *One* does not like *one's* [NOT *his* or *their* ] motives to be doubted.

The use of *his* (for *one's*) to refer back to a preceding *one* is found in respectable writers, but is contrary to the best usage.

For the indefinite use of *we, you, they,* see § 118.

**140.** *All, several, few, many,* and similar words are often classed as indefinites. They may be used as adjectives or as substantives. *Everybody, everything, anybody, anything, somewhat, aught, naught,*[1] etc., are called indefinite nouns.

**141.** Care should be taken in framing such sentences as the following : —

> Everybody has *his* [NOT *their*] faults.
> If anybody wishes to go, *he* [NOT *they*] may.
> If anybody objects, let *him* [NOT *them*] speak.
> Every member of this class must hand in *his* [NOT *their*] composition to-day.
> Each hurries toward *his* [NOT *their*] home.
> Each of us must lead *his* [NOT *their*] own life.

In sentences of this kind, the personal pronoun (*he, his, him*) must be in the singular to agree with its antecedent (*everybody, anybody,* etc.) (see § 113).

NOTE. When the antecedent is of common gender (as in the last example), the personal pronouns (*he, his, him*) may be regarded as of common gender also. In very precise or formal language, one may say *he or she, his or her :* as, — "Each of us must lead *his or her* own life"; but this form of expression is to be avoided unless the distinction is clearly necessary.

**142.** When used as adjectives, none of the indefinites have any forms of inflection. The same is true when they are pronouns, except as follows : —

*Others* is used as the plural of *another.* The possessive forms are : — singular, *another's;* plural, *others'.* The other (possessive, *the other's*) has in the plural *the others* (possessive, *the others'*). *Each other* and *one another* add *'s* in the possessive. *One* has a possessive *one's; the one* becomes *the ones* in the plural.

---

[1] The negative *not* (§ 190, 4) is merely a shortened form of *naught.*

## RELATIVE PRONOUNS

**143.** Relative pronouns have a peculiar function in the sentence, since they serve both as **pronouns** and as **connectives.** Their use may be seen by comparing the two sentences that follow : —

    1. This is the sailor, and he saved my life.
    2. This is the sailor who saved my life.

Each consists of two parts or clauses (§ 44). In No. 1, the two clauses are connected by the conjunction *and,* which belongs to neither ; the pronoun *he,* which stands for *sailor,* is the subject of the second clause. In No. 2, there is no conjunction ; instead, we find the word *who,* which replaces *and he.* This *who* is a **pronoun,** since it stands for *sailor* (precisely as *he* does in No. 1) and (like *he*) is the subject of the verb *saved.* But *who* is also a **connective,** since it joins the two parts of the sentence as *and* does in No. 1. Such words (which serve both as pronouns and as connectives) are called **relative pronouns.**

In No. 1, the two clauses are coördinate. Neither serves as a modifier, and each might stand alone as a complete sentence ("This is the sailor." "He saved my life"). The sentence is compound (§ 44). In No. 2, on the contrary, the clause *who saved my life* is a **subordinate** or **dependent clause,** for it is used as an adjective modifier of the noun *sailor,* which it limits by showing what particular sailor is meant. The sentence is **complex** (§ 44). The dependent clause (*who saved my life*) is connected with the main clause (*this is the sailor*) by the pronoun *who,* which refers to *sailor.*

**144.** Relative pronouns connect dependent clauses with main clauses by referring directly to a substantive in the main clause.[1]

This substantive is the antecedent of the relative (§ 11).

Thus in § 143 the noun *sailor* is the antecedent of *who.*

*Relative* means "carrying back." These pronouns are so called because they carry the mind back directly to the antecedent.

[1] Because of their use as connectives, relative pronouns are sometimes called **conjunctive pronouns.**

**145.** The simple relative pronouns are *who, which, that, as,* and *what.*

*Who* and *which* are declined as follows in both the singular and the plural: —

| | | |
|---|---|---|
| *Nominative* | who | which |
| *Possessive* | whose | whose |
| *Objective* | whom | which |

*That, as,* and *what* are not inflected. They have the same form for both nominative and objective and are not used in the possessive case.

**146.** *As* may be used as a relative pronoun when *such* stands in the main clause.

> Such of you *as* have finished may go.
> I have never seen such strawberries *as* these [are].
> Use such powers *as* you have.

**147.** *As* is often used as a relative after *the same.*

> This color is the same *as* that [is].

Other relatives are also used after *the same.*

> This is the same book *that* (or *which*) you were reading yesterday.
> This is the same man *that* (or *whom*) I saw on the pier last Friday.

**148.** *Who* is either masculine or feminine; *which* and *what* are neuter; *that* and *as* are of all three genders.

> All *who* heard, approved.
> Here is the lad *whose* story interested you.
> The first woman *whom* I saw was Mary.
> He answered in such English *as* he could muster.
> I saw nobody *that* I knew.
> This is the road *that* leads to London.

In older English *the which* is often used for *which :* as, —

> Our foster-nurse of nature is repose,
> The *which* he lacks. — SHAKSPERE.

For other uses of *as,* see §§ 368, 428–429. For *but* in such sentences as "There was nobody *but* believed him," see § 370.

**149.** **A relative pronoun must agree with its antecedent in gender, number, and person.**

The sentences in § 148 illustrate the agreement of the relative with its antecedent in **gender.**

Since relative pronouns have the same form for both numbers and for all three persons, their **number and person** must be discovered, in each instance, by observing the number and person of the **antecedent.**

It is *I who am* wrong. [First person, singular number : antecedent, *I.*]

All *you who are* ready may go. [Second person plural : antecedent, *you.*]

Give help to *him who needs it.* [Third person, singular : antecedent, *him.*]

The *road that leads* to the shore is sandy. [Third person singular : antecedent, *road.*]

The *roads that lead* to the shore are sandy. [Third person plural : antecedent, *roads.*]

To determine the number and person of a relative pronoun is particularly necessary when it is the **subject of the clause,** for the form of the verb varies (as the examples show) according to the number and person of the subject (§ 222). Hence the rule for the agreement of a relative with its antecedent is of much practical importance.

**150.** **The case of a relative pronoun has nothing to do with its antecedent, but depends on the construction of its own clause.**

The servant *who* opened the door wore livery. [*Who* is in the nominative case, being the subject of *opened.*]

He discharged his servant, *who* immediately left town. [*Who* is in the nominative case, since it is the subject of *left,* although its antecedent (*servant*) is in the objective.]

The servant *whom* you discharged has returned. [*Whom* is in the objective case, since it is the direct object of *discharged.* The antecedent (*servant*) is, on the other hand, in the nominative, because it is the subject of *has returned.*]

Here is such money *as* I have. [*As* is in the objective case, being the object of *have.* The antecedent (*money*) is in the nominative.]

**151.** A relative pronoun in the objective case is often omitted.

| | |
|---|---|
| Here is the book *which* you wanted. | Here is the book you wanted. |
| The noise *that* I heard was the wind. | The noise I heard was the wind. |
| The man *whom* I met was a carpenter. | The man I met was a carpenter. |

NOTE. In older English a relative in the nominative is often omitted: as, — "There's two or three of us *have* seen strange sights" (*Julius Cæsar*), that is, "There are two or three of us *who have* seen," etc. The same omission is often made in rapid or careless colloquial speech. It is approved in clauses with *there* in such sentences as "He is one of the best men there are in the world" (§ 232).

**152.** Certain questions of **gender** call for particular attention.

1. *Which* is commonly used in referring to the lower animals unless these are regarded as persons. This is true even when *he* or *she* is used of the same animals (§ 69).

> This is the dog *which* I mentioned. Isn't *he* a fine fellow?
> We have one cow *which* we prize highly. *She* is a Jersey.

2. The possessive *whose* may be used of any object that has life.

> This is the man *whose* watch was stolen.
> I have a cat *whose* name is Tabby.
> This is the tree *whose* leaves were destroyed. *It* is quite dead.

3. In the case of things without animal life, *of which* and *whose* are both common. The tendency is to prefer *of which* in prose, but *whose* is often used because of its more agreeable sound. In poetry, *whose* is especially frequent.

> A broad river, the name *of which* I have forgotten, forms the northern boundary of the province.
> Jack was fishing with a bamboo rod, to the end *of which* he had tied a short piece of ordinary twine.
> She was gazing into the pool, *whose* calm surface reflected her features like a mirror. ["The surface *of which*" would not sound so well.]

NOTE. In older English, *which* is often used for *who* or *whom*: as, — "He *which* hath your noble father slain, pursued my life" (*Hamlet*).

The compounds *whereof, wherefrom, wherewith*, etc., are equivalent to *of which, from which*, etc. (cf. § 124). Thus, — "Esau hated Jacob because of the blessing *wherewith* his father blessed him" (*Genesis* xxvii. 41).

### DESCRIPTIVE AND RESTRICTIVE RELATIVES

**153.** The clause introduced by a relative pronoun is an **adjective clause,** since it serves as an adjective modifier of the antecedent (§ 143). There are two different ways in which the antecedent may be thus modified.

> 1. The Italian, *who wore a flower in his coat,* smiled at me.
> 2. The Italian *who wore a flower in his coat* smiled at me.

In the first sentence, the italicized relative clause serves simply to **describe** the Italian, not to identify him. The flower is a mere detail of the picture.

In the second sentence, the relative clause serves not merely to describe the Italian, but also to distinguish him from all others. The flower is mentioned as a means of **identification.** The relative clause confines or **restricts** the meaning of the antecedent (*Italian*).

**154.** A relative pronoun that serves merely to introduce a descriptive fact is called a descriptive relative.

A relative pronoun that introduces a clause confining or limiting the application of the antecedent is called a restrictive relative.

Thus in the first example in § 153, *who* is a descriptive relative; in the second, it is a restrictive relative.

**155.** Before a descriptive relative we regularly make a pause in speaking, but never before a restrictive relative. Hence the rule : —

A descriptive relative is preceded by a comma; a restrictive relative is not.

Three sailors, *who* were loitering on the pier, sprang to the rescue.

A clumsy weapon, *which* I took for a blunderbuss, hung over the fireplace.

I told the news to the first man *that* (or *whom*) I met.

The coins *that* (or *which*) you showed me are doubloons.

Nothing *that* I have ever read has moved me more profoundly than the third act of " King Lear."

**156.** *Who, which,* and *that* are all used as restrictive relatives; but some writers prefer *that* to *which,* especially in the nominative case.

NOTE. *That* is not now employed as a descriptive relative, though it was common in this use not very long ago. Thus in 1844 Disraeli wrote: "The deer, *that* abounded, lived here in a world as savage as themselves" (*Coningsby,* book iii, chapter 5).

The omission of the relative (§ 151) is possible only when the relative is restrictive.

The boy [*whom*] I saw at your house has left town. [Restrictive.]
Charles, *whom* I saw yesterday, had not heard the news. [Descriptive.]

### THE RELATIVE PRONOUN *WHAT*

**157.** The relative pronoun *what* is equivalent to *that which,* and has a double construction : — (1) the construction of the omitted or implied antecedent (*that*); (2) the construction of the relative (*which*).

$\left.\begin{array}{l}\textit{What}\\\textit{That which}\end{array}\right\}$ was said is true. [Here *what,* being equivalent to *that which,* serves as the subject both of *was said* and of *is.*]

Tom always remembers $\left\{\begin{array}{l}\textit{what}\\\textit{that which}\end{array}\right\}$ is said to him. [Here *what,* being equivalent to *that which,* serves as both the object of *remembers* and as the subject of *is said.*]

Tom always remembers $\left\{\begin{array}{l}\textit{what}\\\textit{that which}\end{array}\right\}$ he learns. [Here *what* serves both as the object of *remembers* and as the object of *learns.*]

In parsing *what,* mention both of its constructions.

NOTE. Another method of dealing with the relative *what* is to regard the whole clause (*what was said; what is said to him; what he learns*) as a noun clause. Thus the clause *what was said* in the first sentence would be the subject of *is;* in the second and third sentences, the clause would be the object of *remembers. What,* in the first sentence, would be parsed as the subject of *was said;* in the second, as the subject of *is said;* and in the third, as the object of *learns.* Neither view is incorrect, and each has its special advantages. The student may well be familiar with both methods, remembering that grammar cannot be treated like mathematics.

## COMPOUND RELATIVE PRONOUNS

**158.** The compound relative pronouns are formed by adding *ever* or *soever* to *who, which,* and *what.*

They are declined as follows : —

SINGULAR AND PLURAL

| | | | |
|---|---|---|---|
| *Nominative* | whoever | (whosoever) | whichever (whichsoever) |
| *Possessive* | whosever | (whosesoever) | —— —— |
| *Objective* | whomever | (whomsoever) | whichever (whichsoever) |

*Whatever* (*whatsoever*) has no inflection. The nominative and the objective are alike, and the possessive is supplied by the phrase *of whatever* (*of whatsoever*).

The phrase *of whichever* (*of whichsoever*) is used instead of *whosever* exactly as *of which* is used instead of *whose* (§ 152).

**159.** The compound relative pronouns may include or imply their own antecedents and hence may have a double construction.

*Whoever* calls, *he* must be admitted. [Here *he*, the antecedent of *whoever*, is the subject of *must be admitted*, and *whoever* is the subject of *calls*.]

*Whoever calls* must be admitted. [Here the antecedent *he* is omitted, being implied in *whoever*. *Whoever* has therefore a double construction, being the subject of both *calls* and *must be admitted*.]

> He shall have *whatever* he wishes.
> I will do *whichever* you say.

In such sentences, care should be taken to use *whoever* and *whomever* correctly. The nominative (*whoever*) is required when the relative is the subject of its own clause.

> He asked *whoever* came.
> He told the story to *whoever* would listen.
> He asked *whomever* he knew.
> He told the story to *whomever* he met.

**160.** The compound relatives are sometimes used without an antecedent expressed or implied.

*Whoever* deserts you, I will remain faithful.
*Whomever* it offends, I will speak the truth.
*Whatever* he attempts, he is sure to fail.
*Whichever* you choose, you will be disappointed.

NOTE. This construction is closely related to that explained in § 159. "Whoever deserts you, I will remain faithful," is practically equivalent to "Whoever deserts you, let him desert you! I will remain faithful." No antecedent, however, is felt by the speaker, and hence none need be supplied in parsing. Compare concessive clauses (§ 401).

**161.** *Which, what, whichever,* and *whatever* are often used as adjectives.

Use *what* (or *whatever*) powers you have.
*Whichever* plan you adopt, you have my best wishes.

**162.** A noun limited by the adjectives *what, whichever,* and *whatever,* may have the same double construction that these relatives have when they are used as pronouns (§ 159). Thus, —

Take *whichever* pen is not in use. [Here *pen* is both the direct object of *take,* and the subject of *is.*]

*Whoso* for *whosoever* and *whatso* for *whatsoever* are common in older English.

## INTERROGATIVE PRONOUNS

**163.** The interrogative pronouns are *who, which,* and *what.* They are used in asking questions.[1]

*Who* is your neighbor?
*Who* goes there?
*Whom* have you chosen?
From *whom* did you learn this?
*Whose* voice is that?

*Which* shall I take?
*Which* is correct?
*What* did he say?
*What* is lacking?
With *what* are you so delighted?

**164.** *Who* has a possessive *whose,* and an objective *whom. Which* and *what* are not inflected.

*Who* may be either masculine or feminine; *which* and *what* may be of any gender.

[1] For indirect questions, see § 441.

**165.** The **objective** *whom* often begins a question (as in the third example in § 163). Care should be taken not to write *who* for *whom*.

**166.** *Which* and *what* are used as **interrogative adjectives.**

> *Which* street shall I take?
> *What* village is this?

**167.** The interrogative adjective *what* may be used in a peculiar form of exclamatory sentence. Thus, —

> *What* a cold night this is!
> *What* courage he must have had!

*What!* by itself often serves as an exclamation: as, — "*What!* do you really think so?" In this use *what* may be regarded as an interjection.

**168.** In **parsing pronouns** the following models may be used:—

**1.** *He* was my earliest friend.

*He* is a personal pronoun of the third person. It is in the masculine gender, the singular number, and the nominative case, being the subject of the verb *was*.

**2.** A policeman *whom* I met showed me the house.

*Whom* is a relative pronoun of the masculine gender, singular number, and third person, agreeing with its antecedent, *policeman*. It is in the objective case, being the direct object of the transitive verb *met*.

**3.** The corporal, *whose* name was Scott, came from Leith.

*Whose* is a relative pronoun of the masculine gender, singular number, and third person, agreeing with its antecedent, *corporal*. It is in the possessive case, modifying the noun *name*.

**4.** *Whose* birthday do we celebrate in February?

*Whose* is an interrogative pronoun in the masculine or feminine gender, singular number, and possessive case, modifying the noun *birthday*.

**5.** He injured *himself* severely.

*Himself* is a compound personal pronoun of the third person, used reflexively. It is of the masculine gender, singular number, and third person, agreeing with its antecedent, *he*. It is in the objective case, being the direct object of the transitive verb *injured*.

# CHAPTER IV

## ADJECTIVES

### CLASSIFICATION OF ADJECTIVES

**169.** An adjective is a word which describes or limits a substantive. An adjective is said to belong to the substantive which it describes or limits.

An adjective which describes is called a descriptive adjective; one which points out or designates is called a definitive adjective (§ 13).

Most adjectives are descriptive: as, — *round, cold, red, angry, graceful, excessive, young, sudden, Roman.*

NOTE. Many descriptive adjectives are compound (see § 64): as, — steadfast, lionlike, fireproof, downright, heartsick, everlasting, brown-eyed, broad-shouldered, ill-tempered, dear-bought, far-fetched, never-ending, self-evident, self-important. "He was a *matter-of-fact* person." "Tom is *hail-fellow-well-met* with everybody." "This is an *out-of-the-way* place." "A dashing, *down-at-the-heel* youth answered my knock."

**170.** A proper noun used as an adjective, or an adjective derived from a proper noun, is called a **proper adjective** and usually begins with a capital letter.

EXAMPLES: a *Panama* hat, *Florida* oranges, a *Bunsen* burner; Virginian, Spenserian, Newtonian, Icelandic, Miltonic, Byronic, Turkish, English, Veronese.

NOTE. Many so-called proper adjectives begin with a small letter because their origin is forgotten or disregarded: as, — *china* dishes, *italic* type, *mesmeric* power, a *jovial* air, a *saturnine* expression, a *mercurial* temperament, a *stentorian* voice.

**171. Definitive adjectives** include: — pronouns used as adjectives (as, *this* opportunity; *those* pictures; *either* table; *what* time is it?); numeral adjectives (as, *two* stars; the *third* year); the **articles,** *a* (or *an*) and *the*.

Pronouns used as adjectives (often called pronominal adjectives) have been studied under Pronouns — demonstratives (§§ 131–134), indefinites (§§ 135–142), relatives (§§ 143–162), interrogatives (§§ 163–167).

Numeral adjectives will be treated, along with other numerals (nouns and adverbs), in §§ 204–208.

The articles will be treated in §§ 173–180.

**172.** Adjectives may be classified, according to their position in the sentence, as **attributive, appositive,** and **predicate adjectives.**

**1.** An **attributive adjective** is closely attached to its noun and regularly precedes it.

> The *angry* spot doth glow on Cæsar's brow.
> O you *hard* hearts, you *cruel* men of Rome!
> *Yond* Cassius has a *lean* and *hungry* look.

**2.** An **appositive adjective** is added to its noun to explain it, like a noun in apposition (§ 88, 5).

| NOUN IN APPOSITION | APPOSITIVE ADJECTIVE |
|---|---|
| The castle, a *ruin*, stood on the edge of the cliff. | The castle, *ancient* and *ruinous*, stood on the edge of the cliff. |
| Bertram, the *ringleader*, refused to surrender. | Bertram, *undaunted*, refused to surrender. |

**3.** A **predicate adjective** completes the meaning of the predicate verb, but describes or limits the subject.

Predicate adjectives are common after *is* (in its various forms) and other copulative verbs, particularly *become* and *seem* (§ 17).

> The sea is *rough* to-day.
> Burton soon became *cautious* in his judgments.
> You seem *anxious* about your future.
> The air grew *hot* and *sultry*.
> Our first experiment proved *unsuccessful*.
> The milk turned *sour*.
> Our agent proved *trustworthy*.

NOTE. The construction of the predicate adjective is similar to that of the predicate nominative (§ 88, 2). Both are known as **complements,** because they complete the meaning of a verb.

After *look, sound, taste, smell, feel,* a predicate adjective is used to describe the subject. Thus, —

> Your flowers look *thrifty.* [NOT: look thriftily.]
> Their voices sound *shrill.* [NOT: sound shrilly.]
> This apple tastes *sweet.* [NOT: tastes sweetly.]
> The air smells *good.* [NOT: smells well.]
> The patient feels *comfortable.* [NOT: feels comfortably.]

For predicate adjectives after passive verbs, see § 492.
For the use of an adjective as predicate objective, see § 104.

## THE ARTICLES

**173.** The adjectives *a* (or *an*) and *the* are called articles.

**1.** The definite article *the* points out one or more particular objects as distinct from others of the same kind.

> *The* train is late.
> Here is *the* key.
> *The* children are in *the* next room.

**2.** The indefinite article *a* (or *an*) designates an object as merely one of a general class or kind.

> Lend me *a* pencil.
> I have *a* cold.
> *A* young man answered my knock.

The article *a* is a fragment of *ān* (pronounced *ahn*), the ancient form of the numeral *one ; an* keeps the *n,* which *a* has lost. *The* is an old demonstrative, related to *that.*

**174.** *The* with a singular noun sometimes indicates a **class** or **kind** of objects.

> *The scholar* is not necessarily a dryasdust.
> *The elephant* is the largest of quadrupeds.
> *The aëroplane* is a very recent invention.
> Resin is obtained from *the pine.*

NOTE. In this use *the* is often called the **generic article** (from the Latin *genus,* "kind" or "sort"). The singular number with the generic *the* is practically equivalent to the plural without an article. Thus in the first example the sense would be the same if we had, "*Scholars* are not necessarily dryasdusts."

**175.** An adjective preceded by *the* may be used as a plural noun.

> *The brave* are honored.
> *The rich* have many cares.
> *The strong* should protect *the weak.*

**176.** *An* **is used before words beginning with a vowel or silent** *h*; *a* **before other words.** Thus, —

> *an* owl; *an* apple; *an* honest man; *a* stone; *a* pear.

**177.** Special rules for *a* or *an* are the following: —

1. Before words beginning with the sound of *y* or *w*, the form *a*, not *an*, is used.

EXAMPLES: a union, a university, a yew, a ewe, a eulogy, a Utopian scheme, such a one.

This rule covers all words beginning with *eu* and many beginning with *u*. Note that the initial sound is a consonant, not a vowel. *An* was formerly common before such words (as, — *an* union, such *an* one), but *a* is now the settled form.

2. Before words beginning with *h* and not accented on the first syllable, *an* is often used. Thus, we say —

> *a* his'tory; BUT, *an* histor'ical novel.

In such cases, the *h* is very weak in sound, and is sometimes quite silent, so that the word practically begins with a vowel. Usage varies, but careful writers favor the rule here given. *An* was formerly more common before *h* than at present.

**178.** With two or more connected nouns or adjectives the article should be repeated whenever clearness requires (cf. § 123).

I have consulted *the* secretary and *the* treasurer. ["The secretary and treasurer" would imply that the same person held both offices.]

I found *an* anchor and *a* chain. ["An anchor and chain" would suggest that the chain was attached to the anchor.]

In some towns there are separate schools for *the* boys and *the* girls; in others *the* boys and girls attend the same schools.

He waved *a* red and white flag.

He waved *a* red and *a* white flag.

**179.** *A* is often used distributively, in the sense of *each.*

> I paid five dollars *a* pair for my shoes.
> The letter-carrier calls twice *a* day.
> My class meets three times *a* week.

In such phrases *a* is better than *per*, except in strictly commercial language.

**180.** When used with adjectives, the articles precede, except in a few phrases : as, —

> Such an uproar was never heard.
> Many a man has tried in vain.

For the adverb *the*, which is quite distinct from the article in use and meaning, see § 195.

For the preposition *a* (as in " He went *a*-fishing "), see § 352.


### COMPARISON OF ADJECTIVES

**181.** In comparing objects with each other, we may use three different forms of the same adjective.

> Thomas is *strong.*
> William is *stronger* than Thomas.
> Herbert is *strongest* of the three.

This inflection of adjectives is called **comparison,** and the three forms are called **degrees of comparison.**

**182.** The degrees of comparison indicate by their form in what degree of intensity the quality described by the adjective exists.

There are three degrees of comparison, — the positive, the comparative, and the superlative.

1. The positive degree is the simplest form of the adjective, and has no special ending.

It merely describes the quality, without expressing or suggesting any comparison.

> Thomas is *strong.*

Thus, the positive degree of the adjective *strong* is *strong.*

**2. The comparative degree of an adjective is formed by adding the termination *er* to the positive degree.**

It denotes that the quality exists in the object described in a higher degree than in some other object.

William is *stronger* than Thomas.

Thus, the comparative degree of the adjective *strong* is *stronger*.

**3. The superlative degree is formed by adding *est* to the positive degree.**

It denotes that the quality exists in the highest degree in the object described.

Herbert is *strongest* of the three.

Other examples of the **comparison of adjectives** are : —

| POSITIVE DEGREE | COMPARATIVE DEGREE | SUPERLATIVE DEGREE |
| --- | --- | --- |
| rich | richer | richest |
| poor | poorer | poorest |
| fast | faster | fastest |
| firm | firmer | firmest |

**183.** RULES OF SPELLING.

**1.** Adjectives ending in silent *e* drop this letter before the comparative ending *er* and the superlative ending *est*. Thus, —

wise, wiser, wisest ; pure, purer, purest ; handsome, handsomer, handsomest.

**2.** Most adjectives ending in *y* change *y* to *i* before the endings *er* and *est*. Thus, —

silky, silkier, silkiest ; glossy, glossier, glossiest ; sorry, sorrier, sorriest.

**3.** Adjectives having a short vowel and ending in a single consonant double this before the endings *er* and *est*. Thus, —

dim, dimmer, dimmest ; sad, sadder, saddest ; fit, fitter, fittest ; big, bigger, biggest ; red, redder, reddest ; hot, hotter, hottest.

**184.** Many adjectives are compared by prefixing the adverbs *more* and *most* to the positive degree.

Many adjectives of two syllables and most adjectives of three or more syllables are so compared. Thus, —

recent, more recent, most recent ; terrible, more terrible, most terrible ; triumphant, more triumphant, most triumphant ; economical, more economical, most economical.

Some adjectives may be compared in either way.

EXAMPLES : intense, intenser, intensest ; OR intense, more intense, most intense. So also — profound, sublime, unkind.

NOTE. The adverbs *less* and *least* may be used with an adjective, if one wishes to run *down* the scale of comparison : as, — *terrible, less terrible, least terrible*. This idiom, however, should not be regarded as comparison of the adjective. "Superlative" means "in the highest degree," and is not applicable to *least terrible*, which means "terrible in the *lowest* degree."

## IRREGULAR COMPARISON

**185.** Several adjectives have irregular comparison.[1]

| POSITIVE | COMPARATIVE | SUPERLATIVE |
|---|---|---|
| bad (evil, ill) | worse | worst |
| far | farther | farthest |
| —— | further | furthest |
| good | better | best |
| late | later, latter | latest, last |
| well (in health) | better | —— |
| little | less, lesser | least |
| much, many | more | most |

*Old* has comparative *older* or *elder*, superlative *oldest* or *eldest*. *Elder* or *eldest* may be used with certain nouns of relationship, or in the phrases *the elder* and *the eldest*.

This is my *elder* brother.　　My brother is *older* than yours.
Jane was the *eldest* of six children.　　I shall wear my *oldest* clothes.

*Elder* is also used as a noun : as, — "You should respect your *elders*."

[1] In some of these cases the comparative and superlative are really different words from the positive.

*Next* is a superlative of *nigh*. It is used only in the sense of "the very nearest."

> I live in the *next* street.
> The *next* time he comes, I shall refuse to see him.

**186.** A few superlatives end in *-most*. With these, one or both of the other degrees are commonly wanting.

| POSITIVE | COMPARATIVE | SUPERLATIVE |
|---|---|---|
| —— | (former) | foremost |
| hind | hinder | hindmost |
| —— | inner | inmost, innermost |
| (out, *adverb*) | { outer | outmost, outermost |
|  | { (utter) | utmost, uttermost |
| (up, *adverb*) | upper | uppermost |
| —— | —— | endmost |
| —— | nether | nethermost |
| top | —— | topmost |
| —— | —— | furthermost |
| north | —— | northmost |
| northern | (more northern) | northernmost |
| south | —— | southmost |
| southern | (more southern) | southernmost |
| east, eastern | (more eastern) | easternmost |
| west, western | (more western) | westernmost |

NOTE. The ending *-most* is not the adverb *most*. It is a very old superlative ending *-mest* changed under the influence of the adverb *most*.

**187.** For adjectives incapable of comparison, see § 202. For special rules for the use of comparative and superlative, see §§ 199–203.

**188.** In **parsing** an adjective, tell whether it is descriptive or definitive, mention the substantive to which it belongs, and specify the degree of comparison.

# CHAPTER V

## ADVERBS

**189. An adverb is a word which modifies a verb, an adjective, or another adverb.**

> The storm ceased *suddenly*.
> A *very* disastrous storm swept the coast.
> The storm ceased *very* suddenly.

**190.** Adverbs are classified according to their meaning as: (1) adverbs of **manner**; (2) adverbs of **time**; (3) adverbs of **place**; (4) adverbs of **degree**.[1]

1. Adverbs of manner answer the question "How?" "In what way?"

They modify verbs or adjectives, rarely adverbs. Most of them are formed from adjectives by adding *ly*.

> Tom answered *courageously*.
> The poor child looked *helplessly* about.
> *Softly* and *silently* fell the snow.
> The pain was *terribly* severe.
> The river rose *surprisingly* fast.

2. Adverbs of time answer the question "When?" They usually modify verbs. Thus, —

> The old castle is *now* a museum.
> He was *recently* promoted.
> I have been disturbed *lately*.
> My friend arrives *to-day*.
> James was *then* a boy of seven.
> I have *already* rung the bell.
> *Afterwards* he regretted his haste.

[1] The four classes are not absolute, for the same adverb may be used in different senses and thus belong to different classes. Sometimes, too, there is room for difference of opinion. Thus in the fourth and fifth examples under 1, *terribly* and *surprisingly* are equivalent to "in a terrible (or surprising) manner," and therefore are classified as adverbs of manner; but they may also be regarded as adverbs of degree.

3. Adverbs of place answer the question " Where ? " They usually modify verbs. Thus, —

> Come *here*.
> *Yonder* stands the culprit.
> An old sailor came *forward*.
> My sister is *out*.
> I was *abroad* that winter.

4. Adverbs of degree answer the question " To what degree or extent ? " They modify verbs, adjectives, and adverbs. Thus, —

> Arthur is *rather* tall.
> Father was *much* pleased.
> Father was *very much* pleased.
> The task seemed *utterly* hopeless.
> That is *hardly* possible.
> That is *not* possible.

**191.** Some adverbs have the same form as the corresponding adjectives.

> You have guessed *right*.
> How *fast* the tide ebbs !
> The horse was sold *cheap*.
> Tired men sleep *sound*.

Other examples are : — wrong, straight, early, late, quick, hard, far, near, slow, high, low, loud, ill, well, deep, close, just, very, much, little.

Under this head come certain adverbs of degree used to modify adjectives.

> His eyes were *dark* blue.   [Compare : *very* blue.]
> That silk is *light* yellow.   [Compare : *rather* yellow.]
> These flowers are *deep* purple.   [Compare : *intensely* purple.]
> The water was *icy* cold.   [Compare : *extremely* cold.]

That *dark*, *light*, etc., are adverbs in this use appears from the fact that they answer the question " How ? " Thus, — "His eyes were blue." " *How* blue ? " " *Dark* blue."

NOTE. In the oldest English many adverbs ended in -*ĕ*, as if formed directly from adjectives by means of this ending. Thus, the adjective for *hot* was *hāt*, side by side with which was an adverb *hātĕ* (dissyllabic), meaning *hotly*. In the fourteenth century this distinction was still kept up. Thus,

Chaucer used both the adjective *hŏt* and the dissyllabic adverb *hŏtĕ*, meaning *hotly*. Between 1400 and 1500 all weak final *e*'s disappeared from the language. In this way the adverb *hotĕ*, for example, became simply *hot*. Thus these adverbs in *-ĕ* became identical in form with the corresponding adjectives. Hence in the time of Shakspere there existed, in common use, not only the adjective *hot*, but also the adverb *hot* (identical in form with the adjective but really descended from the adverb *hotĕ*). One could say not only "The fire is *hot*" (adjective), but "The fire burns *hot*" (adverb of manner).

The tendency in modern English has been to confine the form without ending to the adjective use and to restrict the adverbial function to forms in *-ly*. Thus, a writer of the present time would not say, in prose, "The fire burns *hot*," but "The fire burns *hotly*." Nevertheless, a number of the old adverbs without ending still remain in good use, and must not be regarded as erroneous.

In poetry, moreover, such adverbs are freely employed; as, — "The boy like a gray goshawk stared *wild*." [In prose: stared *wildly*.]

For adverbial phrases, see §§ 41-42, 475.

For the adverbial objective, see § 109.

**192.** *Yes* and *no* are peculiar adverbs used in assenting and denying. Thus, —

> Are you hungry?
> No.

NOTE. As now used, *yes* and *no* stand for complete sentences. Originally, however, they were modifiers, and hence they are still classed as adverbs. The original meaning of *no* was "never." Compare *never* as an emphatic negative in modern English: as, — "Will you surrender?" "*Never!*" The oldest affirmative adverb was *yea*. *Yes* was originally a compound of *yea* with a form of *so*, and was used in emphatic affirmatives (like our *just so!*).

Other adverbs or adverbial phrases are sometimes used like *yes* or *no*. Such are *certainly*, *assuredly*, *by no means*, *not at all*. In these cases, however, the modifying effect of the word or phrase may easily be seen when the sentence is supplied. Thus, — "Will you help me?" "*Certainly* [J will help you]."

**193.** *There* is often used merely to introduce a sentence in the inverted order (§ 5).

> There is a hole in my shoe.
> There are many strangers in town.
> There rose a thick smoke from the volcano.

In this use, *there* is sometimes called an **expletive** (or "filler"). It is unemphatic, and has lost all its force as an adverb of place. Contrast "THERE [emphatic] stood an Indian under a tree" with, "There [unemphatic expletive] stood an Indian under a tree."

## RELATIVE AND INTERROGATIVE ADVERBS

**194.** Relative adverbs introduce subordinate clauses and are similar in their use to relative pronouns.

I know a farmhouse $\left\{ \begin{array}{l} \text{in which} \\ \text{where} \end{array} \right\}$ we can spend the night.

*Where* is an adverb of place, modifying *can spend*. But it also introduces the subordinate clause, as the relative pronoun *which* does. Hence *where* is called a **relative adverb**.

**195.** The principal relative adverbs are: — *where, whence, whither, wherever, when, whenever, while, as, how, why, before, after, till, until, since.*

Because of their similarity to conjunctions, these words are often called **conjunctive adverbs.**

He had a fever *when* he was in Spain.

Work *while* it is day.

*As* the ship passed, we observed that her decks were crowded with Malays. [Time.]

Keep to the right, *as* the law directs. [Manner.]

You started *before* I was ready.

Wait *until* the car stops.

*Since* you came, it has rained constantly.

*As* and *since* in the sense of " because," and *while* in the sense of " although," are classed as conjunctions (§ 368).

The clauses introduced by relative adverbs may be either adjective or adverbial (§§ 49–50, 379–382).

NOTE. In " *The* more you waste, *the* sooner you will want " (and similar sentences) *the* is not an article, but an old case-form of the pronoun *that*, used as an adverb of degree. We may expand the sentence as follows: " *To what extent* you waste more, *to that extent* you will want sooner." Thus it appears that the first *the* has a relative force, and the second *the* a demonstrative force.

**196. An interrogative adverb introduces a question.**

*Where, when, whence, whither, how, why*, may be used as **interrogative adverbs.** Thus, —

*Where* are you going ?

*Why* must you go ?

## COMPARISON OF ADVERBS

**197** Adverbs have three degrees of comparison, — the positive, the comparative, and the superlative.

**1.** Most adverbs are compared by means of *more* and *most*.

> John came *promptly*. [Positive.]
> Richard came *more promptly* than John. [Comparative.]
> Henry came *most promptly* of all. [Superlative.]

**2.** A few adverbs are compared by means of the endings *er* and *est*. Thus, —

| Positive | Comparative | Superlative |
|---|---|---|
| near | nearer | nearest |
| soon | sooner | soonest |

Further examples are: — cheap, dear, early, fast, hard, high, long, loud, quick, slow, deep.[1]

Some adverbs are compared in both ways. Thus,—

> often, oftener *or* more often, oftenest *or* most often.

**198.** Several adverbs have irregular comparison.

| Positive | Comparative | Superlative |
|---|---|---|
| far / forth | farther / further | farthest / furthest |
| ill / badly | worse | worst |
| nigh | nigher | nighest / next |
| well | better | best |
| late | later | latest / last |
| little | less | least |
| much | more | most |

These adverbs in the main have the same forms as the adjectives studied in § 185 above. Note, however: (1) that *good* and *bad* are never adverbs; (2) that *ill* and *well*, *better* and *best*, *worse* and *worst*, may be either adverbs or adjectives. *Rather* is now used in the comparative only.

[1] Many comparatives and superlatives in *er* and *est* that are no longer allowable in prose are still used in poetry.

## USE OF THE COMPARATIVE AND SUPERLATIVE

**199.** The comparative degree, not the superlative, is used in comparing two persons or things.

The superlative is used in comparing one person or thing with two or more.

RIGHT : { Mary is the *more agreeable* of the two.
{ Mary is the *most agreeable* of all the family.

WRONG : { I like both Mary and Jane, but I am *fondest* of Mary.
{ I am studying Latin, history, and geometry, but I dislike
{ the *latter*.

The same principle applies to adverbs.

John runs *faster* than Tom. [Here the acts of two persons are compared.]

Which of you three can run *fastest?* [Here the acts of more than two are compared.]

NOTE. In older English the superlative sometimes occurs when only two objects are thought of. This use is still found in a few proverbial phrases; as, — "Put your *best* foot *foremost*."

**200.** The superlative is sometimes used merely for emphasis, without implying any definite comparison : as, — " My *dearest* Kate ! "

The superlative of emphasis is very common with *most*.

*Most potent, grave,* and *reverend* signiors. — SHAKSPERE.
Justice had been *most cruelly* defrauded. — WORDSWORTH.

Excessive use of this construction (like frequent repetition of *very*) is tiresome and weakens style.

Double comparison (as *more worthier, most unkindest*) is common in older English, but is now a gross error.

**201.** When two adjectives or adverbs are contrasted by means of *than, more* is used with the first.

Such indulgence is *more kind* than wise.
This scheme is *more clever* than honest.
He acts *more boldly* than discreetly.

NOTE. The adverb *rather* is often used with the first adjective or adverb (as, — " *rather* kind than wise " or " kind *rather* than wise "), but in a slightly different sense.

**202.** Many adjectives and adverbs are, from their meaning, incapable of comparison. Such are : —

**1.** Adjectives expressing a quality as absolute or complete, and adverbs derived from such adjectives.

EXAMPLES: unique, universal, single, matchless, instantaneous, triangular, everlasting, infinite, mortal; uniquely, singly, eternally, mortally.

**2.** The adverbs *here, there, then, now, when,* and the like.

NOTE. Words like *perfect, exact, straight,* etc., are commonly said to be incapable of comparison, but this is an error. For each of these words may vary in sense. When *perfect* (for example) denotes *absolute perfection,* it cannot be compared. But *perfect* has also another sense: namely, "partaking in a higher or lower degree of the qualities that make up absolute perfection," so that we may describe one statue as *more perfect* than another, or one of three statues as the *most perfect* of them all. In this use, which is unobjectionable, we simply admit that nothing in the world is absolutely flawless, and assert that the three statues approach ideal perfection in various degrees.

**203.** An adjective phrase may sometimes be compared by means of *more* and *most.*

I was never *more out of humor* [ = more vexed].
I think your last suggestion *most in keeping* [ = most appropriate].

## NUMERALS — ADJECTIVES, NOUNS, AND ADVERBS

**204.** Words indicating number are called numerals. They are adjectives, nouns, or adverbs.

There are *seven* days in the week. [Adjective.]
*Twelve* make a *dozen.* [Noun.]
I have called *twice.* [Adverb.]

**205.** The chief classes of numerals are **cardinals** and **ordinals.**

**1.** Cardinal numeral adjectives (*one, two, three, four,* etc.) are used in counting, and answer the question "How many ?"

I had to pay *three* dollars.
There were *forty-two* vessels in the fleet.

NOTE. In such expressions as "The boy was *sixteen,*" the numeral is a predicate adjective limiting *boy* (§ 172, 3). We need not expand *sixteen* to "sixteen years old."

**2. Ordinal numeral adjectives** (*first, second, third,* etc.) **denote the position or order of a person or thing in a series.**

> Carl plays the *second* violin.
> Your friend is sitting in the *fifth* row.

**206.** All the cardinal and ordinal numerals may become nouns and may take a plural ending in some of their senses.

> *One* is enough.
> *Four* are missing.
> The *nine* played an excellent game.
> Three *twos* are six.
> The men formed by *fours*.
> *Thousands* perished by the way.
> Eight is two *thirds* of twelve. [So regularly **in fractional parts.**]

NOTE. *Hundred, thousand, million* were originally nouns, but are now equally common as adjectives. Other numeral nouns are: — twain, couple, pair, brace, trio, quartette, quintette, foursome, dozen, score, century.

**207.** Certain numeral adjectives (*single, double, triple,* etc.) indicate how many times a thing is taken or of how many like parts it consists.

> A *double* row of policemen stood on guard.
> A *fourfold* layer of chilled steel forms the door.

Some of these words may be used as adverbs.

> The cabman charged *double*.
> His fear increased *tenfold*.

**208.** Certain numeral adverbs and adverbial phrases indicate how many times an action takes place.

> *Once* my assailant slipped.
> I rang the bell *twice*.
> The river hath *thrice* flow'd, no ebb between. — SHAKSPERE.

The only adverbs of this kind in ordinary use are *once* and *twice*. For larger numbers an adverbial phrase (*three times, four times,* etc.) is employed *Thrice*, however, is still common in poetry and the solemn style.

# CHAPTER VI

## VERBS

### CLASSIFICATION OF VERBS

**209.** A verb is a word which can assert something (usually **an** action) concerning a person, place, or thing (§ 14).

Most verbs express **action**. Some, however, merely express **state** or condition. Thus, —

> 1. We *jumped* for joy.
>    Rabbits *burrow* into the sides of hills.
> 2. While memory *lasts,* I can never forget you.
>    This mountain *belongs* to the Appalachian range.

**A verb-phrase is a group of words that is used as a verb (§ 15).**

> The leaves *are turning*.
> The money *has been found*.

**210.** Certain verbs, when used to make verb-phrases, are called auxiliary (that is, "aiding") verbs, because they help other verbs to express action or state of some particular kind (§ 16).

The auxiliary verbs are *is* (*are, was, were,* etc.), *may, can, must, might, shall, will, could, would, should, have, had, do, did.*

> I am writing.          He has forgotten me.
> We must go.            We had failed.
> You will fall.         I do see him.

The auxiliary verb may be separated from the rest of the verb-phrase by other words.

> I *have* always *liked* him.
> I *shall* soon *send* for you.
> Robert *was* completely *bewildered*.
> He *has* hardly ever *spoken* to me.

**211.** Verbs are either **transitive** or **intransitive** (§ 99).

Some verbs may be followed by a substantive denoting that which receives the action or is produced by it. These are called **transitive** verbs. All other verbs are called intransitive.

A substantive that completes the meaning of a transitive verb is called its direct object.

In the following sentences, the first four verbs are **transitive** (with objects), the last five are **intransitive** (without objects) : —

> Lightning *shattered* the oak.
> Clouds *darkened* the sky.
> Chemists *extract* radium from pitchblende.
> The orator *quoted* Tennyson incorrectly.
> Look where he *stands* and *glares!*
> The bankrupt *absconded.*
> The orange sky of evening *died* away.
> The words *differ* in a single letter.

**212.** A verb which is transitive in one of its senses may be intransitive in another.

| TRANSITIVE (WITH OBJECT) | INTRANSITIVE (WITHOUT OBJECT) |
|---|---|
| Boys *fly* kites. | Birds *fly.* |
| The pirates *sank* the ship. | The stone *sank.* |
| I *closed* my eyes. | School *closed* yesterday. |
| Tom *tore* his coat. | The cloth *tore* easily. |

**213.** Many transitive verbs may be used absolutely, — that is, merely to express action without any indication of the direct object.

| TRANSITIVE VERB WITH OBJECT EXPRESSED | TRANSITIVE VERB USED ABSOLUTELY |
|---|---|
| The horses *drank* water. | The horses *drank* from the brook. |
| The farmer *plows* his fields. | The farmer *plows* in the spring. |
| Charles *is drawing* a picture. | Charles *is drawing.* |

There is a sharp contrast between a transitive verb used absolutely and a real intransitive verb. To the former we can always add an object; with the latter no object is possible.

**214.** *Is* (in its various forms) and several other verbs may be used to frame sentences in which some word or words in the predicate describe or define the subject (§ 17).

Such verbs are called **copulative** (that is, "joining") verbs.

*Is* in this use is often called the **copula** (or "link").

> Time *is* money.
> Grant *was* a tireless worker.
> Macbeth *became* a tyrant.
> His swans always *prove* geese.
> The current *is* sluggish.
> Lions *are* carnivorous.
> This village *looks* prosperous.
> The consul's brow *grew* stern.
> The queen *turned* pale.

In the first four examples, the copulative verb (the simple predicate [1]) is followed by a predicate nominative (§ 88, 2); in the last five by a predicate adjective (§ 172, 3).

The copulative verbs are intransitive, since they take no object. Sometimes, however, they are regarded as a third class distinct both from transitive and intransitive verbs.

**215.** The verb *is* is not always a copula. It is sometimes emphatic and has the sense of *exist*.

> I think. Therefore I *am*. [That is, I *exist*.]
> Whatever *is*, is right. [The second *is* is the copula.]

Most of the other copulative verbs may be used in some sense in which they cease to be copulative.

> The lawyer *proved* his case.
> Walnut trees *grow* slowly.
> Mr. Watson *grows* peaches.
> The wheel *turned* slowly on the axle.
> He *turned* his head and *looked* at me.

---

[1] Many grammarians regard *is* and the noun or adjective that follows it (*is money*, etc.) as the simple predicate; but the nomenclature here adopted is equally scientific and more convenient.

### INFLECTION OF VERBS

**216.** Verbs have inflections of **tense, person** and **number, and mood.** They also have the distinction of **voice,** which is expressed by the help of verb-phrases.

**Tense** indicates time; **person** and **number** correspond with person and number in substantives; **mood** shows the manner in which the action is expressed; **voice** indicates whether the subject acts or is acted upon.

### TENSE OF VERBS

**217.** The tense of a verb indicates its time.[1]

Verbs have forms of tense to indicate present, past, or future time.
1. A verb in the present tense refers to present time.
2. A verb in the past tense refers to past time.[2]
3. A verb in the future tense refers to future time.
The present, the past, and the future are called simple tenses.

| Present Tense | Past Tense | Future Tense |
|---|---|---|
| He *lives* here. | He *lived* here. | He *will live* here. |
| The sun *shines*. | The sun *shone*. | The sun *will shine* |
| I *know* him. | I *knew* him. | I *shall know* him. |

### FORMS OF THE PRESENT AND THE PAST

**218.** The **present** and the **past** tense have special forms of inflection.

For the moment we will consider the form which the verb has when its subject is the first personal pronoun *I*.

**In the present tense the verb has its simplest form, without any inflectional ending.**

| | |
|---|---|
| I *like* it. | I *dwell* in the wilderness. |
| I *hope* for the best. | I *find* him amusing. |

---

[1] The word *tense* is simply an English form of the French word for *time*.

[2] The **past tense** is often called the preterite (from a Latin word meaning "gone by"). *Preterite* is in some ways a better name for the tense than *past*, since both the perfect and the pluperfect tenses also refer to past time.

**219.** The past tense is formed in two ways, and a verb is classed as **weak** or **strong** in accordance with the way in which it forms this tense.

1. **Weak verbs form the past tense by adding *ed*, *d*, or *t* to the present.**

EXAMPLES : mend, mended ; select, selected ; fill, filled ; glow, glowed ; talk, talked ; revere, revered ; dwell, dwelt.

2. **Strong verbs form the past tense by changing the vowel of the present, without the addition of an ending.**

EXAMPLES : drink, drank ; begin, began ; come, came ; rise, rose ; bind, bound ; cling, clung ; stick, stuck ; wear, wore.[1]

Weak verbs are sometimes called **regular,** and strong verbs **irregular verbs.**

For a list of the strong verbs see pp. 291–297.

NOTE. The terms **strong** and **weak** were first applied to verbs for a some-what fanciful reason. The strong verbs were so called because they seemed to form the past tense out of their own resources, without calling to their assist-ance any ending. The weak verbs were so called because they could not form the past tense without the aid of the ending *ed*, *d*, or *t*.

**220.** The ending that is written *ed* is fully pronounced only when *d* or *t* precedes (as, — *thread, threaded ; attract, attracted*). Otherwise, *e* is silent, so that the ending becomes, in pronun-ciation, *d* or *t* (as, — *entered*, pronounced *enter'd ; rocked*, pronounced *rockt*).

In poetry and the solemn style, however, the silent *e* in the ending *ed* is sometimes restored to its ancient rights.

**221.** Many **weak verbs** show special irregularities in the past tense.

1. *Make* has *made* in the past, and *have* has *had.*

2. Some verbs in *-nd* and *-ld* form their past tense by chang-ing this *d* to *t.*

EXAMPLES : bend, bent ; send, sent ; lend, lent ; rend, rent ; spend, spent ; build, built.

[1] Silent final *e* is not counted as an ending.

3. A few verbs add *d* or *t* in the past and also change the vowel of the present. Thus, —

| | | | |
|---|---|---|---|
| sell | sold | buy | bought |
| tell | told | catch | caught |
| shoe | shod | seek | sought |
| say | said (pronounced *sed*) | beseech | besought |
| hear | heard (pronounced *herd*) | teach | taught |
| bring | brought | methinks | methought |

*Work* has an old past tense *wrought*, common in poetry; its usual past is *worked*. For *must, would*, etc., see p. 299.

4. Some verbs that have a long vowel sound in the present have in the past a short vowel sound before the ending *t*.

EXAMPLES : creep, crept ; keep, kept ; sleep, slept ; sweep, swept ; weep, wept ; feel, felt ; deal, dealt (pronounced *delt*) ; mean, meant (pronounced *ment*) ; lose, lost ; leave, left.[1]

5. Some verbs in *d* or *t* preceded by a long vowel sound have a short vowel in the past but add no ending.

EXAMPLES : bleed, bled ; breed, bred ; feed, fed ; speed, sped ; lead, led ; read (pronounced *reed*), read (pronounced *red*) ; meet, met ; light, lit (*also* lighted).

6. Some verbs in *d* or *t* have in the past the same form as in the present.

EXAMPLES : shed, *past* shed ; spread, *past* spread ; bet, *past* bet ; hit, *past* hit ; set, *past* set ; put, *past* put ; shut, *past* shut ; cut, *past* cut ; hurt, *past* hurt ; cast, *past* cast.

NOTE. The verbs in 5 and 6 might appear to be strong verbs, since they have no ending in the past and some of them change the vowel. They are, however, all weak verbs. Their lack of ending is due to the fact that the *d* or *t* of the termination has been absorbed in the final *d* or *t* of the verb itself. Thus, the past *set* was originally *settĕ* (dissyllabic), and this form, after the loss of -*ĕ*, became indistinguishable in sound from *set*, the present.

For lists of irregular weak verbs, see pp. 291–299.

[1] Notice also the change from *v* to *f* before *t*.

### PERSON AND NUMBER—THE PERSONAL ENDINGS

**222.** A verb must agree with its subject in number and person.

Verbs, like substantives, have two numbers (singular and plural) and three persons (first, second, and third).

The singular number denotes a single person or thing. The plural number denotes more than one person or thing.

The first person denotes the speaker; the second person denotes the person spoken to; the third person denotes the person or thing spoken of.

**223.** The inflections of **person and number** in verbs may be seen by framing sentences with the personal pronouns as subjects. Thus, —

#### PRESENT TENSE

| SINGULAR | PLURAL |
|---|---|
| 1. I walk. | 1. We walk. |
| 2. Thou walk-*est*. | 2. You walk. |
| 3. He walk-*s* [old form, walk-*eth*]. | 3. They walk. |

#### PAST TENSE

| SINGULAR | PLURAL |
|---|---|
| 1. I walked. | 1. We walked. |
| 2. Thou walked-*st*. | 2. You walked. |
| 3. He walked. | 3. They walked. |

From the sentences it is evident (1) that the **person** and **number** of a verb are usually shown by its subject only, but (2) that some verb-forms have special **endings** which denote person and number.

**224.** The endings by means of which a verb indicates person and number are called personal endings.

**1.** In the present tense a verb has two personal endings, *est* for the second person singular and *s* for the third person singular (old form *eth*).

The first person singular and all three persons of the plural are alike. The simplest form of the verb is used and no personal ending is added.

**2.** The past tense has but one personal ending, — *est* or *st* in the second person singular.[1]

The forms in *est* or *st* are confined to poetry and the solemn style. In ordinary language, the second person plural is used to address a single person.

The following table shows the **personal endings** of the present and the past tense : —

#### PERSONAL ENDINGS

| PRESENT TENSE | | PAST TENSE | |
|---|---|---|---|
| SINGULAR | PLURAL | SINGULAR | PLURAL |
| 1. [*no ending*] | 1. ⎫ | 1. [*no ending*] | 1. ⎫ |
| 2. -est, -st | 2. ⎬ [*no ending*] | 2. -est, -st | 2. ⎬ [*no ending*] |
| 3. -s [*old,* -eth] | 3. ⎭ | 3. [*no ending*] | 3. ⎭ |

#### CONJUGATION OF THE PRESENT AND THE PAST

**225.** The inflection of a verb is called its **conjugation** (§ 53). When we inflect a verb we are said to **conjugate** it.

#### CONJUGATION OF THE WEAK VERB *WALK*

##### PRESENT TENSE

| SINGULAR | PLURAL |
|---|---|
| 1. I walk. | 1. We walk. |
| 2. Thou walkest.[2] | 2. You walk. |
| 3. He walks. | 3. They walk. |

##### PAST TENSE

| SINGULAR | PLURAL |
|---|---|
| 1. I walked. | 1. We walked. |
| 2. Thou walkedst. | 2. You walked. |
| 3. He walked. | 3. They walked. |

---

[1] The ending *ed* indicates tense, not person or number.

[2] The second person singular is often given as "*Thou walkest* or *You walk*," but it is simpler to regard *You walk* in this use as a plural in a singular sense (§ 224).

## CONJUGATION OF THE STRONG VERB *FIND*

### PRESENT TENSE

| SINGULAR | PLURAL |
|---|---|
| 1. I find. | 1. We find. |
| 2. Thou findest. | 2. You find. |
| 3. He finds. | 3. They find. |

### PAST TENSE

| SINGULAR | PLURAL |
|---|---|
| 1. I found. | 1. We found. |
| 2. Thou foundest. | 2. You found. |
| 3. He found. | 3. They found. |

## CONJUGATION OF THE COPULA

### PRESENT TENSE

| SINGULAR | PLURAL |
|---|---|
| 1. I am. | 1. We are. |
| 2. Thou art. | 2. You are. |
| 3. He is. | 3. They are. |

### PAST TENSE

| SINGULAR | PLURAL |
|---|---|
| 1. I was. | 1. We were. |
| 2. Thou wast. | 2. You were. |
| 3. He was. | 3. They were. |

NOTE. The English verb formerly had more personal endings. In Chaucer, for instance, the typical inflection of the present is: —

| SINGULAR | PLURAL |
|---|---|
| 1. I walkë. | 1. We walken (*or* walkë). |
| 2. Thou walkest. | 2. Ye walken (*or* walkë). |
| 3. He walketh. | 3. They walken (*or* walkë). |

The disappearance of all weak final *e*'s in the fifteenth century (§ 191) reduced the first person singular and the whole plural to the single form *walk*. Later, *walks* (a dialect form) was substituted for *walketh*, and still later the second person singular was replaced in ordinary use by the plural. The result has been that in modern speech there are only two common forms in the present tense, — *walk* and *walks*. In poetry and the solemn style, however, *walkest* and *walketh* are still in use. The plural in *en* is frequently adopted by Spenser as an ancient form (or **archaism**): as, — "You *deemen* the spring is come."

### Special Rules of Number and Person

**226.** When the subject is compound (§ 38), the number of the verb is determined by the following rules : —

**1.** A compound subject with *and* usually takes a verb in the plural number.

> My brother and sister *play* tennis.
> The governor and the mayor *are* cousins.

**2.** A compound subject with *or* or *nor* takes a verb in the singular number if the substantives are singular.

> Either my brother or my sister *is* sure to win.
> Neither the governor nor the mayor *favors* this appointment.

**3.** A compound subject with *and* expressing but a single idea sometimes takes a verb in the singular number.

> The sum and substance [= gist] of the matter *is* this.

Note. This construction is rare in modern English prose. It is for the most part confined to such idiomatic phrases as *end and aim* (= *purpose*), *the long and short of it*, etc. The poets, however, use the construction freely (as in Kipling's " The tumult and the shouting dies ").

**4.** If the substantives connected by *or* or *nor* differ in number or person, the verb usually agrees with the nearer.

> Either you or he *is* to blame.
> Neither you nor he *is* an Austrian.
> Neither John nor we *were* at home.
> Neither the mayor nor the aldermen *favor* this law.

But colloquial usage varies, and such expressions are avoided by careful writers. The following sentences show how this may be done : —

> Either you are to blame, or he is.
> One of you two is to blame.
> Neither of you is an Austrian.
> He is not afraid ; neither am I.
> Both John and we were away from home.

**227.** In such expressions as the following, the subject is not compound, and the verb agrees with its singular subject: —

> The *governor* with his staff *is* present.
> *John*, as well as Mary, *is* in London.
> *Tom*, along with his friends Dick and Bob, *is taking* a sail.

**228.** Nouns that are plural in form but singular in sense commonly take a verb in the singular number (§ 84).

> Economics *is* an important study.
> The gallows *has been* abolished in Massachusetts.

In some words usage varies. Thus, *pains*, in the sense of *care* or *effort*, **is** sometimes regarded as a singular and sometimes as a plural.

> Great *pains has* (or *have*) been taken about the matter.

**229. Collective nouns** take sometimes a singular and sometimes a plural verb.

When the persons or things denoted are thought of as *individuals*, the plural should be used. When the collection is regarded as a **unit**, the singular should be used.[1]

**1.** The Senior Class *requests* the pleasure of your company. [Here the class is thought of **collectively**, acting as a unit.]
**2.** The Senior Class *are* unable to agree upon a president. [Here the speaker has in mind the **individuals** of whom the class is composed.]
**3.** The nation *welcomes* Prince Joseph. [The whole nation unites as a single individual to welcome a distinguished guest.]
**4.** The American nation *are* descended from every other nation on earth. [The separate qualities of the individuals who constitute the nation are in the speaker's mind.]

**230.** *A number* in the sense of "several" or "many" regularly takes the plural; *the number* takes the singular

> A number of sailors *were loitering* on the pier.
> The number of tickets *is limited*.

[1] This rule is not absolute. Sometimes the distinction is unimportant, and the feeling of the moment often determines the number of the verb.

**231.** *Half, part, portion,* and the like, take either the sin gular or the plural according to sense.

> *Half* of a circle *is* a semicircle.
> *Half* of the passengers *were* lost.

**232.** A verb which has for its subject a **relative pronoun** is in the same person and number as the antecedent. For examples, see § 149.

Errors are especially common in such sentences as,—

This is one of the strangest sights that ever *were* seen. [The antecedent of *that* is *sights* (not *one*) ; hence the relative (*that*) is plural, and accordingly the verb is plural (*were*, not *was*).]

Mr. Winn's oration was among the most eloquent that *have* [NOT *has*] been delivered in this state for many years.

This is one of the finest paintings there *are* in the hall. [For the omission of the relative, see § 151.]

### THE FUTURE TENSE

**233.** The **future tense** is a verb-phrase consisting of the auxiliary verb *shall* or *will* followed by the infinitive without *to* (§ 29).

The following table shows the form of the **future** for each of the three persons (1) in **assertions** and (2) in **questions** : —

### FUTURE TENSE

#### ASSERTIONS (DECLARATIVE)

| SINGULAR | PLURAL |
|---|---|
| 1. I shall fall. | 1. We shall fall. |
| 2. Thou wilt fall. | 2. You will fall. |
| 3. He will fall. | 3. They will fall. |

#### QUESTIONS (INTERROGATIVE)

| SINGULAR | PLURAL |
|---|---|
| 1. Shall I fall ? | 1. Shall we fall ? |
| 2. Shalt thou fall ? | 2. Shall you fall ? |
| 3. Will he fall ? | 3. Will they fall ? |

**234.** Common errors are the use of *will* for *shall* (1) in the first person in assertions and questions, and (2) in the second person in questions.

In the following sentences the first person of the future tense is correctly formed: —

| | |
|---|---|
| I shall [NOT *will*] drown. | Shall [NOT *will*] I drown ? |
| I shall [NOT *will* ] fail. | Shall [NOT *will*] I fail ? |
| We shall [NOT *will*] sink. | Shall [NOT *will*] we sink ? |

The verb-phrases with *shall* express merely the action of the verb in future time. They do not indicate any willingness or desire on the part of the subject.

Contrast the following sentences, in which *I will* or *we will* is used: —

> I will go with you.
> I will give you what you ask.
> I will not endure it.
> We will allow you to enter.
> We will have the truth.

Here the verb-phrases with *will* do not (as in the previous examples of *I shall*) express the action of the verb in future time. They express the **present willingness** or **desire** or **determination** of the speaker to do something in the future.

Hence such verb-phrases with *will* in the first person are not forms of the future tense. They are special verb-phrases expressing willingness or desire.

**235.** In the first person *shall,* not *will,* is the auxiliary of the future tense in both assertions and questions. It denotes simple futurity, without expressing willingness, desire, or determination.

*Will* in the first person is used in promising, threatening, consenting, and expressing resolution. It never denotes simple futurity.

### I. SIMPLE FUTURITY (FUTURE TENSE)

> *I shall be* eighteen years old in July. [NOT: *will be.*]
> Hurry, or *we shall miss* our train. [NOT: *will miss.*]
> *We shall be* glad to see him. [NOT: *will be.*]

## II. Promises, Threats, etc.

I *will subscribe* to your fund. [Promise.]
We *will do* our best. [Promise.]
I *will discharge* you if you are late again. [Threat.]
We *will permit* you to go. [Consent.]
I *will have* obedience. [Resolution.]

*I'll* and *we'll* are contractions of *I will* and *we will* and can never stand for *I shall* and *we shall*.

*I'll* meet you at noon. [Promise.]
*I'll* never consent. [Resolution.]
*We'll* be revenged on you. [Threat.]

**236.** When willingness is expressed by an **adjective**, *I shall* is correct; when by an **adverb**, *I will*. Thus,—

I *shall be glad* to help you.
I *will gladly* help you.

Note. Such expressions as *I shall be glad, I shall be willing, I shall be charmed to do this*, express willingness not by means of *shall* but in the adjectives *glad, willing, charmed*. To say, "I will be glad to do this," then, would be wrong, for it would be to express volition twice. Such a sentence could only mean "*I am determined* to be glad to do this."

On the other hand, in "I *will gladly help* you," volition is expressed by the verb-phrase *will help* and the adverb merely modifies the phrase by emphasizing the speaker's willingness. Hence *I will* is correct.

**237.** *Will*, when **emphasized**, always expresses determination on the part of the subject, even in the second and third persons.

I will go, no matter what you say.
You will } act foolishly, in spite of my advice.
He will }

**238.** In the second person *Shall you?* not *Will you?* is the proper form of the future tense in questions.

*Will you?* always denotes willingness, consent, or determination, and never simple futurity.

Note that in questions in the second person, the auxiliary used is the same as that expected in the answer.

### I. Future Tense (Simple Futurity)

*Shall* you *be* disappointed if he does not come? [I shall.]
*Shall* you *regret* his absence? [I shall.]
*Shall* you *go* by boat or by train? [I shall go by boat.]

### II. Verb-Phrase denoting Willingness, etc.

*Will* you *write* often? [I will.]
*Will* you *allow* me to help you? [I will.]
*Will* you *be* so kind as to open the window? [I will.]

**239.** *Shall* in the **second** and **third persons** is not the sign of the **future** tense in declarative sentences.

It is used in **commanding, promising, threatening,** and expressing **resolution,** the volition being that of the speaker.

Thou *shalt* not *kill.* [Command.]
You *shall have* the hat before Monday. [Promise.]
You *shall pay* for this insult! [Threat.]
She *shall* not *regret* her generosity. [Resolution.]

In prophetic language, *shall* is common in the second and third persons, even when there is no idea of commanding or the like.

The sun *shall be turned* into darkness and the moon into blood.— *Joel* ii. 31.

**240.** In military orders and official communications, custom permits the more courteous *will* in the place of *shall* in the second and third persons.

You *will* immediately report for orders.
Heads of Departments *will submit* their estimates before January first.

For *shall* and *will* in subordinate clauses, see pp. 130–132.

**241.** Future time may also be expressed by the present tense, or by *about* or *going* with the infinitive (§ 319).

We *sail* for Havana on Tuesday.
They are *about to begin* the study of Greek.

## COMPLETE OR COMPOUND TENSES

**242.** Completed action is denoted by special **verb-phrases** made by prefixing to the **past participle** some form of the auxiliary verb *have*.

These are called the **complete** or **compound tenses.**

There are three **complete** or **compound** tenses, — the **perfect** (or **present perfect**), the **pluperfect** (or **past perfect**), and the **future perfect.**

1. **The perfect (or present perfect) tense denotes that the action of the verb is complete at the time of speaking. It is formed by prefixing** *have* **(***hast, has***) to the past participle.**

> I *have learned* my lesson.
> He *has convinced* me.

NOTE. With several verbs of motion the auxiliary *be* is sometimes used instead of *have:* as, — "My friends *are gone*" (or "*have gone*"); "Your time *is come*" (or "*has come*").

2. **The pluperfect (or past perfect) tense denotes that the action was completed at some point in past time. It is formed by prefixing** *had* **(***hadst***) to the past participle.**

> Before night fell, I *had finished* the book.
> When Blake *had spoken*, Allen rose to reply.

3. **The future perfect tense denotes that the action will be completed at some point in future time. It is formed by prefixing the future tense of** *have* **(***shall have***, etc.) to the past participle.**

> Before I hear from you again, I *shall have landed* at Naples.

The future perfect tense is rare except in very formal writing.

**243.** The forms of the past participle will be studied in § 334. Meanwhile, the following practical rule will serve every purpose : —

**The past participle is that verb-form which is used after *I have*.**

EXAMPLES: [I have] mended, tried, swept, bought, broken, forgotten, found, sunk, dug.

**244.** A verb-phrase made by prefixing *having* to the past participle is called the **perfect participle**.

*Having reached* my destination, I stopped.

A verb-phrase made by prefixing *to have* to the past participle is called the **perfect infinitive**.

I am sorry *to have missed* you.

**245.** Three forms of the verb are so important that they are called the **principal parts**. These are:—

(1) the first person singular of the present;
(2) the first person singular of the past;
(3) the past participle.

| PRESENT | PAST | PAST PARTICIPLE |
|---|---|---|
| (I) walk | (I) walked | walked |
| (I) think | (I) thought | thought |
| (I) see | (I) saw | seen |
| (I) come | (I) came | come |
| (I) make | (I) made | made |

## VOICE — ACTIVE AND PASSIVE

**246.** Voice is that property of verbs which indicates whether the subject acts or is acted upon.

There are two voices, active and passive.

**1. A verb is in the active voice when it represents the subject as the doer of an act.**

Richard *shot* the bear.
Mr. Hardy *builds* carriages.
Dr. Wilson *has cured* my father.

**2. A verb is in the passive voice when it represents the subject as the receiver or the product of an action.**

The bear *was shot* by Richard.
Carriages *are built* by Mr. Hardy.
My father *has been cured* by Dr. Wilson.

**247.** The passive voice of a verb is expressed by a verb-phrase made by prefixing some form of the copula (*is, was,* etc.) to the past participle.

In the passive voice of the **complete tenses,** the past participle *been* follows the proper form of the auxiliary *have* (as in the third example in § 246, 2).

The passive of the **infinitive** is made by prefixing *to be* (perfect, *to have been*) to the past participle. Thus, —

> PRESENT INFINITIVE PASSIVE: to be struck.
> PERFECT INFINITIVE PASSIVE: to have been struck.

**248.** The following table gives the **conjugation** of the verb *strike* in the active and passive of the six tenses : —

| ACTIVE VOICE | PASSIVE VOICE |
|---|---|

PRESENT TENSE

SINGULAR

| | |
|---|---|
| 1. I strike. | 1. I am struck. |
| 2. Thou strikest. | 2. Thou art struck. |
| 3. He strikes. | 3. He is struck. |

PLURAL

| | |
|---|---|
| 1. We strike. | 1. We are struck. |
| 2. You strike. | 2. You are struck. |
| 3. They strike. | 3. They are struck. |

PAST TENSE

SINGULAR

| | |
|---|---|
| 1. I struck. | 1. I was struck. |
| 2. Thou struckest. | 2. Thou wast (*or* wert) struck. |
| 3. He struck. | 3. He was struck. |

PLURAL

| | |
|---|---|
| 1. We struck. | 1. We were struck. |
| 2. You struck. | 2. You were struck. |
| 3. They struck. | 3. They were struck. |

| ACTIVE VOICE | PASSIVE VOICE |
|---|---|

## FUTURE TENSE

### SINGULAR

| | |
|---|---|
| 1. I shall strike. | 1. I shall be struck. |
| 2. Thou wilt strike. | 2. Thou wilt be struck. |
| 3. He will strike. | 3. He will be struck. |

### PLURAL

| | |
|---|---|
| 1. We shall strike. | 1. We shall be struck. |
| 2. You will strike. | 2. You will be struck. |
| 3. They will strike. | 3. They will be struck. |

## PERFECT (OR PRESENT PERFECT) TENSE

### SINGULAR

| | |
|---|---|
| 1. I have struck. | 1. I have been struck. |
| 2. Thou hast struck. | 2. Thou hast been struck. |
| 3. He has struck. | 3. He has been struck. |

### PLURAL

| | |
|---|---|
| 1. We have struck. | 1. We have been struck. |
| 2. You have struck. | 2. You have been struck. |
| 3. They have struck. | 3. They have been struck. |

## PLUPERFECT (OR PAST PERFECT) TENSE

### SINGULAR

| | |
|---|---|
| 1. I had struck. | 1. I had been struck. |
| 2. Thou hadst struck. | 2. Thou hadst been struck. |
| 3. He had struck. | 3. He had been struck. |

### PLURAL

| | |
|---|---|
| 1. We had struck. | 1. We had been struck. |
| 2. You had struck. | 2. You had been struck. |
| 3. They had struck. | 3. They had been struck. |

| ACTIVE VOICE | PASSIVE VOICE |
|---|---|

### FUTURE PERFECT TENSE

#### SINGULAR

| | |
|---|---|
| 1. I shall have struck. | 1. I shall have been struck. |
| 2. Thou wilt have struck. | 2. Thou wilt have been struck. |
| 3. He will have struck. | 3. He will have been struck. |

#### PLURAL

| | |
|---|---|
| 1. We shall have struck. | 1. We shall have been struck. |
| 2. You will have struck. | 2. You will have been struck. |
| 3. They will have struck. | 3. They will have been struck. |

### USE OF THE PASSIVE VOICE

**249.** Any sentence of which the predicate is a transitive verb followed by an object, may be changed from the active to the passive form without affecting the sense.

> ACTIVE.    Richard *shot* the bear.
> PASSIVE.   The bear *was shot* by Richard.

In this change, (1) *bear*, the object of the active verb *shot*, becomes the subject of the passive verb *was shot ;* and (2) *Richard*, the subject of the active verb *shot*, becomes *by Richard*, an adverbial phrase, modifying the passive verb *was shot*. Thus we have the rule : —

**The object of the active verb becomes the subject of the passive, and the subject of the active verb becomes in the passive an adverbial phrase modifying the predicate verb.**

| ACTIVE VOICE | PASSIVE VOICE |
|---|---|
| My cat caught a bird. | A bird was caught by my cat. |
| Austin thanked Charles. | Charles was thanked by Austin. |
| The bullet penetrated a tree. | A tree was penetrated by the bullet. |
| Sargent painted that portrait. | That portrait was painted by Sargent. |
| The fireman had saved the child. | The child had been saved by the fireman. |

**250.** **Intransitive verbs** are ordinarily used in the active voice only.

The bystanders *laughed.*     The watchdogs *bark.*     Snow *is falling.*

**251.** An intransitive verb followed by a preposition is often used in the passive, the object of the preposition becoming the subject of the verb.

| ACTIVE VOICE | PASSIVE VOICE |
|---|---|
| Everybody *laughed at* him. | He *was laughed at* by everybody. |
| The attorney general *has* not yet *passed upon* this bill. | This bill *has* not yet *been passed upon.* |
| He *has tampered with* this lock. | This lock *has been tampered with.* |
| The cart *ran over* me. | I *was run over* by the cart. |

Other examples are: talk about (= discuss), look or inquire into (= investigate), look upon (= regard), jeer at (= deride), reason with, object to, insist upon, act upon.

NOTE. In this idiom, the preposition is treated like an **ending** attached to the verb to make it transitive. In other words, *laugh at, pass upon,* etc., are treated as compound verbs, and the object of the preposition is, in effect, the object of the compound. In the passive, this object becomes the subject and the preposition (now lacking an object) remains attached to the verb. The passive construction is well established, but not always graceful.

**252.** The passive of some verbs of *choosing, calling, naming, making,* and *thinking* may be followed by a **predicate nominative** (§ 88, 2).

| ACTIVE VOICE | PASSIVE VOICE |
|---|---|
| (PREDICATE OBJECTIVE) | (PREDICATE NOMINATIVE) |
| We elected John *president.* | John was elected *president.* |
| The Roman people called the chief *friend.* | The chief was called *friend* by the Roman people. |
| The herald proclaimed him *emperor.* | He was proclaimed *emperor* by the herald. |

NOTE. In the active voice, these verbs may take two objects referring to the same person or thing, — a direct object and a predicate objective (§ 104). In the passive, the direct object becomes the subject, and the predicate objective becomes a predicate nominative, agreeing with the subject (§ 88, 2).

### Object of the Passive

**253.** When a verb takes both a **direct** and an **indirect object,** one of the two is often retained after the passive, the other becoming the subject. Thus, —

### 1. The **indirect object** is retained.

| Active Voice | Passive Voice |
|---|---|
| My aunt gave *me* this watch. | This watch was given *me* by my aunt. |
| We allowed *them* free choice. | Free choice was allowed *them*. |
| He allowed each *speaker* an hour. | An hour was allowed each *speaker*. |
| Congress granted *me* a pension. | A pension was granted *me*. |

NOTE. The preposition *to* is often inserted in the passive construction, especially with a noun; as, — "A small pension was granted *to Dr. Johnson.*"

### 2. The **direct object** is retained.

| Active Voice | Passive Voice |
|---|---|
| We allowed them their *choice*. | They were allowed their *choice*. |
| He allowed each speaker an *hour*. | Each speaker was allowed an *hour*. |
| They showed me the *way*. | I was shown the *way*. |
| Experience has taught me *wisdom*. | I have been taught *wisdom* by experience. |

The direct object after a passive verb is often called the retained object.

NOTE. This construction, though common, is avoided by many careful writers, except in a few well-established idioms. Its habitual use gives one's style a heavy and awkward air. Instead of "He was given permission," one may say "He received permission"; instead of "I was given this watch by my aunt," either "It was my aunt who gave me this watch" or "This watch was a present from my aunt."

**254.** The verb *ask*, which may take two direct objects, — one denoting the person, the other the thing, — sometimes retains its second object in the passive construction (§ 103).

> ACTIVE.   We asked *him* his *opinion*.
> PASSIVE.  He was asked his *opinion*.

## PROGRESSIVE VERB-PHRASES

**255.** In addition to the tense-forms already described, verbs have so-called **progressive forms.**

**The progressive form of a tense represents the action of the verb as going on or continuing at the time referred to.**

I *ate* my dinner.
I *was eating* my dinner.
While I *was* quietly *reading* by my fireside, strange things *were taking* place in the square.

Both *ate* and *was eating* are in the past tense. But *ate* merely expresses a past action, whereas *was eating* describes this action as continuing or in progress in past time.

**256.** The progressive form is a verb-phrase made by prefixing to the present participle some form of the verb *to be*.

### PROGRESSIVE FORM

#### ACTIVE VOICE

##### PRESENT TENSE

| SINGULAR | PLURAL |
|---|---|
| **1.** I am striking. | 1. We are striking. |
| **2.** Thou art striking. | 2. You are striking. |
| **3.** He is striking. | 3. They are striking. |

So in the other tenses :

| | |
|---|---|
| PAST | I was striking, etc. |
| FUTURE | I shall be striking, etc. |
| PERFECT | I have been striking, etc. |
| PLUPERFECT | I had been striking, etc. |
| FUTURE PERFECT | I shall have been striking, etc. |

#### PASSIVE VOICE

| | |
|---|---|
| PRESENT | I am being struck, etc. |
| PAST | I was being struck, etc. |

**257.** In the passive, the progressive forms are confined to the present and the past tense.

> He *is being helped* by his brother. [Present.]
> I *am being trained* by Arthur Ray. [Present.]
> When I called, tea *was being served*. [Past.]

**258.** In subordinate clauses, the verb *is* (in its various forms) with its subject is often omitted in progressive phrases.

While *waiting* for the train, I bought a newspaper. [That is, While I was waiting.]

Though [he was] *swimming* vigorously, he could not stem the tide.

When [I am] *reading*, I like to have the light shine over my left shoulder.

In parsing, the omitted words should be supplied.

**259.** For such progressive forms as *is building* for *is being built*, see § 352.

### EMPHATIC VERB-PHRASES

**260.** The present or the past of a verb in the active voice may be expressed with emphasis by means of a verb-phrase consisting of *do* or *did* and the infinitive without *to*.

Such a phrase is called the emphatic form of the present or past tense.

" I do see you " and " I did go " differ from " I see you " and " I went " merely in emphasis. Hence *do see* is called the emphatic form of the present tense of *see*, and *did go* the emphatic form of the past tense of *go*.

**261.** In questions and in negative statements the emphatic forms are used without the effect of emphasis.

> Did you go ?          I did not go.

NOTE. *Do* often stands for some other verb which has just been used: as, — " Jack *swims* better than I *do*," " You *looked* as tired as she *did*." This idiom comes from the omission of the infinitive in the verb-phrase: — " Jack swims better than I *do* [*swim*]."

In poetry and older English the verb-phrase with *do* or *did* in declarative sentences often carries no emphasis, but merely takes the place of the present or past: as, — " The serpent beguiled me, and I *did eat*."

## MOOD OF VERBS

**262.** Mood is that property of verbs which shows the manner in which the action or state is expressed.

Mood (or mode) is derived from the Latin word *modus*, "manner."

Compare the following sentences, noting the form of the verb in each : —

> Richard *is* quiet.
> *Is* Richard quiet ?
> If Richard *were* quiet, I might study.
> Richard, *be* quiet.

In the first and second sentences, the form *is* is used to assert or question a fact; in the third, the form *were* expresses a condition or supposition that is contrary to fact; in the fourth, the form *be* expresses a command or request.

The difference in form seen in the verb in these sentences is called a difference of mood.

**263.** There are three moods, — the indicative, the imperative, and the subjunctive.

1. The indicative is the mood of simple assertion or interrogation, but it is used in other constructions also.

2. The imperative is the mood of command or request.

3. The subjunctive mood is used in certain special constructions of wish, condition, and the like.

Thus, in the examples in § 262, *is* is in the **indicative**, *were* in the **subjunctive**, and *be* in the **imperative** mood.

### I. INDICATIVE MOOD

**264.** The ordinary forms of the indicative mood in the active and the passive voice and in all six tenses, — present, past, future, perfect (or present perfect), pluperfect (or past perfect), and future perfect, — may be seen in the table on pp. 108–110.

For the progressive form of the indicative, see § 256; for the emphatic form, see § 260

**265.** The commonest uses of the indicative mood are in statements or questions as to matters of fact; but it may express almost any other form of thought. Thus, —

> Time and tide *wait* for no man. [Assertion.]
> How *goes* the world with you ? [Interrogation.]
> How it *rains !* [Exclamation.]
> If the river *rises*, the dam will be swept away. [Supposition.]
> I suspect that he *has absconded*. [Doubt.]
> I hope that John *will come* soon. [Desire.]
> Though Ellen *dislikes* algebra, she never shirks. [Concession.]
> You *will report* for duty immediately. [Command.]
> *Will* you *allow* me to use your knife ? [Request.]

NOTE. The indicative and the subjunctive were originally quite distinct in form, and each had its own set of constructions. But, as our language has grown simpler in its structure, the forms of these two moods have become almost identical, and the uses of the indicative have been greatly multiplied at the expense of the subjunctive. Indeed, there is scarcely any variety of thought expressed by the subjunctive or the imperative for which the indicative cannot also be employed. It is therefore impossible to frame any satisfactory definition of the indicative. Its functions are too varied to be included in one general statement. The indicative is often described as the mood which asserts thought *as a fact*, and the subjunctive as the mood which expresses thought as supposition (or *as mere thought*). But the indicative, as well as the subjunctive, may express supposition, condition, doubt, desire, concession, etc. Hence the definitions in § 263 are as exact as the facts of the language allow. All the efforts of grammarians to devise more " accurate " definitions break down when tested by actual usage.

### II. IMPERATIVE MOOD

**266.** The imperative is the mood of command or request.

| | |
|---|---|
| *Hurry !* | *Light* the lamp. |
| *Lie* down. | *Show* us the way. |
| *Shut* the door. | *Wait* a moment. |
| *Have* patience. | *Come* to dinner. |

The imperative has both voices, active and passive, but only one tense, — the present. It has both numbers, the singular and the plural, but only one person, the second. It has the same form for both the singular and the plural.

**267.** 1. **The imperative active is the verb in its simplest form.**

For examples, see § 266.

The imperative of the verb *to be* is *be*. Thus, —

| | |
|---|---|
| *Be* brave. | *Be* sure you are right. |
| *Be* careful. | *Be* here at noon. |

**2. The imperative passive is a verb-phrase consisting of *be* and a past participle.**

> *Be trusted* rather than feared.
> Study your failures and *be instructed* by them.

**268. The subject of an imperative is seldom expressed unless it is emphatic.**

The subject, when expressed, may precede the imperative: as, — *You sit here.*

NOTE. In older English, the subject often followed the imperative: as, — *Go thou, Go you, Hear ye.* This use is now confined to the solemn style and to poetry.

**269.** The **emphatic form** of the imperative consists of the imperative *do*, followed by the infinitive without *to*.

> *Do tell* me what he said.
> *Do stand* still.

The form with *do* is often used when the subject is expressed: as, — *Do you remain.*

**270.** Prohibition (or **negative command**) is commonly expressed by means of the form with *do*.

> *Do* not *open* a closed door without knocking.
> *Do* not *forget* to say "thank you."

In poetry and the solemn style prohibition is often expressed by the simple imperative with *not*.

> *Tell* me *not* what too well I know.
> *Devise not* evil against thy neighbor.
> *Seek not* to learn my name.

**271.** Commands are sometimes expressed in the indicative by means of *shall* or *will* (§§ 239–240).

> Thou *shalt* not *steal.*
> You *will leave* the room immediately.

For such expressions as "Forward!" "Off with you!" and the like, see § 530.

For the imperative in conditions, see § 418.

### III. SUBJUNCTIVE MOOD

#### FORMS OF THE SUBJUNCTIVE

**272. The subjunctive mood is used in certain special constructions of wish, condition, and the like.**

In older English the subjunctive forms were common in a variety of uses, as they still are in poetry and the solemn style. In ordinary prose, however, subjunctive forms are rare, and in conversation they are hardly ever heard, except in the case of the copula *be.*

The subjunctive forms of *be* are the following : —

#### SUBJUNCTIVE MOOD

##### PRESENT TENSE

| SINGULAR | PLURAL |
|---|---|
| 1. If I be. | 1. If we be. |
| 2. If thou be. | 2. If you be. |
| 3. If he be. | 3. If they be. |

##### PAST TENSE

| SINGULAR | PLURAL |
|---|---|
| 1. If I were. | 1. If we were. |
| 2. If thou wert. | 2. If you were. |
| 3. If he were. | 3. If they were. |

##### PERFECT (OR PRESENT PERFECT) TENSE

| SINGULAR | PLURAL |
|---|---|
| 1. If I have been. | 1. If we have been. |
| 2. If thou have been. | 2. If you have been. |
| 3. If he have been. | 3. If they have been. |

PLUPERFECT (OR PAST PERFECT) TENSE

| SINGULAR | PLURAL |
|---|---|
| 1. If I had been. | 1. If we had been. |
| 2. If thou hadst been. | 2. If you had been. |
| 3. If he had been. | 3. If they had been. |

*If* is used in the paradigm because it is in clauses beginning with *if* that the subjunctive is commonest in modern English; but *if* is of course no part of the subjunctive inflection.

**273.** In other verbs, the **subjunctive active** has the same forms as the **indicative**, except in the **second** and **third persons singular** of the **present** and the **perfect**, which are like the **first** person : —

| PRESENT | PERFECT |
|---|---|
| 1. If I strike. | 1. If I have struck. |
| 2. If thou strike. | 2. If thou have struck. |
| 3. If he strike. | 3. If he have struck. |

In the **passive subjunctive**, the subjunctive forms of the copula (§ 272) are used as auxiliaries : — present, *If I be struck;* past, *If I were struck;* perfect, *If I have been struck;* pluperfect, *If I had been struck.* (See table, p. 304.)

**274.** **Progressive verb-phrases** in the subjunctive may be formed by means of the copula : — present, *If I be striking;* past, *If I were striking.* The present is rare ; the past is common.

USES OF THE SUBJUNCTIVE

**Subjunctive in Wishes and Exhortations**

**275.** The subjunctive is often used in wishes or prayers.

> Angels and ministers of grace *defend* us !
> Heaven *help* him !
> The saints *preserve* us !
> God *bless* you !
> Long *live* the king !
> O that I *had listened* to him !
> O that we *were* rid of him !

In the first five examples, the wish is expressed in an independent sentence. In the last two, the construction is subordinate, — the *that*-clause being the object of an unexpressed " I wish " (§ 407).

**276.** The subjunctive *be* is often omitted when it may easily be supplied.

> Peace [*be*] to his ashes !
> Honor [*be*] to his memory !
> Honor [*be*] to whom honor is due !

**277.** Wishes are often introduced by *may* or *would*.

> *May* you never want !
> *Would* that he *were* safe !
> *Would* you *were* with us ! [For *Would that.*]

*May* and *would* in such expressions were originally subjunctives; *would* stands for *I would*, that is, *I should wish*. *Want* in the first example is an infinitive without *to* (§ 311). For wishes expressed by the infinitive, see § 320.

**278.** Exhortations in the first person plural sometimes take the subjunctive in elevated or poetical style.

> *Hear we* the king !
> *Join we* in a hymn of praise !

Exhortation is ordinarily expressed by *let us* followed by the infinitive without *to*.

> Let us join hands.
> Let us have peace.
> Let 's camp here.

*Let* is a verb in the imperative mood, *us* is its object, and the infinitive (*join, have, camp*) depends on *let*.

### Subjunctives in Concessions, Conditions, etc.

**279.** The subjunctive is used after *though, although,* to express an admission or concession not as a fact but as a supposition.

> Though he *slay* me, yet will I trust in him.
> Though he *were* to beg this on his knees, I should still refuse

When the concession is stated as an admitted **fact, the indicative** is regular.

> Although he *is* a foreigner, he speaks good English.
> Though he sometimes *sings*, he is not now in good voice.

**280.** After *if* and *unless*, expressing **condition,** the **subjunctive**
may be used in a variety of ways.

1. If this *be* gold, our fortune is made. [It may or may not be gold.]
2. If he *confess*, I shall overlook the offence. [He may or may not
confess.]
3. Unless he *confess*, he cannot be convicted. [He may or may not
confess.]
4. If this *were* gold, our fortune would be made. [It is *not* gold ; hence
our fortune is not made.]
5. If he *stood* before me at this moment, I should tell him my opinion. [He does *not* stand before me ; hence I do not tell him.]
6. If he *had confessed*, I should have overlooked his fault. [He did
not confess ; hence I did not overlook it.]
7. Unless he *had confessed*, he could not have been convicted. [He
did confess ; hence he was convicted.]

In conditional clauses, the **present subjunctive** denotes either
**present** or **future** time. It puts the supposed case doubtfully, but
not necessarily as improbable. (See examples 1–3.)

The **past subjunctive** refers to **present** time. It implies that
the supposed case **is not now a fact.** (See examples 4 and 5.)

The **pluperfect** (or **past perfect**) **subjunctive** refers to **past** time.
It implies that the supposed case **was not a fact.** (See 6 and 7.)

For details of conditional sentences, see pp. 167–172.

**281.** Concession or condition may be expressed by the **subjunctive**
without *though* or *if*, the verb preceding the subject, which is
sometimes omitted.

### I. Concession

> *Try* as we may, we cannot swim to that rock.
> *Say* what he will, he can never convince me.
> *Come* what will, I 'll stand my ground.
> *Be* that as it may, my mind is made up.

## II. Condition

*Were* I asked, I could tell all the facts. [If I were asked, etc.]
*Had* I known, I would have written to you. [If I had known, etc.]
I shall be twenty years old, *come* Tuesday. [If Tuesday come, etc.]
I will go, *rain* or *shine*. [If it rain, or if it shine, etc.]
*Be* he prince or *be* he pauper, every guest is welcome here.

NOTE. The subjunctive in these concessive and conditional uses is really the same as that in exhortations (§ 278). "*Try* [*we*] as we may" means literally, "*Let us try* as hard as we can," and this has the force of "*However* hard we try" or "*Although we try* ever so hard."

**282.** After *as if* (*as though*), the **past subjunctive** is used.

He looks as if he *were* about to speak. [NOT: as if he *was* about to speak.]
I act as if I *were* crazy. [NOT: as if I *was* crazy.]

**283.** The **subjunctive** may express not what **is** or **was**, but what **would be** or **would have been**, the case.

It *were* safer to travel by day. [It would be safer, etc.]
I *had been* wiser had I forded the river. [I should have been wiser if I had.]

This construction is old-fashioned. Modern English commonly uses *should* (or *would*) *be, should* (or *would*) *have been,* instead.

**284.** The **subjunctive** is occasionally used after *that, lest, before, until,* etc., in subordinate clauses referring to the future and commonly expressing **purpose** or **expectation**.

Take heed that he *escape* not. [Purpose.]
Give him food lest he *perish*. [Purpose.]
Let us tarry until he *come*. [Expectation.]

This construction is confined to poetry and the solemn or formal style. In ordinary language the indicative or a verb-phrase with *may* is used.

Take heed that he *does* not *escape*.
Give him food in order that he *may* not *perish*.
Let us wait till he *comes*.

**285.** The **past subjunctive** *had* is common in *had rather* and similar phrases.

> I *had rather* wait a day.
> You *had better* leave the room.
> He *had as lief* go as stay.

NOTE. *Had* in this construction is sometimes condemned as erroneous or inelegant; but the idiom is well-established.

*Might better, would better,* and *would rather* may be used instead of *had better,* etc.; but *would better* is improper in the first person.

**286.** The subjunctive forms are often replaced by verb-phrases containing the auxiliaries *may, might, could, would, should.*

**1.** In wishes (§ 277).

> *May* you *live* long and *prosper!*
> *May* he never *repent* this act !
> Ah, *could* I but *live* a hundred years !

**2.** In concessions and conditions (§§ 279–280).

> Though $\begin{Bmatrix} \text{I} \\ \text{you} \\ \text{he} \end{Bmatrix}$ *should fail,* there would still be hope.

> If $\begin{Bmatrix} \text{I} \\ \text{you} \\ \text{he} \end{Bmatrix}$ *should fail,* all would be lost.

**3.** In sentences expressing not what **is** or **was,** but **what would be** or **would have been,** the case (§ 283).

> $\begin{Bmatrix} \text{I } should \\ \text{You } would \\ \text{He } would \end{Bmatrix}$ *write* to Charles if I knew his address.
> It *would have been* better to telegraph.

**4.** In subordinate clauses introduced by *that, lest, before, until,* etc. (§ 284).

> I will take care that nothing *may prevent.*
> I took care that nothing $\begin{Bmatrix} might \\ should \end{Bmatrix}$ *prevent.*
> The general determined to wait until fresh troops *should arrive.*

## POTENTIAL VERB-PHRASES

### USE OF MODAL AUXILIARIES

**287.** Several auxiliary verbs are used to form verb-phrases indicating ability, possibility, obligation, or necessity.

Such verb-phrases are called **potential phrases,** that is, " phrases of possibility."

The auxiliary verbs used in **potential phrases** are : — *may, can, must, might, could, would,* and *should.* They are called **modal auxiliaries** and are followed by the infinitive without *to.*

> We *may ask* him a few questions.
> I *can manage* a motor car.
> You *must inquire* the way.
> He *might give* you a chance.
> I *could show* you his house if you *would permit* me.
> I *should enjoy* a sea-voyage.

NOTE. The fact that *give*, etc., in such phrases as *can give*, are infinitives may be seen by comparing " I can *strike* " with " I am able *to strike*," " I may *strike* " with " I am permitted *to strike*," " I must *strike* " with " I am obliged *to strike*," and so on. In earlier periods of the language, when the infinitive had a special ending (*-an* or *-en*), the nature of the construction was unmistakable.

**288.** Potential phrases may be arranged in tables of conjugation, like that on pp. 108–110. They are often called, collectively, the **potential mood.**

### ACTIVE VOICE

#### PRESENT TENSE

| SINGULAR | PLURAL |
|---|---|
| 1. I may strike.[1] | 1. We may strike. |
| 2. Thou mayst strike. | 2. You may strike. |
| 3. He may strike. | 3. They may strike. |

#### PAST TENSE

| | |
|---|---|
| 1. I might strike.[2] | 1. We might strike. |
| 2. Thou mightst strike. | 2. You might strike. |
| 3. He might strike. | 3. They might strike. |

[1] So *I can strike*, etc.
[2] So *I could strike*, etc.

### Perfect (or Present Perfect) Tense

| SINGULAR | PLURAL |
|---|---|
| **1.** I may have struck.[1] | **1.** We may have struck. |
| **2.** Thou mayst have struck. | **2.** You may have struck. |
| **3.** He may have struck. | **3.** They may have struck. |

### Pluperfect (or Past Perfect) Tense

| | |
|---|---|
| **1.** I might have struck.[2] | **1.** We might have struck. |
| **2.** Thou mightst have struck. | **2.** You might have struck. |
| **3.** He might have struck. | **3.** They might have struck. |

### Passive Voice

#### Present Tense

I may be struck, etc.          We may be struck, etc.

#### Past Tense

I might be struck, etc.          We might be struck, etc.

#### Perfect (or Present Perfect) Tense

I may have been struck, etc.          We may have been struck, etc.

#### Pluperfect (or Past Perfect) Tense

I might have been struck, etc.          We might have been struck, etc.

**289.** *Can* (past tense, *could*) regularly indicates that the subject **is able** to do something.

> John *can* ride a bicycle.
> Harry *could* swim.

**290.** *May* (past tense, *might*) indicates (1) **permission,** (2) **possibility** or doubtful intention, (3) a **wish.**

> (1) You *may* borrow my pencil.
> I told him that he *might* join our party.
> (2) He *may* accept my offer.
> You *might* not like it.
> (3) *May* good fortune attend you !

---

[1] So *I can have struck*, etc.     [2] So *I could have struck*, etc.

**291.** In asking permission, the proper form is "*May* I?" not "*Can* I?" With negatives, however, *can* is more common than *may*, except in questions. Thus, —

> QUESTION. *May* I (or *may* n't I) play ball this morning?
> ANSWER. No, you *cannot;* but you *may* play this afternoon.

**292.** *Must* expresses **necessity** or **obligation.**

> We *must* all die sometime.
> You *must* wait for the train.
> You *must* not be discouraged by failure.

NOTE. *Must*, though originally a past tense, is in modern English almost always used as a present. Past necessity may be expressed by *had to* with the infinitive: as, — "I *had to wait* for the train."

**293.** *Ought* with the **present infinitive,** expresses a present duty or moral obligation; with the **perfect infinitive,** a past duty or obligation. *Should* is often used in the same sense.

> I *ought to write* that letter. [Present.]
> You *ought* not *to object.* [Present.]
> This roof *ought to be mended.* [Present.]
> I *ought to have known* better. [Past.]
> Your dog *ought* not *to have been unleashed.* [Past.]
> You *should be* careful. [Present.]
> The garden *should have been weeded* yesterday. [Past.]

NOTE. *Ought* is really an old past tense of the verb *owe*, but is now always a present. Its former meaning may be seen in Dame Quickly's "You *ought* him a thousand pound" (SHAKSPERE, *1 Henry IV*, iii. 3. 152).

*Had* should never be prefixed to *ought*.

| CORRECT | INCORRECT |
|---|---|
| You *ought* to stay at home. | You had ought to stay at home. |
| We *ought* n't to make so much noise. | We had n't ought to make so much noise. |
| John ought to begin, *ought* n't he? | John ought to begin, had n't he? |

**294.** *Should* and *ought* sometimes express what would certainly be expected in the case supposed.

Three weeks $\left\{\begin{array}{l} should \\ ought\ to \end{array}\right\}$ suffice.

If the train is on time, he $\left\{\begin{array}{l} should \\ ought\ to \end{array}\right\}$ arrive at six.

**295.** *Would* in all three persons sometimes indicates **habitual action** in the past.

*I would* gaze at the sea for hours at a time.

Whenever we asked Edward about his adventures, *he would begin* to talk of something else.

## SPECIAL RULES FOR *SHOULD* AND *WOULD*

**296.** *Should* is the past tense of *shall*, and *would* is the past tense of *will*. Hence the rules for *should* and *would* are similar to those for *shall* and *will* (§§ 233–239). But there is much variation, especially in subordinate clauses.

### I. IN SIMPLE SENTENCES AND INDEPENDENT CLAUSES

**297.** Except in certain kinds of subordinate clauses, the distinction between *should* and *would* is practically the same as that between *shall* and *will*.

When the auxiliary verb expresses **futurity** without any idea of **wishing, consenting,** or the like, the forms are as follows : —

#### ASSERTIONS (DECLARATIVE)

| SINGULAR | PLURAL |
|---|---|
| **1.** I should fall. | **1.** We should fall. |
| **2.** Thou wouldst fall. | **2.** You would fall. |
| **3.** He would fall. | **3.** They would fall. |

#### QUESTIONS (INTERROGATIVE)

| SINGULAR | PLURAL |
|---|---|
| **1.** Should I fall ? | **1.** Should we fall ? |
| **2.** Shouldst thou fall ? | **2.** Should you fall ? |
| **3.** Would he fall ? | **3.** Would they fall ? |

**298.** Common errors are the use of *I would* for *I should* in assertions, and that of *Would I?* and *Would you?* for *Should I?* and *Should you?* in questions.

The correct forms are shown in the following sentences.

I. *I should (we should)* and *I would (we would)* in **assertions** : --

1. *I should* break my neck if I fell.
2. *I should* hesitate to try this experiment.
3. *I should*n't wonder if he escaped.
4. *We should* regret any misunderstanding.
5. *I should* wish to examine the plans again before deciding.
6. *I should* be glad to accept any fair offer.
7. *I would* give five dollars for a ticket.
8. *I would* help you if I could.
9. *I would* never agree to such a proposition.
10. *We would* rather die than surrender.
11. *We would* pay our bill to-day if we had the money.
12. *I would* gladly accept any fair offer.

In the first six examples, *I* (or *we*) *should* is correct, because the auxiliary gives no suggestion of the speaker's will (or volition). In the last six, on the contrary, the speaker's willingness or desire is plainly expressed by the auxiliary, and *I* (or *we*) *would* is therefore used.

NOTE. In such sentences as the fifth, — "I should wish to examine the plans again before deciding," — *wish* expresses volition. Hence "I *would* wish" is incorrect, for it expresses volition twice and can mean only "I desire to wish." On the same principle we say "I should prefer," "I should be glad," etc. (see § 236).

Sometimes either *I would* or *I should* may be used, but with a difference in meaning. Thus, in the eighth example, "I should help you" might be substituted for "I would help you." This change, however, makes the remark sound less cordial and sympathetic; for *I should* (unlike *I would*) gives no hint of the speaker's desire to be of service.

II. *Should I* (or *we*)? in **questions** : —

1. *Should I* break my neck if I fell?
2. *Should I* be poisoned if I ate those berries?
3. *Should I* take cold without my overcoat?
4. *Should I* disturb you if I were to practise my music lesson?
5. *Should we* run aground if we missed the channel?

NOTE. *Would I?* is confined, for the most part, to questions in which one repeats the words or thought of another. Thus, — "*You would* give five dollars for a ticket." "*Would I?* No, I would n't!" In this use it is chiefly colloquial.

III. *Should you?* and *Would you?* in questions : —

1. *Should you* drown if the boat were to capsize ? [Yes, *I should* drown, for I do not know how to swim.]

2. *Should you* despair if this plan were a failure ? [No, *I should* not, for I have other resources.]

3. *Should you* think that ten yards of velvet would be enough ? [Yes, *I should* think so.]

4. *Should you* be offended if I were to speak frankly ? [No, *I should* not be offended.]

5. *Should you* wish to examine the plans again before deciding ? [Yes, *I should* (see note under I, above).]

6. *Would you* wear a hat or a cap ? [*I would* wear a cap if I were you.]

7. *Would you* study Greek if you were in my place ? [Yes, *I would.*]

8. *Would you* accept my apology if it were offered ? [Certainly, *I would* accept it gladly.]

9. *Would you* be so kind as to lend me your compasses? [Certainly *I would* lend them, if I had not lost them.]

10. *Would you* allow me to use your name as a reference ? [*I would.*]

The choice between *should* and *would* in these sentences corresponds to the form expected in the answer (§ 238).

**299.** The chief occasions on which *Would you?* is correct are : — (1) in **asking advice** in a matter of doubt, and (2) in **asking consent** or **permission**.

In examples 6 and 7 in § 298, III, the speaker asks advice ; in 8, 9, and 10, he asks consent or permission.

**300.** Note that the proper forms are *I should like, Should I like?* and *Should you like?*

*I should* like to read that book.
*Should I* like to go to Rome ? Indeed, *I should.*
*Should you* like to receive a copy of our catalogue ? [*I should* like to receive one.]

NOTE. *Would* is very common in these phrases, even among writers of repute, but it is still contrary to the best usage. The reason for *should* is the same as in *I should wish* (§ 298, I, note).

**301.** *I'd* and *we'd* are contractions of *I would* and *we would*. Hence they can never stand for *I should* and *we should* (§ 235).

**302.** *Should* in the **second** and **third persons** may be used in simple declarative sentences and independent clauses to express the will of the speaker (§ 239).

If I had my way, *you should* be prosecuted. [That is: I would take care that you were prosecuted.]

If I had the money, *you should* be paid immediately. [Compare: *You shall* be paid.]

If I were you, *she should* not regret her generosity. [Compare: *She shall* not regret it.]

## II. *SHOULD* AND *WOULD* IN SUBORDINATE CLAUSES

**303.** In some kinds of **subordinate clauses,** the use of *should* and *would* differs considerably from that in simple sentences and principal clauses.

The following classes require attention : — (1) clauses of purpose or expectation (§ 304), (2) conditional and concessive clauses (§ 305), (3) clauses expressing volition not that of the subject (§ 306), (4) clauses stating something as an idea (§ 307), (5) indirect discourse (§ 308).

**304.** In subordinate clauses expressing the **purpose** or **expectation** with which anything is done, *shall* and *should* are used in all three persons.

Carleton took great pains that $\begin{Bmatrix} I \\ you \\ they \end{Bmatrix}$ *should* understand the details of the treaty.

Scott $\begin{Bmatrix} is \\ was \end{Bmatrix}$ very careful that *nothing* $\begin{Bmatrix} shall \\ should \end{Bmatrix}$ interfere with his plans.

They took every precaution lest $\begin{Bmatrix} I \\ you \\ he \end{Bmatrix}$ *should* suspect the plot.

Anderson waited patiently until $\begin{Bmatrix} I \\ you \\ they \end{Bmatrix}$ *should* arrive with the horses.

We strained every nerve to reach the cave before the *storm should* break.

**305.** In conditional or concessive clauses expressing a future supposed case doubtfully, *shall* and *should* are used in all three persons; but *will* and *would* are proper when the subject is thought of as wishing or consenting.

**1.** What would happen if $\begin{Bmatrix} I \\ you \\ he \end{Bmatrix}$ *should* not carry out the commander's instructions?

**2.** If $\begin{Bmatrix} I \\ you \\ he \end{Bmatrix}$ *should* miss the steamer, our friends would be alarmed.

**3.** *Whoever* $\begin{Bmatrix} shall \\ should \end{Bmatrix}$ violate this law $\begin{Bmatrix} shall \\ should \end{Bmatrix}$ pay the penalty. [That is: If anybody shall violate, etc.]

**4.** Whenever $\begin{Bmatrix} I \\ you \\ he \end{Bmatrix}$ *shall* find an opportunity, let us try the experiment. [That is: If ever I shall find, etc.]

**5.** He promised to assist you whenever *you should* need help. [Whenever = if ever.]

**6.** Though $\begin{Bmatrix} we \\ you \\ they \end{Bmatrix}$ *should* fail, others would make the attempt. [Concession.]

**7.** Though *Evans should* disappoint me, I should not lose confidence in him.

**8.** Vernon will do his part if $\begin{Bmatrix} I \\ you \\ they \end{Bmatrix}$ *will* coöperate with him.

**9.** If $\begin{Bmatrix} I \\ you \\ he \end{Bmatrix}$ *will* only make the effort, success is certain.

**10.** Edmund would reveal the secret if $\begin{Bmatrix} I \\ you \\ they \end{Bmatrix}$ *would* assist him in his search for the treasure.

**11.** If *we would* take pains, our parents would be satisfied.

**12.** *Whoever will* join us may be sure of a pleasant and profitable journey. [That is: If any one will join us, he may be sure, etc.]

When a future supposed case is admitted or conceded as certain, *will* may be used in the second and third persons to denote mere futurity.

Though $\begin{Bmatrix} you \\ he \end{Bmatrix}$ *will* certainly fail, $\begin{Bmatrix} you \\ he \end{Bmatrix}$ may make the attempt.

Though the *ship will* not sink for some hours, let us take to the boats.

**306.** *Shall* and *should* are often used in the second and third persons in subordinate clauses to express volition which is not that of the subject.

> Templeton insists that *you shall* accompany him.
> This letter directs where *you shall* station yourself.
> We gave orders that the *gates should* be closed.
>
> My wish is that $\left\{ \begin{array}{l} you \\ he \end{array} \right\}$ *should* remain at home.
>
> The law prescribed when and to whom the *tax should* be paid.

**307.** When a clause with *that* states something, not as a fact but as an **idea** to be considered, *should* is the proper auxiliary in all three persons.

> I am not surprised that you *should* find your lesson rather difficult. [That is : " When I consider the matter, I do not find the idea surprising." In " I am not surprised *that you find*," etc., the subordinate clause makes the statement **as a fact.**]
>
> It is strange that Tom *should* neglect his swimming lessons. [Contrast : It is strange that Tom *neglects*.]
>
> That Napoleon *should* have chafed at captivity is only natural. [Contrast : That Napoleon *chafed*.]

**308.** For *shall* and *will*, *should* and *would*, in **indirect discourse**, see §§ 438–439.

### THE INFINITIVE

**309.** The **infinitive** is a **verb-form** that has some of the properties of a noun (§ 28). Its two-sided character comes out clearly when it is used as the subject of a sentence.

> 1. *To hope* is our only resource.
> 2. *To flatter* is not my custom.
> 3. *To sleep* was an impossibility.
> 4. *To surrender* seemed disgraceful.
> 5. *To choose* wisely was my greatest difficulty.
> 6. *To scale* the wall was the work of a moment.

Each of these infinitives (*to hope*, *to flatter*, etc.) is a **noun,** for each is the simple subject of a sentence. Besides, an ordinary noun may be substituted for each infinitive with no change in meaning; as, — "*Hope* is our only resource"; "*Flattery* is not my custom"; "*Sleep* was an impossibility."

But each of these infinitives is also a **verb**, — for (1) it expresses action; (2) it may be modified by an adverb, as in No. 5; (3) it takes an object if it is transitive, as in No. 6.

An infinitive (as the examples show) has regularly no subject and therefore lacks both number and person. Hence it is not bound by the general rule for the agreement of a verb with its subject (§ 222). From this fact it derives its name, **infinitive,** which means "unrestricted" or "free from limitations." [1]

**310.** The infinitive is a verb-form which partakes of the nature of a noun. It expresses action or state in the simplest possible way, without person or number.

It is commonly preceded by the preposition *to,* which is called the sign of the infinitive.

*To* is not, in strictness, a part of the infinitive, but it may be so regarded for convenience, since the infinitive, in most of its uses, is preceded by *to*.

NOTE. *To* sometimes stands for an infinitive in careless speech: as, — "You may go if you wish *to*" (that is, "if you wish *to go*"). Such expressions are to be avoided. It is better to say, "You may go if you wish."

**311.** The infinitive often lacks *to*, especially in verb-phrases with the auxiliaries *will, shall, may, can, must, might, could, would, should, do, did.* For examples, see pp. 102, 114, 124.

**312.** The infinitive has two tenses, — the **present** and the **perfect.**

1. The **present infinitive** is the verb in its simplest form, usually preceded by *to :* as, — *to live, to teach, to bind, to strike.*

2. The **perfect infinitive** is made by prefixing the infinitive of the auxiliary verb *have* to the past participle (§ 243): as, — *to have lived, to have taught, to have bound, to have struck.*

[1] For the so-called **infinitive clause,** in which the infinitive has a subject of a peculiar kind, see §§ 324-328.

**313.** An infinitive may be modified by an **adverb**, an **adverbial phrase**, or an **adverbial clause**.

To write *legibly* is a valuable accomplishment.
It would be useless to search *longer*.
They allowed him to go *in peace*. [Adverbial phrase.]
To dive *among those weeds* would be folly.
Theodore promises to come *when I send for him*. [Adverbial clause.]

**No modifier should be inserted between *to* and the infinitive.**

I beg you to inquire carefully into this matter. [NOT: to carefully inquire.]
Mr. Harris moved to postpone the question indefinitely. [NOT: to indefinitely postpone.]
I expect always to be poor. [NOT: to always be poor.]

NOTE. Careless writers pay slight attention to this rule, and some good writers and speakers defy it, hoping to break it down. But it is unquestionably still in accord with the best usage.

**314. The infinitive may take an object if its meaning allows.**

I long to visit *Italy*.
My mother feared to enter the *house*.
To launch a *boat* was impossible.
To grant your *request* is a pleasure.
To give *him money* is useless. [*Money* is the direct object of *to give*, and *him* the indirect object.]

**315.** The infinitive is used in a variety of constructions, — (1) as a **noun**, (2) as an **adjective modifier** or **adverbial modifier**, (3) in the so-called **infinitive clause**.

### I. THE INFINITIVE AS NOUN

**316.** The infinitive is used in various **noun constructions**, — as subject, as predicate nominative, as nominative of exclamation, as appositive, as object of certain prepositions, as modifier.

**317. An infinitive with or without a complement or modifiers, may be used as the subject of a sentence, as a predicate nominative, or as an appositive.**

*To descend* was extremely difficult. [Subject.]

*To secure* a seat was impossible.

*To sing* well requires practice.

His delight was *to travel.* [Predicate nominative.]

The governor's policy is *to wait.*

My wish is *to see* you immediately.

*To decide* was *to act.* [The first infinitive is the subject, and the second is a predicate nominative.]

Both alternatives, *to advance* and *to retreat*, seemed equally hazardous. [Apposition with the subject.]

My first plan, *to tunnel* under the wall, proved a failure.

He has but one aim in life, *to succeed.* [Apposition with the object.]

I have written with a definite purpose, *to dissuade* you.

I give you three choices, — *to buy*, *to lease*, or *to build.*

**318.** An infinitive in the predicate is often in apposition with the expletive subject *it*.

It was a pleasure *to see* him. [Instead of: To see him was a pleasure.]

It is easy *to understand* you.

It will be impossible *to forget.*

It proved very difficult *to find* evidence against him.

In this use the infinitive, though grammatically in apposition with *it*, is really the subject of the thought (see § 120, 2).

**319.** The infinitive may be used as the **object of the prep-**ositions *but, except, about.*

> There was nothing to do but *walk* (or *to walk*).
> He will do anything except *resign* (or except *to resign*).
> We are about *to object.* [An idiom expressing futurity.]
> The train is about *to start.*

NOTE. *Can but* and *cannot but* are distinct idioms. (1) In "I *can but* thank you," *but* is an adverb (= *only*). The sentence means: "I can *only* thank you — simply that and nothing more!" (2) In "I *cannot but* thank you," *but* is a preposition (= *except*). The idiom is shortened from "I cannot *choose but* thank you," — that is, "I have *no choice except* to do so," or, in other words, "I cannot help it."

The infinitive after *for* (now a gross error) was once in good use: as, —

> What sweeter music can we bring
> Than a carol *for to sing.* — HERRICK.

**320.** The infinitive may be used as a **nominative of exclamation** (§ 88, 4).

> *To sleep!* perchance *to dream!*
> *To suffer* and *be* silent!
> O *to be* a boy again! [A wish.]
> O *to have lived* in the brave days of old!

## II. THE INFINITIVE AS A MODIFIER

**321.** An infinitive may be used as an adjective modifier of a noun or as an adverbial modifier of an adjective.

In this use the infinitive is said to depend on the word which it modifies.

| WITH NOUNS (ADJECTIVE MODIFIER) | WITH ADJECTIVES (ADVERBIAL MODIFIER) |
| --- | --- |
| An opportunity *to advance* came. | The men are ready *to advance.* |
| Determination *to win* brings success. | John is eager *to win.* |
| Willingness *to oblige* makes friends. | I shall be glad *to oblige* you. |
| I wish I had the ability *to swim.* | We are all able *to swim.* |
| His anxiety *to please* us was laughable. | He is anxious *to please* everybody. |

NOTE. This use is due to the fact that the infinitive with *to* is really a prepositional phrase (§ 42). Thus, "determination *to win*" is equivalent to "determination *for victory*," and "eager *to win*" to "eager *for victory*." The adjective force of the infinitive comes out clearly in "nothing *to eat*," where *to eat* is practically synonymous with *eatable*.

In its adjective use, the present infinitive sometimes shows no distinction in voice, so that the active and the passive are interchangeable: as, — "a house *to let*" or "*to be let*"; "an axe *to grind*" or "*to be ground*." In such expressions the active form is usually preferable.

**322.** The infinitive without *to* may be used as an adjective modifier after the direct object of *see, hear, feel,* and some other verbs of like meaning.

> I saw the policeman *arrest* him.
> Hear the sea *roar!*
> Can you feel the ground *tremble?*
> Ruth watched the tide *come* in.

In this use the infinitive is practically equivalent to a participle. Compare "I heard him *shout*" with "I heard him *shouting.*" Hence the substantive may be regarded as an object, and the infinitive as its modifier. But the construction closely approaches that of an infinitive clause (§§ 324–325).

**323.** An infinitive may modify a verb (1) by completing its meaning, or (2) by expressing the purpose of the action.

### I. Complementary Infinitive

The ship began *to roll*.
The rain continued *to fall* heavily.
Every boy desires *to succeed*.
The officer neglected *to watch* his men.
The prisoners attempted *to escape*.
You promised *to come* to-night.

After *dare*, the complementary infinitive may or may not have *to*. Thus, — "I dare not *do* it"; "Who will dare *to speak?*"

### II. Infinitive of Purpose

He went to New York *to study* medicine.
He opened his lips *to speak*.
She closed her eyes *to shut* out the sight.
Elsa lifted the cover *to see* what was inside.
The conductor signalled *to stop* the train.
Harold waited *to assist* his teacher.

Both the **complementary infinitive** and the **infinitive of purpose** may be regarded as **adverbial phrases** modifying the verb.

NOTE. After some verbs the infinitive approaches the construction of a pure noun and is often regarded as an object. Thus, — "I desire *to see* you" (compare "I desire a *sight* of you"). It is simpler, however, to regard all such infinitives as complementary and to treat them as adverbial modifiers. For it is impossible to distinguish the construction of the infinitive after certain adjectives (as in "I am eager *to see* you") from its construction after such verbs as *wish* and *desire*.

### III. THE INFINITIVE CLAUSE

**324.** A peculiar infinitive construction often replaces a *that*-clause as the object of a verb. Thus, —

I wished $\begin{cases} \textit{that he should go.} \\ \textit{him to go.} \end{cases}$

In the first sentence, the noun clause *that he should go* is the object of *wished;* in the second, this clause is replaced by *him to go*, but without any change in meaning. This expression consists of two parts : — (1) *him*, a pronoun in the objective case, which replaces the subject *he ;* and (2) an infinitive *to go*, which replaces the predicate *should go*. Thus it is plain that *him to go* is also a noun clause, of which *him* is the subject, and *to go* the predicate. Such an expression is called an **infinitive clause.**

**325.** A kind of clause, consisting of a substantive in the objective case followed by an infinitive, may be used as the object of certain verbs.

Such clauses are called infinitive clauses, and the substantive is said to be the subject of the infinitive.

The subject of an infinitive is in the objective case.

**Infinitive clauses** are used (1) after verbs of *wishing, commanding, advising,* and the like, and (2) after some verbs of *believing, declaring,* and *perceiving.*[1] Thus, —

> The colonel commanded *them to charge* [ = that they should charge].
> I believe *him to be trustworthy* [ = that he is trustworthy].
> The judge declared *him to be a dangerous man* [ = that he was, etc.].

After a few verbs the infinitive without *to* is used in infinitive clauses.

> Mr. Esmond bade his servant *pack* a portmanteau and *get* horses. [Compare : ordered his servant *to pack*, etc.]
> What makes him *cry ?* [Compare : What causes him *to cry ?*]
> I let him *sleep*. [Compare : I allowed him *to sleep*.]

NOTE. Ordinarily the infinitive cannot assert and hence has no subject (§ 309). The infinitive clause is, therefore, a peculiar exception, for *him to go* makes an assertion as clearly as *that he should go* does. That *him* is really the subject of *to go* and not the object of *wished* is manifest, for *I wished him* makes no sense. The object of *wished* is the whole clause (*him to go*).

Originally, to be sure, the noun or pronoun in the objective was felt to be the object of the main verb, and this relation may still be felt in "I ordered him to go"; but even here the real object of *ordered* is the clause (as may be seen in "I ordered the castle to be blown up"). The substantive has come to be the real subject of the infinitive, and should be so treated in parsing.

[1] After verbs of *wishing*, etc., they express purpose (§ 403) ; after verbs of *believing*, etc., they are in indirect discourse (§ 431).

**326.** A predicate pronoun after *to be* in an infinitive clause is in the objective case, agreeing with the subject of the infinitive.

Care should be taken not to confuse this construction with the predicate nominative (§ 88, 2).

| PREDICATE PRONOUN AFTER *TO BE* | PREDICATE NOMINATIVE |
|---|---|
| I believed it to be *her*. | I believed that it was *she*. |
| We know the author to be *him*. | We know that the author is *he*. |
| | The author is known to be *he*. |
| He thought Richard to be *me*. | He thought that Richard was *I*. |
| | Richard was thought to be *I*. |
| We suspected the intruders to be *them*. | We suspected that the intruders were *they*. |

Note the case of the **relatives** and of the **predicate pronouns** in the following sentences : —

A boy *whom* I thought to be honest deceived me. [*Whom* is the subject of the infinitive *to be* and is therefore in the objective case.]

A boy *who*, I thought, was honest deceived me. [*Who* is the subject of *was* and is therefore nominative. *I thought* is parenthetical (§ 502).]

A boy *whom* I believe to be *him* just passed me.

A boy *who*, I believe, was *he*, just passed me.

**327.** An infinitive clause may be the object of the preposition *for*. Thus, —

I wrote for *him to come*. [The clause *him to come* is the object of *for; him* is the subject of *to come*.]

> They are waiting on the shore
> For *the bark to take them home*. — NOEL.

> I long for *him to come back*.

**328.** An infinitive clause with *for* may be used as a subject, as a predicate nominative, or as the object of a preposition.

*For us to delay* would be fatal to your enterprise. [Compare : *Our delay* would be fatal.]

Our best plan is *for the boat to shoot the rapids*. [Predicate nominative agreeing with the subject *plan*.]

I see no way out of the difficulty except *for them to offer an apology* [Compare : except the *offer* of an apology on their part.]

## PARTICIPLES

**329.** Certain words unite in themselves some of the properties of **adjectives** with some of the properties of **verbs.** Such words are called **participles** (§ 31). Thus, —

*Shattered* and *sinking*, but gallantly *returning* the enemy's fire, the frigate drifted out to sea.

*Shattered, sinking,* and *returning* are verb-forms which are in some respects similar to infinitives : for (1) they express action ; (2) they have no subject to agree with, and hence have neither person nor number ; and (3) one of them takes a direct object. They differ from infinitives, however, in that they resemble, not nouns, but adjectives, for they describe the substantive *frigate* to which they belong.

Such verb-forms are called **participles,** because they share (or participate in) the nature of adjectives.

**330.** The participle is a verb-form which has no subject, but which partakes of the nature of an adjective and expresses action or state in such a way as to describe or limit a substantive.

Who *thundering* comes on blackest steed ? — BYRON.
*Clinging* to the horns of the altar, voiceless she stood. — DE QUINCEY.
*Deserted, surrounded, outnumbered,* and with everything at stake, he did not even deign to stand on the defensive. — MACAULAY.
*Shrouded* in such baleful vapors, the genius of Burns was never seen in clear azure splendor, *enlightening* the world. — CARLYLE.

### FORMS OF PARTICIPLES

**331.** Verbs have three participles, — the **present,** the **past,** and the **perfect.**

**332.** The **present participle** ends in *-ing.* It usually describes an action as taking place at the same time with some other action.

Tom came *sauntering* up the path.
The beggar shambled down the steps, *grumbling.*
*Reaching* for the flower, I lost my balance.

**333.** The present participle often refers to time preceding that denoted by the predicate verb.

*Rising* from his chair, he bowed. [That is, when he had risen.]
*Learning* that your brother was in trouble, I hastened to his aid.

**334.** The past participle is always associated with the idea of past time or completed action.

**1.** The past participle of a weak verb has the same form as the past tense.[1]

| PRESENT TENSE | PAST TENSE | PAST PARTICIPLE |
|---|---|---|
| I *mend* chairs. | I *mended* the chairs. | The chairs are *mended*. |
| I *sweep* the rooms. | I *swept* the rooms. | The rooms are *swept*. |
| I *seek* treasure. | I *sought* treasure. | Treasure is *sought*. |
| I *lose* money. | I *lost* money. | The money is *lost*. |

**2.** The past participle of strong verbs shows a change from the vowel of the present tense.

All strong verbs had originally the ending *en* (*n*) in the past participle, but this ending has been lost in many verbs.

| PRESENT TENSE | PAST TENSE | PAST PARTICIPLE |
|---|---|---|
| He *speaks*. | He *spoke*. | (He has) *spoken*. |
| He *draws*. | He *drew*. | (He has) *drawn*. |
| He *sings*. | He *sang*. | (He has) *sung*. |
| He *wins*. | He *won*. | (He has) *won*. |

The forms show great variety and must be learned by practice. (See pp. 291–297 for a list.)

**335.** The **perfect participle** is made by prefixing *having* to the past participle.

*Having mended* the watch, I sent it to the owner.
*Having lost* his money, James was forced to walk home.

**336.** The present participle is used in forming the progressive verb-phrases (§§ 255–259).

The past participle is used in forming the complete tenses (§§ 242–244) and the passive voice (§ 247).

---

[1] The only exceptions are trifling differences in spelling.

## CONSTRUCTIONS OF PARTICIPLES

**337.** Since the participle has adjective properties, its constructions are in the main like those of adjectives.

**338. A participle is said to belong to the substantive which it describes or limits.**

Rupert, *missing* his companion, stepped to the door. [The present participle *missing* belongs to the subject *Rupert*.]

*Rising*, she opened the window. [*Rising* belongs to *she*.]

I heard the rain *falling*. [*Falling* belongs to the object *rain*.]

Tom's arm, *broken* by the blow, hung useless. [The past participle *broken* belongs to the subject *arm*.]

*Having climbed* the hill with great difficulty, I stopped to rest. [The perfect participle *having climbed* belongs to the subject *I*.]

**339. A participle should not be used without some substantive to which it may belong.**

RIGHT: *Entering* the room, we saw a strange sight. [The participle *entering* belongs to the pronoun *we*.]

WRONG: *Entering* the room, a strange sight was seen. [Since there is no substantive to which *entering* can belong, it has no construction.]

Apparent exceptions are *concerning, considering, pending, generally speaking*, etc. The first three may be classed as prepositions (§ 355), the last as an independent participle.

We fought every day, and, *generally speaking*, twice every day. — DE QUINCEY.

NOTE. The rule in § 339 does not apply to such phrases as *on entering, after investigating*, etc., in which the words in *-ing* are not participles, but verbal nouns (§ 348). Thus the following sentences are grammatical: — "*On entering* the room, a strange sight appeared"; "*After investigating* the subject, the plan was adopted." Such expressions, however, should be used with caution, since they are sometimes awkward or ambiguous.

**340. A participle may be modified by an adverb, an adverbial phrase, or an adverbial clause.**

Smiling *brightly*, she extended her hand. [Adverb.]

He leaped forward, shrieking *with all his might*. [Adverbial phrase.]

Laughing *until he cried*, he sank into a chair. [Adverbial clause.]

**341.** A participle may take an object if its meaning allows.

I found the old man mending his *net*.
Lifting the *box*, he moved toward the door.
Giving *me* a friendly *nod*, he passed on. [Here *nod* is the direct object of *giving*, and *me* is the indirect object.]

The participle, with its modifiers and such other words as are attached to it, is sometimes called a **participial phrase.**

**342.** A participle may be used as a pure adjective.

A *grinning* boy confronted me.
A *battered* hat hung on the peg.
Kate was playing with a *broken* doll.
We could hear a *rushing* stream.
*Willing* hands make light work.
He was struck by a *spent* ball.

**343.** The past participle is often used as a **predicate adjective** expressing state or condition.

This construction is easily confused with the passive of verbs. The distinction may be seen in the following examples: —

The rain began to fall heavily, and every time a gust of wind struck us we *were drenched* by it.
When the rain at last ceased, we were *drenched* [that is, *very wet*].

In the first sentence, *were drenched* is the past passive of the verb *drench* (compare the active "every time a gust of wind struck us, it *drenched* us"). In the second, the participle *drenched* expresses mere condition, and is therefore a predicate adjective. The distinction, however, is not always sharp, and in cases of doubt the phrase may be taken together as a passive verb.

NOTE. The real test is the following. Whenever a person or thing is distinctly present to the mind as the doer of the action, we have a passive verb-phrase. Whenever, on the other hand, the participle merely describes condition with no thought of its being the result of an antecedent act, the construction is that of a predicate adjective (§ 172, 3).

### Nominative Absolute

**344.** A substantive, with the participle belonging to it, is often used to make a peculiar form of adverbial modifying phrase: as, —

> *The wind failing*, we lowered the sail.

Here *the wind failing* is equivalent to an adverbial phrase (*on the failure of the wind*) or an adverbial clause (*when the wind failed*). It defines the time of the action.

> *The wind failing,*
> *On the failure of the wind,* } we lowered the sail.
> *When the wind failed,*

**345.** A substantive, with a participle, may express the cause, time, or circumstances of an action.

This is called the absolute construction.

The substantive is in the nominative case and is called a nominative absolute.

*My knife slipping*, I cut myself severely. [The phrase *my knife slipping* is equivalent to *because my knife slipped:* it expresses cause.]

*Two days having elapsed*, we again set forward. [The phrase in italics is equivalent to *when two days had elapsed:* it expresses time.]

Evenings he read aloud, *his wife sewing by his side.* [The phrase expresses one of the circumstances that attended the reading.]

*This done*, proceed to business. [The phrase *this done* is equivalent to the clause *since* (or *when*) *this is done*, and indicates cause or time.]

Note. This construction is called absolute (that is, "free" or "loosened") because the substantive is not in any one of the constructions (subject, object, apposition, etc.) which ordinarily attach nouns grammatically to other words in the sentence. Nevertheless, the whole phrase, though standing apart from the rest of the sentence, is in meaning an adverbial modifier of some verb.

**346.** The participle *being* is sometimes omitted in the absolute construction.

Allen once mayor, my chance of advancement would be ruined. [That is: *Allen* once *being mayor.*]

Peter stood before me, his hands in his pockets.

His clothing in shreds, he presented a sorry sight.

## VERBAL NOUNS IN *-ING* (PARTICIPIAL NOUNS)

**347.** English has a large and important class of **verbal nouns** that end in *-ing*, and that serve as the **names of actions.**

These are identical in form with **present participles,** for which they are frequently mistaken. The distinction, however, is clear, for the present participle is never used as the name of an action. Hence no such word in *-ing* that is a subject or an object, or stands in any other noun construction, can be a participle.

While I was *travelling* in Mexico, I met with an accident. [Participle.]
*Travelling* broadens the mind. [Verbal noun, used as subject.]
He enjoys *travelling*. [Verbal noun, used as object of a verb.]
He spends his time in *travelling*. [Verbal noun, object of a preposition.]
Tom's favorite exercise is *swimming*. [Verbal noun, predicate nominative.]
This sport, *fishing*, has been called the contemplative man's recreation. [Verbal noun, in apposition with *sport*.]

That nouns in *-ing* are real nouns may be proved by putting ordinary nouns in their place.

| | |
|---|---|
| *Travelling* broadens the mind. | *Travel* broadens the mind |
| *Talking* is useless. | *Talk* is useless. |
| He is afraid of *falling*. | He is afraid of a *fall*. |

**348.** From nearly every English verb there may be formed a **verbal noun in *-ing*.**

Verbal nouns in *-ing* have the form of present participles, but the construction of nouns.

They are often called **participial nouns.**

Such nouns are freely used, either by themselves or in a series along with ordinary nouns.

*Mining* is a dangerous occupation.
*Painting* and *sculpture* are sister arts.
The Indians of Massachusetts spent their time in *hunting*, *fishing*, *agriculture*, and *warfare*.
*Reading*, *writing*, and *arithmetic* are jocosely called "the three r's."

**349.** Verbal nouns in *-ing* have certain properties of the verb.

**1. Verbal nouns in *-ing* may take a direct or an indirect object if their meaning allows.**

Digging *gold* seems to the uninitiated like finding buried *treasure*.

Lending *him money* is useless; it merely fosters his unthrifty habits. [Here the noun *lending*, which is the simple subject of the sentence, takes both a direct object (*money*) and an indirect object (*him*), precisely as the verb *lend* might do.]

**2. A verbal noun in *-ing* may take an adverbial modifier.**

Speaking *extemporaneously* is good practice. [Here the verbal noun *speaking* is the simple subject; but it is modified by the adverb *extemporaneously*, precisely as if it were a verb.]

But verbal nouns in *-ing*, like other nouns, may be modified by **adjectives**.

*Extemporaneous* speaking is good practice.

**3. To the verbal nouns *being* and *having*, past participles may be attached, so as to give the effect of voice and tense.**

After *being instructed* in my duties, I was ordered to wait on the king.

There were grave doubts expressed as to his *having seen* the mastodon.

After *having been treated* in so harsh a fashion, I had no wish to repeat the interview.

Such expressions are **verbal noun-phrases**.

**350.** Verbal nouns in *-ing* are similar in some of their constructions to infinitives used as nouns (p. 135).

| Infinitive as Noun | Verbal Noun in *-ing* |
|---|---|
| *To swim* was difficult. | *Swimming* was difficult. |
| My business is *to make* shoes. | My business is *making* shoes. |
| *To see* is *to believe*. | *Seeing* is *believing*. |

Nouns in *-ing* are sometimes called **infinitives** or **gerunds**.

**351.** A noun in *-ing* may be used as an **adjective**, or as the adjective element in a **compound noun** (§ 64).

The *sleeping* car was completely wrecked.

William has plenty of *spending* money.

NOTE. Other examples are: — *a working day, an ironing board, drinking water, smelling salts, marching orders, a walking tour, a swimming race, a vaulting pole.* In such cases it makes little difference whether the two nouns are taken together as a compound, or whether the first is regarded as an adjective modifying the second. The difference between this use and that of the participle is perfectly clear. A *"sleeping dog"* is a dog *that sleeps;* a *"sleeping car"* is a car *for sleeping.* Sometimes, indeed, either explanation is possible. Thus, a *"hoisting engine"* may be understood either as an *"engine that hoists,"* or as an *"engine for hoisting."* But it is better to class these exceptions with the nouns in *-ing.*

**352.** When a verbal noun in *-ing* is preceded by an article or any other adjective, it cannot take an object.

Shooting song-birds  
The shooting *of* song-birds } is forbidden.

Launching a ship  
The launching *of* a ship } requires care and skill.

Drawing maps  
The drawing *of* maps } is a useful exercise.

Eating confectionery constantly  
Constant eating *of* confectionery } is bad for the teeth.

My business is { driving wells.  
the driving *of* wells.

Observe that, in each instance, the **object** (*song-birds, ship, maps, confectionery, wells*) is replaced by a **prepositional phrase** when an article or other adjective precedes the verbal noun.

NOTE. In such expressions as "I went a-fishing," *a* is a shortened form of the preposition *on*, and *fishing* is a verbal noun used as its object. When *a* is omitted we have "I went fishing," "The house is building," and the like, in which the word in *-ing* seems to be a participle, but is really the object of the omitted *a* (= *on*).

**353.** The possessive case of a noun or pronoun may be used to limit a verbal noun in *-ing.*

I was sure of its *being* he. [NOT: *it.*]  
I heard of Allen's *being* elected. [NOT: *Allen.*]

# CHAPTER VII

## PREPOSITIONS

**354.** A preposition is a word placed before a substantive to show its relation to some other word in the sentence.

The substantive which follows a preposition is called its object and is in the objective case.

A phrase consisting of a preposition and its object, with or without other words, is called a prepositional phrase.

> *On* the floor lay a heap *of* nuts.
> He stood *behind* the tree *for* some time.
> *From* morning *till* night he remained *at* his post.
> The fire destroyed everything *except* a few articles *of* furniture.

A **prepositional phrase** may be either adjective or adverbial.

Thus, in the first example, *of nuts* is an adjective phrase modifying the noun *heap*, and *on the floor* is an adverbial phrase modifying the verb *lay*. In the second sentence, the verb *stood* is modified by two adverbial phrases, *behind the tree* and *for some time*.

**355.** The following list includes most of the prepositions:

| | | |
|---|---|---|
| aboard | because of | considering |
| about | before | despite |
| above | behind | down |
| according to | below | during |
| across | beneath | ere |
| after | beside, besides | except, excepting |
| against | between | for |
| along | betwixt | for the sake of |
| along with | beyond | from |
| amid, amidst | but (= except) | from among |
| among, amongst | by | from between |
| apart from | by dint of | from under |
| around | by means of | in |
| as for, as to | by reason of | in accordance with |
| at | by virtue of | in addition to |
| athwart | by way of | in case of |
| barring | concerning | in compliance with |

| | | |
|---|---|---|
| in consequence of | on | throughout |
| in consideration of | on account of | to, unto |
| in front of | out of | touching |
| in lieu of | outside (outside of) | toward, towards |
| in opposition to | over | under |
| in place of | over against | underneath |
| in preference to | past | until, till |
| in regard to | pending | up |
| in spite of | regarding | upon |
| inside (inside of) | respecting | with |
| instead of | round | within |
| into | round about | without |
| notwithstanding | save, saving | with reference to |
| of | since | with regard to |
| off | through | with respect to |

NOTE. Such expressions as *by means of, in accordance with, in spite of,* etc., are really phrases, but may be regarded as compound prepositions.

Several participles like *concerning, considering, pending,* are common in a prepositional use and are therefore included in the list (§ 339).

For *a* (a form of *on*) in *abed, asleep, afire, a-fishing,* etc., see § 352.

*Per* is confined to the strictly commercial style except in such expressions as *perforce, per cent, per annum* (§ 179).

**356.** A preposition may stand at the end of a sentence or clause.

*Whom* did you ask *for?* [Compare : *For whom* did you ask ?]

The box *which* it came *in* has been destroyed. [Compare : The box *in which* it came.]

NOTE. This order, though informal, is common in the best authors; but, if carelessly used, it may result in awkwardness of style. Sometimes a relative which is the object of the preposition is omitted (see § 151). Thus, in the second sentence, *which* might be dropped, and the object of *in* would then be "*which,* understood." For "He was laughed at," and the like, see § 251.

In poetry a preposition sometimes follows its object directly : as, — "Barefoot plod I the cold ground *upon*" (SHAKSPERE).

**357.** Certain adverbial expressions like "on Sunday," "on March first," occur both with and without the preposition.

He came Sunday (*or*, on Sunday).
We sail March first (*or*, on March first).

NOTE. The forms without *on* are good colloquial English, but are avoided in the more formal style. No preposition need be supplied in parsing. The noun is an adverbial objective (§ 109).

**358.** Care is required in the use of **pronouns** as the **objects of prepositions.**

He has been very friendly
The old house will seem lonely } to you and *me*. [NOT: you and *I*.]
That makes no difference

Tom's carelessness makes trouble
There are letters at the post office } for you and *me*.

I have invitations for { you and *him*.
you and *her*.

He will divide the reward between you and *me*.

*Whom* are you waiting for ?
*Whom* were you speaking to ? } [NOT: *who*.]

**359.** Several words are used either as **adverbs** or **prepositions.**

| As Adverb | As Preposition |
|---|---|
| I fell *down*. | I fell *down* the steps. |
| Stand *by* ! | He stood *by* the window. |
| A big dog ran *behind*. | A dog ran *behind* the carriage. |
| Keep *off* ! | Keep *off* the grass. |

Other examples are : — aboard, above, after, along, before, below, beneath, beside, between, beyond, ere, in, inside, on, outside, past, round, since, under, up, within, without.

For words used either as prepositions or as conjunctions, see pp. 152-154.

**360.** Prepositions show various distinctions in use and meaning which must be learned by practice and by the study of synonyms in a large dictionary.

The following groups afford opportunity for such study : — at, in ; in, into ; between, among, amid ; on, upon ; from, off ; round, around, about ; to, with ; beside, besides ; agree with, agree to ; change for, change with ; disappoint in, of ; differ with, from ; confide in, to ; correspond with, to ; part from, with ; compare to, with ; join with, to ; connect with, to ; come up with, to ; talk to, with ; speak to, with ; hang on, from, to ; live at, in, on ; argue with, against ; contend with, against ; depart from, for, at, on, in.

# CHAPTER VIII

## CONJUNCTIONS

**361.** Conjunctions connect words or groups of words.

Conjunctions are either coördinate or subordinate.[1]

**1. A coördinate conjunction connects words or groups of words that are independent of each other.**

1. Hay *and* grain are sold here.
2. Will you take tea *or* coffee?
3. He was pale *but* undaunted.
4. The messenger replied courteously *but* firmly.
5. The troops embarked rapidly *but* without confusion.
6. Noon came, *and* the task was still unfinished.
7. We must hide here until night falls *and* the street is deserted.

In each of the first four sentences, the conjunction (*and, or, but*) connects single words that are in the same construction (subjects, objects, predicate adjectives, adverbs). In the fifth, *but* connects an adverb with an adverbial phrase (both being modifiers of the verb *embarked*). In the sixth, *and* joins the two coördinate clauses of a compound sentence (§ 44). In the seventh, *and* joins two coördinate clauses which, taken together, make up the subordinate clause *until . . . deserted ;* this clause may therefore be called a compound subordinate clause (see § 454).

**2. A subordinate conjunction connects a subordinate clause with the clause on which it depends.**

> Harmon did not quail, *though* he saw the danger.
> Take this seat, *if* you prefer.
> I hesitated *because* I remembered your warning.
> *Unless* you reform, your career will be ruined.

---

[1] Coördinate conjunctions are also called **coördinating**, and subordinate conjunctions are also called **subordinating**.

**362.** The chief **coördinate conjunctions** are : —

| | |
|---|---|
| and (both . . . and) | moreover |
| not only . . . but also | therefore |
| or (either . . . or) | then |
| nor (neither . . . nor) | yet |
| but | still |
| for | nevertheless |
| however | notwithstanding |

Several of these are much used for **transition**, whether from sentence to sentence or from one paragraph to another.

Such are : — however, moreover, therefore, then, nevertheless, notwithstanding, yet, still.

**363.** *Then* is an adverb when it denotes time, a conjunction when it denotes consequence or the like.

*Then* the boat glided up to the pier. [Time.]
Men are imperfect creatures : we must not, *then*, expect them to be angels. [Consequence.]

**364.** *Yet* and *still* are adverbs when they express time or degree, conjunctions when they connect.

We have not started *yet*. [Time.]
It is *still* raining. [Time.]
This hatchet is dull, but that is duller *still*. [Degree.]
I miss him, *yet* I am glad he went. [Conjunction.]
I like dogs ; *still* I do not care to own one. [Conjunction.]

**365.** *For* and *notwithstanding* may be either prepositions or conjunctions.

| PREPOSITIONS | CONJUNCTIONS |
|---|---|
| I am waiting *for* you. | We must go, *for* it is late. |
| Jane is coming, *notwithstanding* the storm. | It is a hard storm. She will come, *notwithstanding*. |

NOTE. *For* is sometimes classified as a subordinate conjunction, but the fact that it may be used to begin an independent sentence (even when such a sentence opens a paragraph) justifies its inclusion among the coördinates.

**366.** The chief **subordinate conjunctions** are : —

| | | |
|---|---|---|
| although, though | if | that |
| as | lest | unless |
| as if (as though) | since (= because) | whereas |
| because | than | whether (whether . . . or) |

A few phrases may be regarded as compound conjunctions. Such are: — *in order that, so that, provided that, in case that, but that, as if, as though, even if. Provided,* and *in case* (without *that*) may also be used as conjunctions: as, — " I will go *provided* it does n't rain."

**367.** The subordinate conjunction *that* is often omitted when it may readily be supplied.

> He said [that] he was starving.
> They feared [that] they were betrayed.
> I cannot believe [that] you would try to injure me.

NOTE. This omission is similar to that of the relative pronoun (§ 151). It is extremely common, not only in colloquial language but also in literature, whether prose or verse.

**368.** *As* and *since* in the sense of " because," and *while* in the sense of " though," are conjunctions.

When denoting **time,** *as* is an adverb, *while* is a noun or an adverb, and *since* is an adverb or a preposition.

> *As* (or *since*) you will not listen, I will say no more. [Conjunction.]
> *As* we crossed the bridge, I looked down at the rushing stream. [Adverb.]
> Ten years have passed *since* my uncle went to sea. [Adverb.]
> The house has been empty *since* Christmas. [Preposition.]

**369.** Conjunctions used in pairs are called **correlative conjunctions.**

The chief correlatives are : —

| | |
|---|---|
| both . . . and | though . . . yet (still) |
| not only . . . but also | although . . . yet (still) |
| either . . . or | since . . . therefore |
| neither . . . nor | if . . . then |

Examples of correlatives may be seen in the following sentences : —

*Both* lions *and* wolves are carnivorous.

The culprit looked *both* angry *and* ashamed.

William II is *not only* German Emperor *but also* King of Prussia.

*Either* brass *or* copper will do.

*Neither* Keats *nor* Shelley lived to be old.

He asked me *whether* I was an Austrian *or* a Russian.

*Though* the roads were very bad, *yet* he managed to reach Utíca before midnight.

*Although* he has wronged me, *still* I cannot believe he is my enemy.

*Since* four is the square of two, *therefore* two is the square root of four.

*If* Allen's testimony is true, *then* Gilbert's must be false.

**370.** *But* is used as a subordinate conjunction in the sense of *but that* or *unless*.

There is no doubt *but that* they are murderers. — SHELLEY.

Your uncle must not know *but* [ = *but that*] you are dead. — SHAKSPERE.

Ne'er may I look on day *but* [ = *unless*] she tells your highness the truth. — SHAKSPERE. [This use is obsolete.]

There is not a wave of the Seine *but* is associated in my mind with the first rise of the sandstones and forest pines of Fontainebleau. — RUSKIN.

There was nobody *but* loved her.

NOTE. In the last two examples the subject of the subordinate clause is omitted : — "There is not a wave *but* [*it*] is associated," "There was nobody *but* [*he*] loved her." In such cases, *but* is sometimes regarded as a relative pronoun.

*Notwithstanding* is used as a subordinate conjunction in the sense of *though*.

I shall go, *notwithstanding* the road is said to be impassable.

**371. Relative adverbs** are similar in their use to conjunctions, and are therefore often called **conjunctive adverbs** (§§ 194–195).

NOTE. Most conjunctions, historically considered, are merely adverbs (or adverbial phrases) which have come to be used in so peculiar a way as to form a special class among the parts of speech. Thus the adverbs *since* and *while* become conjunctions when they cease to denote time; *because* is a corruption of the phrase *by cause* ; *but* is developed from an old adverb meaning "outside."

# CHAPTER IX

## INTERJECTIONS

**372.** An interjection is a cry or other exclamatory sound expressing surprise, anger, pleasure, or some other emotion or feeling.

EXAMPLES : O (*or* oh), ah, hullo (holloa, halloo), bah, pshaw, fie, whew, tut-tut, st (*often spelled* hist), ha, aha, ha ha, ho, hey, hum, hem, heigh-ho (heigh-o), alas, bravo, lo.

When written, interjections are often followed by an exclamation point (!).

**373.** Among interjections are properly included calls to animals (like "whoa!") and imitations of sounds such as "mew!" "cock-a-doodle-do!" "ding dong!" "swish!" "tu-whit-tu-who!"

**374.** Interjections usually have no grammatical connection with the phrases or sentences in which they stand.

Hence they are counted among the "independent elements" of a sentence (§ 501).

Sometimes, however, a substantive is connected with an interjection by means of a preposition. Thus, —

> *O for* a camera!
> *Alas for* my hopes!

Adjectives and adverbs are also found in this use: as, — "Good for you!" "Up with it!"

NOTE. All such expressions are often regarded as elliptical sentences, as if "O for a camera!" stood for "O, I wish for a camera!" and "Good for you!" for "That is good for you!" But it is better to treat them as exclamatory phrases.[1] Other exclamatory phrases are "Dear me!" "Goodness gracious!" "O my!" and the like.

---

[1] Compare the exclamatory sentence (§ 3) and the exclamatory nominative (§ 88, 4).

**375.** Almost any part of speech may be used **as an ex-**clamation.

| | |
|---|---|
| *Nonsense!* I do not believe it. | On! |
| Fire! | Away! |
| Halt! | *Back*, villains! |
| *Good!* I like that! | *I!* not a bit of it! |
| Forward! | But——! |

Such words are often called interjections, but it is better to describe them as nouns, adjectives, etc., used in exclamation, and to confine the term **interjection** to words which belong to no other part of speech.

NOTE. Thus *nonsense!* and *fire!* are nouns in the exclamatory nominative; *I!* is a pronoun in the same construction; *halt!* is a verb in the imperative (compare *hark! hush! behold! look!*); *good!* is an adjective; *forward! on! away!* and *back!* are adverbs; *but!* is a conjunction.

The following examples illustrate various **exclamatory expressions,** — words, phrases, and sentences : —

1. How late I shuddered on the brink ! — YOUNG.
2. "Right! right!" a thousand tongues exclaimed. — SOUTHEY.
3. The pale stars are gone ! — SHELLEY.
4. Poor widowed wretch ! 't was there she wept in vain.—CAMPBELL.
5. O heartfelt raptures ! Bliss beyond compare ! — BURNS.
6. 'T is done ! dread Winter spreads his latest glooms. — THOMSON.
7. Heigh-ho ! sing heigh-ho ! unto the green holly. — SHAKSPERE.
8. I had — ah ! have I now ? — a friend. — BYRON.
9. "To arms !" cried Mortimer, and couched his quivering lance.
   GRAY.
10. O for the gentleness of old Romance ! — KEATS.
11. "Run !" exclaims she, with a toss of indignant astonishment.
   CARLYLE.
12. Can he keep himself still if he would ! Oh, not he !—WORDSWORTH.

# CHAPTER X

## CLAUSES AS PARTS OF SPEECH

**376.** A clause is a group of words that forms part of a sentence and that contains a subject and a predicate.

A clause used as a part of speech is called a subordinate clause (§ 46).

**377.** A subordinate clause may be introduced by (1) a relative or an interrogative pronoun, (2) a relative or an interrogative adverb, (3) a subordinate conjunction.

The **relative pronouns** are: *who, which, what, that* (= *who* or *which*), *as* (after *such* or *same*), and the compound relatives *whoever, whichever, whatever.* Their uses have already been studied (pp. 66–73).

The chief **relative adverbs** are: *where, whence, whither, wherever, when, whenever, while, before, after, till, until, since, as, how, why* (p. 86).

The **interrogative pronouns** are: *who, which, what* (§§ 163–165).

The **interrogative adverbs** are: *where, when, whence, whither, how, why.*

The most important **subordinate conjunctions** are: *because, since* (= *because*), *though, although, if, unless, that* (in order that, so that), *lest, as, as if, as though, than, whether* (whether . . . or).

**378.** According to their use as parts of speech, subordinate clauses are **adjective, adverbial,** or **noun clauses.**

### I. ADJECTIVE CLAUSES

**379.** A subordinate clause that modifies a substantive is called an **adjective clause** (§ 47).

> *Able* men
> Men *of ability*        } can always find employment.
> Men *who show ability*

> *Treeless* spots
> Spots *without trees*        } were plainly visible.
> Spots *where no trees grew*

In each of these groups, a noun (*men, spots*) is modified (1) by an adjective, (2) by an adjective phrase, (3) by an adjective clause. The sense remains unchanged.

**380.** Adjective clauses may be introduced (1) by **relative pronouns**, (2) by **relative adverbs** of place (*where, whence, whither,* etc.) or time (*when, while,* etc.).

## II. ADVERBIAL CLAUSES

**381. A subordinate clause that serves as an adverbial modifier is called an adverbial clause (§ 47).**

Jack spoke $\begin{cases} \textit{thoughtlessly.} \\ \textit{without thinking.} \\ \textit{before he thought.} \end{cases}$

The schoolhouse stands $\begin{cases} \textit{there.} \\ \textit{at the crossroads.} \\ \textit{where the roads meet.} \end{cases}$

We pay our rent $\begin{cases} \textit{monthly.} \\ \textit{on the first of every month.} \\ \textit{when the first of the month comes.} \end{cases}$

In each of these groups, the verb (*spoke, stands, pay*) is modified (1) by an adverb, (2) by an adverbial phrase, (3) by an adverbial clause.

**382.** Adverbial clauses may be introduced (1) by relative adverbs (*when, where, before,* etc.); (2) by subordinate conjunctions (*if, though, because,* etc.); (3) by relative or interrogative pronouns.

**383.** Adverbial clauses oftenest modify verbs, but they are also common as modifiers of adjectives and adverbs.

Angry *because he had failed,* he abandoned the undertaking. [The clause modifies *angry.*]

I am uncertain *which road I should take.* [The clause modifies *uncertain.*]

Farther *than eye could see* extended the waste of tossing waters. [The clause modifies *farther.*]

Here, *where the cliff was steepest,* a low wall protected the path. [The clause modifies *here.*]

**384.** An adverbial clause with *that* may be used to modify verbs and adjectives.

He rejoiced *that the victory was won.*
I am glad *that you are coming.*
He was positive *that no harm had been done.*
They were unwilling *that the case should be brought to trial.*

NOTE. In this use *that* is equivalent either to "because" or to "as to the fact that." The clause may be explained as a noun clause in the **adverbial objective** construction (§ 109).

For the classification of adverbial clauses according to their meaning (place, time, cause, concession, etc.), see pp. 163–182.

## III. NOUN (OR SUBSTANTIVE) CLAUSES

**385.** A subordinate clause that is used as a noun is called **a noun (or substantive) clause** (§ 47).

*Agreement*
*To agree*  ⎫ seemed impossible.
*That we should agree* ⎭

*Victory*
*To win* ⎫ was out of the question.
*That we should win* ⎭

The merchant feared ⎧ *loss.*
⎨ *to lose.*
⎩ *that he might lose money.*

I expect ⎧ *success.*
⎨ *to succeed.*
⎩ *that I shall succeed.*

In each of these groups a noun (*agreement, victory,* etc.) is replaced (1) by an infinitive, (2) by a noun clause. In the first two examples, the noun clause is the subject; in the last two, it is the object of a verb (*feared, expect*).

**386.** Noun clauses may be used in any of the more important constructions of nouns : — (1) as **subject,** (2) as **direct object** of a transitive verb, (3) **in apposition** with a substantive, (4) as **a predicate nominative.**

*That Milton was spared* has often caused surprise. [Subject.]
Brutus said *that Cæsar was a tyrant.* [Object of *said.*]

Cæsar commanded *that the prisoners should be spared.* [Object.]

I wish *that you would work harder.* [Object.]

The traveller inquired *where he could find the inn.* [Object.]

He asked me *what my name was.* [Second object of *asked.*]

My fear *that the bridge might fall* proved groundless. [Apposition with *fear.*]

One fact is undoubted, — *that the state of America has been kept in continual agitation.* — BURKE. [Apposition with *fact.*]

The old saying is *that misery loves company.* [Predicate nominative.]

**387.** Noun clauses may be introduced (1) by the subordinate conjunctions *that, whether (whether . . . or),* and *if* (in the sense of *whether* ); (2) by the interrogative pronouns *who, which, what ;* (3) by the interrogative adverbs *where, whence, whither, how, why, when* (§ 196).

**388.** Noun clauses are common as objects of verbs (1) of *commanding, desiring,* etc.; (2) of *telling, thinking,* etc.; (3) of *asking, doubting,* etc.

See (1) clauses of purpose (§ 406); (2) indirect discourse (§§ 431–437); (3) indirect questions (§ 443).

Object clauses frequently omit *that* (§ 367).

> Charles said [that] *he was sorry.*
> I hope *you will come.*
> I wish *he would help me.*

For the infinitive clause replacing a *that*-clause as object, see §§ 324–325.

**389.** A noun clause may be used as the **retained object** of a passive verb (§ 253).

| ACTIVE VOICE (CLAUSE AS OBJECT) | PASSIVE VOICE (RETAINED OBJECT) |
|---|---|
| They informed me *that the train was late.* | I was informed *that the train was late.* |
| Charles told us *that the ice was thin.* | We were told *that the ice was thin.* |
| They asked me *whether* (or *if* ) *I liked tennis.* | I was asked *whether I liked tennis.* |

**390.** A noun clause may be the object of a preposition.

I see no reason for a lawsuit except *that both parties are stubborn.*
[Compare : except the *stubbornness* of both.]

She never studies, except *when she can find nothing else to do.*

I could say nothing but [= except] *that I was sorry.*

Justice was well administered in his time, save *where the king was party.* — BACON.

She could see me from *where she stood.*

There is a dispute as to *which of the miners first staked out the claim.*

For a noun clause used as an adverbial objective, see § 384.

**391.** Noun clauses with *that* are common in the predicate when the expletive *it* is the grammatical subject (§ 120, 2).

It was plain *that war was at hand.*

It was clear *that this administration would last but a very short time.*

It must be admitted *that there were many extenuating circumstances.*

It was by slow degrees *that Fox became a brilliant and powerful debater.*

It was under the command of a foreign general *that the British had triumphed at Minden.*

In such sentences the real subject of the thought is the clause. This, however, may be regarded as grammatically in apposition with *it,* as if one said " *It* (that war was at hand) was plain."

NOTE. This useful idiom enables us to adopt a kind of inverted order (§ 5), and thus to shift the emphasis. Contrast " *That war was at hand* was plain " with " *It was plain* that war was at hand." In the former sentence, the noun clause is made prominent; in the latter, the adjective *plain.*

**392.** The following sentences, taken from distinguished authors of different periods, illustrate the usefulness of the noun clause in its various constructions.

**1.** That the king would ever again have received Becket into favor is not to be believed. — SOUTHEY.

**2.** That in education we should proceed from the simple to the complex is a truth which has always been to some extent acted on. — SPENCER.

**3.** How great his reputation was, is proved by the embassies sent to him. — COLERIDGE.

**4.** It vexed old Hawkins that his counsel was not followed. — FULLER.

**5.** It became necessary, at last, that I should arouse both master and valet to the expediency of removing the treasure. — POE.

**6.** There is no doubt that breeds may be made as different as species in many physiological characteristics. — HUXLEY.

**7.** The main definition you could give of old Marquis Mirabeau is, that he was of the pedant species. — CARLYLE.

**8.** The fact seems to be that we have survived the tremendous explosion. — BROUGHAM.

**9.** The question is, whether the feigned image of poesy, or the regular instruction of philosophy, have the more force in teaching. — SIDNEY.

**10.** I feared that some serious disaster had befallen my friend. — POE.

**11.** I think with you that the most magnificent object under heaven is the great deep. — COWPER.

**12.** Aureolus soon discovered that the success of his artifices had only raised up a more determined adversary. — GIBBON.

**13.** Harold alleged that he was appointed by Edward. — TEMPLE.

**14.** That we shall die, we know. — SHAKSPERE.

**15.** Her Majesty has promised that the treaty shall be laid before her Parliament. — SWIFT.

**16.** Deerslayer proposed that they should circle the point in the canoe.
COOPER.

**17.** I remembered how soft was the hand of Sleep. — LANDOR.

**18.** I cannot see what objection can justly be made to the practice.
REYNOLDS.

**19.** No man knew what was to be expected from this strange tribunal.
MACAULAY.

**20.** We may imagine with what sensations the stupefied Spaniards must have gazed on this horrid spectacle. — PRESCOTT.

**21.** Observe how graciously Nature instructs her human children.
COLERIDGE.

**22.** My friend asked me if there would not be some danger in coming home late. — ADDISON.

**23.** A message came that the committee was sitting at Kensington Palace. — THACKERAY.

**24.** Jeffreys had obtained of the king a promise that he would not pardon her. — BURNET.

**25.** The present age seems pretty well agreed in an opinion that the utmost scope and end of reading is amusement only. — FIELDING.

**26.** He suddenly alarmed me by a startling question — whether I had seen the show of prize cattle that morning in Smithfield. — LAMB.

**27.** I am told that the Lancashire system is perfect. — KINGSLEY.

# CHAPTER XI

## THE MEANINGS OF SUBORDINATE CLAUSES

**393.** Subordinate clauses may be classified not only according to their use as parts of speech, but also, in quite a different way, in accordance with their **various meanings**. These distinctions in idea are of capital importance for the accurate and forcible expression of thought.

**394.** The variety of meanings which subordinate clauses may express is great, but most of these meanings come under the following heads : — (1) **place** or **time**, (2) **cause**, (3) **concession**, (4) **purpose**, (5) **result**, (6) **condition**, (7) **comparison**,[1] (8) **indirect discourse**, (9) **indirect question**.

The general meaning of the clause is usually indicated by the word which introduces it.

### I. CLAUSES OF PLACE AND TIME

**395.** An adjective or an adverbial clause may express place or time.

#### I. Adjective Clauses

The house *where the robbery occurred* is No. 14.
The bridge *over which we rode* is in ruins.
There is a point *beyond which you cannot go.*
The day *when* (or *on which*) *I was to sail* arrived at last.
The day *before you came* was rainy.
His terror *while it thundered* was pitiable.

#### II. Adverbial Clauses

Remain *where I can see you.*
That belongs *where you found it.*
*Whithersoever I go,* fear dogs my steps.
*Whenever the bell rings,* you must take down the receiver.
Esmond heard the chimes *as he sat in his own chamber.*
I have lived in Cairo *since my father died.*

[1] Including clauses of **manner and degree** (§§ 428–429).

**396.** Adjective clauses of place and time may be introduced by relative pronouns (see examples above).

Adjective and adverbial clauses of place and time may be introduced by relative adverbs. Thus, —

PLACE : where, whence, whither, wherever, whithersoever, wherefrom, whereto, etc.

TIME : when, whenever, while, as, before, after, until, since.

For *as* and *since* in causal clauses, see § 398; for *while* in concessive clauses, see § 399.

**397.** Clauses of time are sometimes shortened by the omission of the copula and its subject.

When [*he was*] rescued, he was almost dead.
Tom was attacked by cramp *while swimming* across the river.

## II. CAUSAL CLAUSES

**398.** An adverbial clause may express cause.

Causal clauses are introduced by the subordinate conjunctions *because, since, as, inasmuch as,* and sometimes *that.*

> I came home *because I was tired.*
> *As the day was clear,* we decided to climb the mountain.
> *Since you will not relent,* you must take the consequences.
> We were glad *that the wreck was no worse.*
> Tom was delighted *that his friend was safe.*

*Since* is a preposition or an adverb when it denotes **time**; **as** is an adverb when it denotes **time**. Both *since* and *as* are conjunctions when they express **cause.** For *as* used as a relative pronoun, see § 147.

## III. CONCESSIVE CLAUSES

**399.** An adverbial clause may express concession.

A **concessive clause** is usually introduced by a subordinate conjunction, *though, although,* or *even if.* It **admits** (or concedes) some fact or supposition **in spite of which** the assertion in the main clause is made.

*Although I do not like his manners*, I respect his character.
We won the game, *though we expected to lose*.
*Even if you fail*, you will have gained experience.
*Even if you were a king*, you would find somebody or something **more** powerful than yourself.
*Though he should read books forever*, he would not grow wise.

NOTE. *While* is often used as a weaker or more courteous synonym for *although*.

The main clause, when it follows the concessive clause, may be emphasized by means of *yet, still, nevertheless*.

Although the task was heavy, *yet* his courage never failed. [*Although* and *yet* are correlative conjunctions (§ 369).]
Though his reputation was great at home, *yet* it was greater abroad.

Concessive clauses sometimes omit the copula and its subject.

*Though* [*he was*] *tired*, he was not disheartened.
This punishment, *though perhaps necessary*, seems rather severe.

**400.** For the distinction between the indicative and the subjunctive in concessive clauses, see § 279; for that between *should* and *would*, see § 305.

**401.** A concessive clause may be introduced by the conjunction *as*, or by a relative pronoun or a relative adverb.

*Whatever* you say,
*Whichever* argument you present, } he will carry his point.
*However* much you object,
*Weak as I am*, I will make the effort.
*Gay as the scene was*, 't was but a dreary place for Mr. Esmond.

NOTE. The adverbial use of *however* is quite distinct from its use as a coördinate conjunction (§ 362).

**402.** Concession is sometimes expressed by a subjunctive clause without a conjunction to introduce it (§ 281).

*Be it ever so humble*, there's no place like home.
I will help you, *cost what it may!*

## IV-V.  CLAUSES OF PURPOSE AND OF RESULT

**403.**  A subordinate clause may express purpose or result.

### I. CLAUSES OF PURPOSE

These men died *that we might live.*

I will take care *that you are not harmed.*

John worked day and night *that the plans might be ready in time.*

We threw our ballast overboard, *so that the airship might clear the treetops.*

All our arrangements have been made with the utmost precision, *in order that the ship may be launched promptly and without accident.*

### II. CLAUSES OF RESULT

He has recovered his strength, *so that he can now work.*

The town stood at the foot of the volcano, *so that every building was destroyed.*

Quentin started *so* suddenly *that he almost dropped his weapon.*

His rancor against the duke was *so* apparent *that one saw it in the first half-hour's conversation.*

Their minds were *so* much embittered *that they imputed to each other nothing less than deliberate villany.*

You make *such* a noise *that I cannot hear the music.*

**404.**  Clauses of purpose may be introduced by the subordinate conjunction *that* or by a phrase containing it (*so that, in order that, to the end that,* etc.).

Negative clauses of purpose may be introduced by *that . . . not* or by *lest.*  For *lest* with the subjunctive, see § 284.

> Take heed *lest thou fall.*
> I feared *lest I might anger thee.* — SHAKSPERE.

**405.**  Clauses of result may be introduced by the phrase *so that,* consisting of the adverb *so* and the subordinate conjunction *that ;* or by *that* alone, especially when *so, such,* or some similar word stands in the main clause.

**406.**  A clause of **purpose** or of **result** may be either an **adverbial clause** (as in § 403) or a **substantive clause.**

I intend *that you shall be elected.* [Object.]
My intention is *that you shall be appointed.* [Predicate nominative.]
The result is *that he is bankrupt.* [Predicate nominative.]
His exertions had this effect, *that the vote was unanimous.* [Appositive.]

**407.** A substantive clause of purpose is often used as the object of a verb of *commanding, desiring,* or the like.

> The general ordered *that the fort should be blown up.*
> The prisoner begged *that his fetters might be struck off.*

**408.** For subordinate clauses with *shall* or *should,* implying purpose or expectation, see § 304.

**409.** Purpose may be expressed by the infinitive with *to* or *in order to,* and result by the infinitive with *to* or *as to.*

He abandoned his profession *to* [or *in order to*] *become a missionary.* [Purpose.]

He was kind enough *to help me.* [Result. Compare: He was so kind *that he helped me.*]

He was so kind *as to help me.* [Result.]

**Negative result** is often expressed by the adverb *too* and the infinitive.

Iron is *too heavy to float.* [Compare: Iron is so heavy *that it does not float.*]

**410.** Purpose may be expressed by an **infinitive clause** (§ 325).

The teacher intended *us to finish the book.* [Compare: The teacher intended *that we should finish the book.*]

The foreman ordered *the engine to be stopped.* [Compare: The foreman ordered *that the engine should be stopped.*]

## VI.  CONDITIONAL SENTENCES

**411.** A clause that expresses a condition introduced by *if,* or by some equivalent word or phrase, is called a conditional clause.

A sentence that contains a conditional clause is called a conditional sentence.

> *If it rains,* we shall remain at home.
> I shall attend the convention *if I am in town.*
> I will take this book, *if you please.*

**412.** A conditional sentence in its simplest form consists of two parts : —

(1) A subordinate (adverbial) clause, commonly introduced by *if*, and expressing the condition.

(2) A main clause expressing the conclusion, that is, the statement which is true in case the condition expressed in the *if*-clause is true.

Thus in the first example in § 411, the condition is *if it rains;* the conclusion is *we shall remain at home.*

Either the condition or the conclusion may come first.

The conditional clause is often called the protasis, and the conclusion is often called the apodosis.

The conclusion of a conditional sentence may be declarative, interrogative, imperative, or exclamatory.

If you go to Philadelphia, *where shall you stay?* [Interrogative.]
*Sit here*, if you wish. [Imperative.]
If you win the prize, *how glad I shall be!* [Exclamatory.]

**413.** A conditional clause may be introduced by *provided* (or *provided that*), *granted that*, *supposing* (or *suppose*), *on condition that*.

I will permit you to go, *on condition that* you come home early.
You may have the money, *provided* you will put it in the bank.
*Supposing* (or *suppose*) it rains, what shall we do?

*Suppose* is really an imperative and *supposing* a participle, the clause being the object.

**414.** A negative condition is commonly introduced by *if . . . not* or *unless.*

I will wait for him, *if* you do *not* object.
*Unless* you overcome that habit, you will be ruined.

**415.** Double (or alternative) conditions may be introduced by *whether . . . or.*

*Whether* he goes *or* stays, he must pay a week's board. [Compare : *If* he goes *or if* he stays, etc.]
He is determined to buy that car, *whether* you approve *or* not. [That is : *if* you approve *or if* you do not approve.]

**416.** A conditional clause may be introduced by *whoever,* *whenever,* or some similar compound (§§ 159, 195).

*Whoever* offends, is punished. [Compare: *If anybody* offends, he is punished.]
*Whoever* shall offend, shall be punished.
*Whomever* you ask, you will be disappointed. [Compare: If you shall ask anybody.]
He will come *whenever* [= *if ever*] he is called.

NOTE. In older English and in poetry, *who* is common in this construction: as, — " *Who* [= *whoever*] steals my purse, steals trash" (SHAKSPERE).

**417.** A conditional clause sometimes omits the copula and its subject.

> I will go if [*it is*] necessary.
> If [*it is*] possible, come to-morrow.

The *if*-clause is sometimes used as an exclamation, with the conclusion omitted.

> If I only had a rifle!

**418.** A condition may be expressed by means of an assertion, a question, an imperative, or the absolute construction (§ 345).

We take the receiver from the hook, and the operator answers. We replace it, and the connection is broken. [Compare: If we take the receiver from the hook, the operator answers, etc.]
Press that button, and the bell will ring.
Do you refuse? Then you must take the consequences.
We shall sail on Monday, weather permitting.

NOTE. In such cases, there is no subordinate conditional clause. Thus, in the first example, we have two independent coördinate clauses, making a compound sentence (§ 44).

### FORMS OF CONDITIONS

**419.** Conditional sentences show great variety of form, but it is easy to classify them according to the **time** of the supposed case and the **degree of doubt** that the speaker expresses.

**420.** Conditions may be **present, past, or future.**

### Present and Past Conditions

**421.** Present and past conditions may be either (1) **non-committal** or (2) **contrary to fact**.

1. A condition is **non-committal** when it implies nothing as to the truth or falsity of the case supposed.

*If James is angry*, I am sorry. [Perhaps James is angry, perhaps not.]

2. A condition is **contrary to fact** when it implies that the supposed case is not or was not true.

*If James were angry*, I should be sorry. [James is *not* angry.]

**422.** In a **non-committal present condition**, the *if*-clause[1] takes the present indicative; in a **non-committal past condition**, the past, the perfect, or the pluperfect.

The conclusion may be in any form that the sense allows.

### I. Present Condition, Non-committal

*If this pebble is a diamond,*
- it is valuable.
- guard it carefully.
- you have made a great discovery.
- you will get a large sum for it.
- why are you so careless of it?
- what a prize it is!

*If it is raining*, shut the window.

*If Jack lives in this house,*
- he is a lucky boy.
- ring the bell.
- he has moved since last **May**.

### II. Past Condition, Non-committal

*If that pebble was a diamond,*
- it was valuable.
- why did you throw it away?
- go back and look for it.

*If Tom has apologized,*
- he has done his duty.
- you ought to excuse him.
- forgive him.

*If John had reached home before we started*, he must have made a quick journey.

By "*if*-clause" is meant the protasis, whatever the conjunction.

In each of these examples, the speaker declines to commit himself as to the truth of the supposed case. Perhaps the pebble was a diamond, perhaps not; Tom may or may not have apologized; whether or not John had reached home, we cannot tell.

**423.** In a **condition contrary to fact**, the *if*-clause takes the past subjunctive when the condition refers to present time, the pluperfect subjunctive when it refers to past time.

The conclusion regularly takes *should* or *would* (§ 286, 3).

If John *were* here, I *should recognize* him. [Present condition, present conclusion.]

If John *were* here, I *should have recognized* him before this. [Present condition, past conclusion.]

If I *had offended* him, I *should have regretted* it. [Past condition, past conclusion.]

If I *had* then *offended* him, I *should regret* it now. [Past condition, present conclusion.]

In each of these sentences, the speaker distinctly implies that the supposed case (or **condition**) *is* (or *was*) *not a fact.* It follows, of course, that the **conclusion** is not a fact: — John is *not* here; therefore I *do not* recognize him.

**424.** In conditions contrary to fact, the subjunctive without *if* is common. In this use, the subject follows the verb (§ 281).

*Were* he my friend, I should expect his help. [ = If he *were* my friend. Present condition, contrary to fact.]

*Had* he *been* my friend, I should have expected his help. [ = If he *had been* my friend. Past condition, contrary to fact.]

NOTE. In older English, the subjunctive may be used in both clauses: as, — "He *were* no lion, *were* not Romans hinds" (SHAKSPERE).

## FUTURE CONDITIONS

**425.** **Future conditions** always imply **doubt,** for no one can tell what may or may not happen to-morrow.

**426.** In all future conditions, some verb-form denoting future time is used in both clauses.

1. In a future condition which suggests nothing as to the probability or improbability of the case supposed, the present indicative is regularly used in the *if*-clause, and the future indicative in the conclusion.

> If it *rains* to-morrow. I *shall* not *go*.

In very formal or exact language a verb-phrase with *shall* may be used in the *if*-clause: as, — "If it *shall rain* to-morrow, I shall not go."

2. The present subjunctive is sometimes used in the *if*-clause. This form commonly suggests more doubt than the present indicative.

> If it *rain* to-morrow, I shall not go.

3. In a future condition which puts the supposed case rather vaguely, often with a considerable suggestion of doubt, a verb-phrase with *should* or *would* is used in both clauses.

> If it *should rain* to-morrow, I *should* not *go*.

For the use of *should* or *would* in such clauses, see § 305.

A phrase with *were to* may replace the *should*-phrase in the *if*-clause. This form often emphasizes the suggestion of doubt.

> If it *were to rain* to-morrow, I should not go.

The past subjunctive may stand in the *if*-clause instead of the *should*-phrase.

> If it *rained* to-morrow, I should not go.

NOTE. The comparative amount of doubt implied in the different kinds of future conditions cannot be defined with precision; for it varies with the circumstances or the context, and often depends on emphasis or the tone of the voice. Thus, in "if it should rain to-morrow," *should* may be so emphasized as to make the supposed case seem highly improbable, whereas an emphasis on *to-morrow* would have a very different effect. As to the subjunctive, its use is often due rather to the writer's liking for that mood than to any special doubt in his mind.

**427.** For *even if* in concessive clauses, see § 399; for *as if* in clauses of comparison, see § 428; for *if* (in the sense of *whether*) in indirect questions, see § 442.

## VII. CLAUSES OF COMPARISON

**428.** An adverbial clause introduced by *as if* may express comparison.[1]

> You speak *as if you were angry*.[2]
> He breathes *as if he were exhausted*.
> She cared for me *as if I had been her son*.

*As though* is also used, but *as if* is now preferred by most writers.

The subjunctive *were*, not the indicative *was*, is used after *as if* (§ 282).

**429.** *As* and *than*, as subordinate conjunctions, introduce clauses of comparison or degree.

> You are as old *as he* [*is*].
> I am younger *than you* [*are*].
> He weighs as much *as I* [*weigh*].
> I pity you more *than* [*I pity*] *her*.

When the verb is omitted, the substantive that follows *as* or *than* is in the same case in which it would stand if the verb were expressed. Thus, —

> You are stronger than *he*. [NOT: than *him*.]
> I see you oftener than *him*. [NOT: than *he*.]
> He plays a better game than *I*. [NOT: than *me*.]
> They will miss John more than *me*. [That is: more than they miss *me*.]

## VIII. INDIRECT DISCOURSE

**430.** A quotation may be direct or indirect.

A direct quotation repeats a speech or thought in its original form.

> I replied: "I am sorry to hear it."
> "Henceforth," he explained, "I shall call on Tuesdays."
> "You must see California," she insisted.

---

[1] Clauses introduced by *as* are often called clauses of manner.
[2] Such sentences are elliptical in origin. Thus, "The man acts as if he were crazy" is equivalent to "The man acts as [he would act] if he were crazy." But it is not necessary to supply the ellipsis in analyzing.

> "Elizabeth no longer lives here," he said.
> "I know nothing about it," was the witness's reply.
> "Where," thought I, "are the crew?" [1]

An **indirect quotation** repeats a speech or thought in substance, but usually with some change in its form.

An indirect quotation, when a statement, is a subordinate clause dependent on some word of *saying* or *thinking*, and introduced by the conjunction *that*.

> I replied *that I was sorry to hear it.* [Direct: I am sorry.]
> He explained *that henceforth he should call on Tuesdays.*
> She insisted *that I must see California.*

**A direct quotation** begins with a **capital letter,** unless it is a fragment of a sentence. It is enclosed in **quotation marks.**

**An indirect quotation** begins with a **small letter.** It usually has no quotation marks.

**431.** A substantive clause introduced by *that* may be used with verbs and other expressions of *telling, thinking, knowing,* and *perceiving,* to report the words or thought of a person in substance, but usually with some change of form.

Such clauses are said to be in the indirect discourse.

For distinction, a remark or a thought in its original form (as in a direct quotation) is said to be in the direct discourse.

**432.** Statements in **indirect discourse,** being substantive clauses, may be used in various noun constructions: (1) as **object** of some verb of *telling, thinking,* or the like, (2) as **subject,** (3) as **predicate nominative,** (4) as **appositive.**

He said *that the box was empty.* [Object.]
*That the box was empty* was all he could say. [Subject.]
My remark was *that the bill is a menace.* [Predicate nominative.]
Your remark, *that the bill is a menace,* has aroused vigorous protest. [Apposition.]

---

[1] In analyzing, the direct quotation may be regarded as the object of the verb of saying, etc. (or the subject, if that verb is passive); and if it forms a complete sentence, this may be analyzed as if it stood by itself. It is not proper to regard the direct quotation as a subordinate clause.

**433.** The conjunction *that* is often omitted.

Jack said [*that*] he was sorry.
I hope [*that*] you can come.
I know he is too busy a man to have leisure for me. — Cowper.

**434.** In indirect discourse, after the past or the pluperfect tense, the present tense of the direct discourse becomes past, and the perfect becomes pluperfect.

1. Direct: I *am* tired.
   Indirect: John $\left\{ \begin{array}{l} \text{said} \\ \text{had said} \end{array} \right\}$ that he *was* tired.

2. Direct: I *have won*.
   Indirect: John $\left\{ \begin{array}{l} \text{said} \\ \text{had said} \end{array} \right\}$ that he *had won*.

But a general or universal truth always remains in the present tense.

Direct: Air *is* a gas.
Indirect: I told him that air *is* a gas.
Indirect: I had told him a hundred times that air *is* a gas.

**435.** The clause with *that* in indirect discourse is sometimes replaced by an infinitive clause (§ 325).

The jury declared *him to be innocent*. [Compare: The jury declared *that he was innocent*.]
Morton admitted *them to be counterfeit*. [Compare: Morton admitted *that they were counterfeit*.]

In these sentences, *him* and *them* are, of course, the subjects of the infinitives, not the objects of *declared* and *admitted*.

**436.** When the verb of *telling* or *thinking* is in the **passive voice**, three constructions occur : —

1. A clause with *that* is used as the subject of the passive verb.

That Rogers desires the office is commonly reported.

2. The expletive *it* is used as the grammatical subject, and a *that*-clause follows the passive verb.

It is commonly reported that Rogers desires the office.

3. The subject of the *that*-clause becomes the subject of the passive verb, and the verb of the clause is replaced by an infinitive.

> Rogers is commonly reported to desire the office.

The choice among these three idioms is largely a matter of emphasis or euphony. The first may easily become heavy or awkward, and it is therefore less common than either of the others.

NOTE. The third of these idioms is often called the **personal construction**, to distinguish it from the second, in which the grammatical subject is the impersonal *it* (§ 120, 1). The infinitive in this third idiom may be regarded as a peculiar adverbial modifier of the passive verb.

Further examples of the three constructions with passive verbs of *telling, thinking,* etc., are the following: —

That in vivacity, humor, and eloquence, the Irish stand high among the nations of the world is now universally acknowledged. — MACAULAY.

It is admitted that the exercise of the imagination is most delightful.
SHELLEY.

It must be owned that Charles's life has points of some originality.
STEVENSON.

Porto Bello is still said to be impregnable, and it is reported the Dutch have declared war against us. — GRAY.

He was generally believed to have been a pirate. — LYTTON.

Pope may be said to write always with his reputation in his head.
JOHNSON.

She was observed to flutter her fan with such vehement rapidity that the elaborate delicacy of its workmanship gave way. — HAWTHORNE.

This is said to be the only château in France in which the ancient furniture of its original age is preserved. — LONGFELLOW.

**437.** A substantive clause with *that* is common after *it seems, it is true, it is evident,* and similar expressions.

> It seems *that Robert has lost all his money.*
> It is true *that genius does not always bring happiness with it.*
> It is evident *that Andrews tells the truth.*

This construction is really the same as that in § 436, 2.

**438.** The uses of *shall* and *will*, *should* and *would*, in **in**-direct discourse are the same as in the **direct**,[1] with the following exception : —

When the first person with *shall* or *should* in direct discourse becomes the second or third person in the indirect, *shall* or *should* is retained.

DIRECT:       You say, "*I shall* die."
INDIRECT:    You say that *you shall* die.

DIRECT:       You said, "*I shall* die."
INDIRECT:    You said that *you should* die.

DIRECT:       He says, "*I shall* die."
INDIRECT:    He says that *he shall* die.

DIRECT:       He said, "*I shall* die."
INDIRECT:    He said that *he should* die.

The reason for the retention of *shall* or *should* is that, in such cases, the second or third person of the indirect discourse represents the first person of the direct.

The change from *shall* (after *says*) to *should* (after *said*) is a mere change of tense, according to the rule in § 434.

NOTE. The general principle is, to retain in the indirect discourse the auxiliary of the direct, simply changing the tense if necessary (§ 434). This principle of course covers the use of *you* or *he shall* or *should* to represent *1 shall* or *should*. There is, however, one important exception to the general principle: when its application would result in the use of *I will* or *I would* to express mere futurity, *I shall* or *I should* is employed. Thus, John says to Charles, "If you fall overboard, *you will* drown; but Charles, reporting this, must say, "John tells me that, if I fall overboard, *I shall* [NOT *will*] drown." The general rule, then, may be stated as follows: The indirect discourse retains the auxiliary of the direct (with a change in tense, if necessary), unless such retention makes *will* or *would* express simple futurity in the first person, — in that case, *shall* or *should* is used.

**439.** The following sentences illustrate the correct use of *shall* and *will*, *should* and *would*, in the indirect discourse : —

1. He writes me that he believes *he shall* be at Eton till the middle of November. — GRAY. [Direct: I shall be at Eton.]

[1] See pp. 102–105, 127–132.

**2.** He that would pass the latter part of his life with honor and decency, must, while he is young, consider that *he shall* one day be old. — JOHNSON. [Direct: I shall one day be old.]

**3.** Could he but reduce the Aztec capital, he felt that *he should* be safe. — PRESCOTT. [Direct: I shall be safe.]

**4.** Plantagenet took it into his head that *he should* like to learn to play at bowls. — DISRAELI. [Direct: I should like.]

**5.** He answered that *he should* be very proud of hoisting his flag under Sir John's command. — SOUTHEY. [Direct: I shall (*or* should) be, etc.]

**6.** He knew that if he applied himself in earnest to the work of reformation, *he should* raise every bad passion in arms against him. — MACAULAY. [Direct: If I apply myself . . ., I shall raise, etc.]

**7.** He was pleased to say that *he should* like to have the author in his service. — CARLYLE. [Direct: I should like.]

**8.** Mr. Tristram at last declared that *he* was overcome with fatigue, and *should* be happy to sit down. — HENRY JAMES. [Direct: I should be happy.]

**9.** She vowed that unless he made a great match, *she should* never die easy. — THACKERAY. [Direct: Unless you make a great match, I shall never die easy.]

**10.** You think now *I shall* get into a scrape at home. You think *I shall* scream and plunge and spoil everything. — GEORGE ELIOT. [Direct: She will get into a scrape, etc.]

**11.** You in a manner impose upon them the necessity of being silent, by declaring that *you will* be so yourself. — COWPER. [Determination: I will be silent.]

**12.** He [Swift] tells them that *he will* run away and leave them, if they do not instantly make a provision for him. — JEFFREY. [Threat: I will run away.]

**13.** The king declared that *he would* not reprieve her for one day. — MACKINTOSH. [Direct: I will not.]

**14.** Horace declares that *he would* not for all the world get into a boat with a man who had divulged the Eleusinian mysteries. — COWPER. [Direct: I would not.]

**15.** I called up Sirboko, and told him, if *he would* liberate this one man to please me, *he should* be no loser. — SPEKE. [Direct: If you will liberate, etc., you shall be no loser.]

**16.** We concluded that, if we did not come at some water in ten days' time, *we would* return. — DE FOE. [Direct: If we do not, etc., we will return.]

**17.** With a theatrical gesture and the remark that *I should* see, he opened some cages and released half a dozen cats. — W. J. LOCKE. [Direct: You shall see.]

## IX. INDIRECT QUESTIONS

**440.** A question expressed in the form actually used in asking it is called a direct question.

> What is your name ?
> " What is your name ? " he asked.

The direct form may be retained when the question is quoted or reported, as in the second example above. Often, however, a question is quoted or reported, not in the direct form, but in the form of a **subordinate clause** : as, —

> He asked *what my name was.*

Such a clause is called an **indirect question.**

**441.** An indirect question expresses the substance of a direct question in the form of a subordinate clause.

Indirect questions depend on verbs or other expressions of *asking, doubting, thinking, perceiving,* and the like.

Franklin asked *where the difficulty lay.* [Direct question : " Where does the difficulty lie ? "]

The sergeant wondered *how he should escape.* [Direct question : " How shall I escape ? "]

I have not decided *which train I shall take.* [Direct question : " Which train shall I take ? "]

**442.** Both **direct** and **indirect questions** may be **introduced** (1) by the interrogative pronouns *who, which, what ;* (2) by the interrogative adverbs *when, where, whence, whither, how, why.*

**Indirect questions** may be introduced by the **subordinate** conjunctions *whether (whether . . . or)* and *if.*

The use of **tenses** in indirect questions is **the** same as in the indirect discourse (§ 434).

The constable inquired *whether* (or *if*) *I lived in Casterbridge.* [His question was : Do you live in Casterbridge ?]

Your father wishes to know *if you have been playing truant.* [Direct question : Have you been playing truant ?]

I considered *whether I should apply to Kent or to Arnold.* [Direct question : Shall I apply to Kent or to Arnold ?]

**443.** Indirect questions are usually noun clauses. They may be used in various noun constructions : (1) as **object** of some verb **of asking** or the like, (2) as **subject**, (3) as **predicate nominative**, (4) as **appositive**, (5) as **object** of a preposition.

The skipper asked *what had become of the cook.* [Object.]

He was asked *what his profession was.* [Retained object after the passive (§§ 253, 389).]

*How we could escape* was a difficult question. [Subject.]

The problem was *how they should find food.* [Predicate nominative.]

The question *who was to blame* has never been settled. [Apposition with *question.*]

They all felt great perplexity as to *what they should do.* [Object of a preposition.]

An indirect question may be an adverbial clause.

They were uncertain *what course they should take.* [The clause modifies *uncertain.*]

Edmund was in doubt *where he should spend the night.* [The clause modifies the adjective phrase *in doubt.*]

**444.** Since the pronouns *who, which,* and *what* may be either interrogative or relative, an indirect question may closely resemble a relative clause. These two constructions, however, are sharply distinguished. A relative clause always **asserts** something. An indirect question, on the contrary, has an **interrogative** sense which may be seen by turning the question into the direct form.

The sailor *who saved the child* is a Portuguese. [The clause *who saved the child* is a relative clause, for it makes a distinct assertion about the sailor, — namely, that he saved the child. *Who* is a relative pronoun and *sailor* is its antecedent.]

I asked

I do not know

It is still a question } *who saved the child.*

It is doubtful

[Here the clause *who saved the child* makes no assertion. On the contrary, it expresses a question which may easily be put in a direct form with an interrogation point : " Who saved the child ? " *Who* is an interrogative pronoun. It has no antecedent.]

The following examples further illustrate the difference between these two constructions : —

1. I foresee the course *which he will take*. [Relative clause.]
   I foresee *which course he will take*. [Indirect question.]
2. I heard *what he said*. [Relative clause. *What* = "that which."]
   I wondered *what he said*. [Indirect question. *What* is an interrogative pronoun.]
3. This is the man *who brought the news*. [Relative clause.]
   The king asked *who brought the news*. [Indirect question.]
4. Here is a paper *which you must sign*. [Relative clause.]
   The clerk will tell you *which paper you must sign*. [Indirect question.]

NOTE. In such a sentence as " Tom knows *who saved the child*," the indirect question may at first appear to be a relative clause with an omitted antecedent (*the man*, or *the person*). If, however, we insert such an antecedent ("Tom knows *the man* who saved the child"), the meaning is completely changed. In the original sentence, it is stated that Tom knows the answer to the question, " Who saved the child ? " In the new form of the sentence, it is stated that Tom is acquainted with a certain person, and to this is added an assertion about this person in the form of a relative clause.

**445.** An indirect question is sometimes expressed by means of an interrogative pronoun or adverb followed by an infinitive.

*Whom to choose* is a serious question. [Direct question : Whom shall we choose ?]
John asked *what to do*. [John's question was : What shall I do ?]
I know *where to go*. [Direct question : Where shall I go ?]
Tell me *when to strike the bell*.
I was at a loss *how to reply*.
I am in doubt *how to begin this essay*.

In the first four examples the italicized phrase is used as a noun (either as subject or object). In the fifth, the phrase *how to reply* is adverbial, modifying the adjective phrase *at a loss*.

**446.** The subjunctive was formerly common in indirect questions, and is still occasionally used after *if* or *whether*.

I doubt if it *be* true.
Elton questioned whether the project *were* wise.

**447.** The rule for *shall* (*should*) and *will* (*would*) in indirect questions is, to retain the auxiliary used in the direct question, merely changing the tense (*shall* to *should ; will* to *would*) when necessary (§ 442).

## I. Mere Futurity

**1. Direct :** What *shall I* do ?

   **Indirect :** I wonder what *I shall* do.

               You ask me what *you shall* do.

               He asks me what *he shall* do.

               I wondered what *I should* do.

               You asked me what *you should* do.

               He asked me what *he should* do.

**2. Direct :** *Shall you* lose your position ?

   **Indirect :** I ask ⎱ you if *you shall* lose your position.
               He asks ⎰

               I asked ⎱ you if *you should* lose your position.
               He asked ⎰

**3. Direct :** *Will Charles* lose his position ?

   **Indirect :** I ask if *Charles will* lose his position.

               I ⎱
               You ⎬ asked if *Charles would* lose his position.
               Tom ⎰

## II. Volition

**4. Direct :** *Will you* help me ?

   **Indirect :** You ask if *I will* help you.

               He asks if *I will* help him.

               You asked if *I would* help you.

               He asked if *I would* help him.

               I asked him ⎱        ⎧ help me.
               You asked him ⎬ if *he would* ⎨ help you.
               Tom asked him ⎰       ⎩ help him.

Note. There is a single exception to the rule in § 447. When, in changing from a direct to an indirect question, the third person with *will* or *would* becomes the first, *shall* or *should* is substituted unless volition is expressed. Thus, John says to Thomas, " *Will Charles* die of his wound?" Charles, reporting John's question, says, "John asked Thomas whether *I should* die of my wound." Compare § 438, note.

# PART THREE

## ANALYSIS

### CHAPTER I

#### THE STRUCTURE OF SENTENCES

**448.** **Analysis** is a Greek word which means "the act of dissolving or breaking up." In grammar it is applied to the separation of a sentence into its constituent parts, or **elements**. To dissect a sentence in this way is to **analyze** it.

The elements which make up a **sentence** are: (1) the **simple subject**; (2) the **simple predicate**; (3) **modifiers**; (4) the **complements**, — direct object, predicate objective, predicate adjective, predicate nominative; and (5) the so-called **independent elements**, — the interjection, the vocative (or nominative of direct address), the exclamatory nominative, and various parenthetical expressions (§ 501).

**449.** The absolute essentials for a sentence are a **substantive as subject** and a **verb as predicate** (§ 35). By combining these two indispensable elements, in various ways, with **modifiers** and **complements**, the sentence may be extended to any length desired. Indeed, the sole limits are the constructive skill of the writer and the hearer's ability to follow the thought without losing the thread.

In the present chapter, we shall consider how sentences are built up, or constructed. Our starting point in this study will be the **simple sentence**.

## SIMPLE SENTENCES

**450.** The following statement is a **simple sentence,** for it con tains but **one subject** and **one predicate** (§ 46) : —

The polar bear | lives in the Arctic regions.

The framework or skeleton of this simple sentence consists of the subject noun *bear* (the simple subject) and the predicate verb *lives* (the simple predicate). To make the **complete subject,** *bear* takes as **modifiers** the two adjectives *the* and *polar ;* to make the **complete predicate,** *lives* takes as **modifier** the adverbial phrase *in the Arctic regions.*

By attaching another simple subject to *bear* we make a **compound subject.** Similarly, we make a **compound predicate** by adding another verb (§ 38).

The polar *bear* and the *walrus* | *live* and *thrive* in the Arctic regions.

The compound subject is *bear and walrus ;* the compound predicate is *live and thrive.* Both verbs are modified by the adverbial phrase *in the Arctic regions.* The sentence itself is still a simple sentence.

In each of the following simple sentences either the subject or the predicate or both are compound : —

Games and carols closed the busy day. — ROGERS.

The stars leap forth, and tremble, and retire before the advancing moon. — GEORGE MEREDITH.

Madame Defarge knitted with nimble fingers and steady eyebrows, and saw nothing. — DICKENS.

Work or worry had left its traces upon his thin, yellow face. — DOYLE.

Crows flutter about the towers and perch on every weathercock.
IRVING.

He gained the door to the landing, pulled it open, and rushed forth.
LYTTON.

Countrymen, butchers, drovers, hawkers, boys, thieves, idlers, and vagabonds of every low grade, were mingled together in a dense mass.
DICKENS.

There stood the broad-wheeled wains and the antique plows and the harrows. — LONGFELLOW.

Both Augustus and Peters joined with him in his design and insisted upon its immediately being carried into effect. — POE.

Women and children, from garrets alike and cellars, through infinite London, look down or look up with loving eyes upon our gay ribbons and our martial laurels. — DE QUINCEY.

## COMPOUND SENTENCES

**451.** If we attach another simple sentence to that in § 450, the result is a **compound sentence**.

The polar bear | lives in the Arctic regions, || but || it | sometimes reaches temperate latitudes.

This is manifestly a **compound sentence**, for it consists of two coördinate clauses, joined by the conjunction *but* (§ 46).

The framework of the second clause consists of the subject *it* and the simple predicate *reaches*. To make the complete predicate, the verb *reaches* takes not only a modifier (the adverb *sometimes*), but a **complement**, — the direct object *latitudes*, which completes the meaning of the verb. This noun is itself modified by the adjective *temperate*. Both clauses are **simple**, for each contains but one subject and one predicate.

**452.** Obviously, almost any number of simple sentences may be joined (with or without conjunctions) to make one compound sentence.

The quiet August noon has come ;
A slumberous silence fills the sky ;
The fields are still, the woods are dumb,
In glassy sleep the waters lie. — BRYANT.

States fall, arts fade, but Nature does not die. — BYRON.

The court was sitting ; the case was heard ; the judge had finished ; and only the verdict was yet in arrear. — DE QUINCEY.

He softly blushed ; he sighed ; he hoped ; he feared ; he doubted ; he sometimes yielded to the delightful idea. — THACKERAY.

A mob appeared before the window, a smart rap was heard at the door, the boys hallooed, and the maid announced Mr. Grenville.—COWPER.

His health had suffered from confinement ; his high spirit had been cruelly wounded ; and soon after his liberation he died of a broken heart.
MACAULAY.

## COMPLEX SENTENCES

**453.** The simple sentence in § 450 may be made **complex** by means of a **subordinate clause** used as a **modifier** (§ 47).

The polar bear, *which lives in the Arctic regions*, sometimes reaches temperate latitudes.

The polar bear sometimes reaches temperate latitudes *when the ice drifts southward*.

In the first example, the simple subject (*bear*), besides its two adjective modifiers (*the* and *polar*), takes a third, the adjective clause *which lives in the Arctic regions* (§ 47). The sentence, then, is **complex**: the main clause is *the polar bear sometimes reaches temperate latitudes*; the subordinate clause is *which lives in the Arctic regions*.

The second sentence is also complex. The main clause is the same as in the first (*the polar bear sometimes reaches temperate latitudes*). The subordinate clause is *when the ice drifts southward*, an **adverbial modifier** of the predicate verb *reaches*.

## COMPOUND AND COMPLEX CLAUSES

**454.** Two or more **coördinate clauses** may be joined to make one **compound clause**.

The polar bear, *which lives in the Arctic regions and whose physical constitution is wonderfully adapted to that frigid climate*, sometimes reaches temperate latitudes.

The polar bear sometimes reaches temperate latitudes *when the floes break up and when the ice drifts southward*.

In the first example, the italicized words form a **compound adjective clause,** modifying the noun *bear*. It consists of two **coördinate adjective clauses** joined by *and*. These clauses are coördinate because they are of the same **order** or **rank** in the sentence (§ 46), each being (if taken singly) an adjective modifier of the noun.

In the second example, the predicate verb *reaches* is modified by a **compound adverbial clause,** similarly made up.

**455**. A clause is **complex** when it contains a modifying clause.

The polar bear, *which lives in the Arctic regions when it is at home*, sometimes reaches temperate latitudes.

Here the **adjective clause** *which lives in the Arctic regions when it is at home* is **complex**, for it contains the adverbial clause *when it is at home*, modifying the verb *lives*.

## COMPOUND COMPLEX SENTENCES

**456**. Two or more independent complex clauses may be joined to make a **compound complex sentence**.

The brown bear, of which there are several varieties, is common in the temperate regions of the Eastern Hemisphere; || and || the polar bear sometimes reaches temperate latitudes when the ice drifts southward.

This is a **compound complex sentence**, for it consists of two complex clauses joined by the coördinate conjunction *and*. Each of these two clauses is independent of the other, for each might stand by itself as a complex sentence.

The first complex clause contains an adjective clause, *of which there are several varieties*, modifying *bear;* the second contains an adverbial clause, *when the ice drifts southward*, modifying *reaches*.

**457**. A sentence consisting of two or more independent clauses is also classed as a compound complex sentence if any one of these is complex.

The brown bear is common in the temperate regions of the Eastern Hemisphere; || and || the polar bear sometimes reaches temperate latitudes when the ice drifts southward.

The brown bear, of which there are several varieties, is common in the temperate regions of the Eastern Hemisphere; || and || the polar bear sometimes reaches temperate latitudes.

Both of these are compound complex sentences. In one, the first clause is simple (§ 451) and the second is complex. In the other, the first clause is complex and the second is simple.

## CHAPTER II

### ANALYSIS OF SENTENCES

#### SIMPLE SENTENCES

**458.** In analyzing a simple sentence, we first divide it into the complete subject and the complete predicate. Then we point out the simple subject with its modifiers, and the simple predicate with its modifiers and complement (if there is one). If either the subject or the predicate is compound, we mention the simple subjects or predicates that are joined.

1. The polar bear lives in the Arctic regions.

This is a simple sentence. The complete subject is *the polar bear;* the complete predicate is *lives in the Arctic regions.* The simple subject is the noun *bear;* the simple predicate is the verb *lives. Bear* is modified by the adjectives *the* and *polar;* *lives* is modified by the adverbial phrase *in the Arctic regions.* This phrase consists of the preposition *in;* its object, the noun *regions;* and the adjectives *the* and *Arctic,* modifying *regions.*

2. The polar bear and the walrus live and thrive in the Arctic regions.

The complete subject is *the polar bear and the walrus.* Two simple subjects (*bear* and *walrus*) are joined by the conjunction *and* to make a compound subject, and two simple predicates (*live* and *thrive*) are joined by *and* to make a compound predicate. *Live* and *thrive* are both modified by the adverbial phrase *in the Arctic regions.*

#### COMPOUND SENTENCES

**459.** In analyzing a compound sentence we first divide it into its coördinate clauses, and then analyze each clause by itself. Thus, —

The polar bear lives in the Arctic regions, but it sometimes reaches temperate latitudes.

This is a compound sentence consisting of two coördinate clauses joined by the conjunction *but:* (1) *the polar bear lives in the Arctic regions* and (2) *it sometimes reaches temperate latitudes.* The complete subject of the first clause is *the polar bear* [and so on, as in § 458, above]. The subject of the second clause is *it;* the complete predicate is *sometimes reaches temperate latitudes.* The simple predicate is *reaches,* which is modified by the adverb *sometimes* and is completed by the direct object *latitudes.* The complement *latitudes* is modified by the adjective *temperate.*

## COMPLEX SENTENCES

**460.** In analyzing a complex sentence, we first divide it into the main clause and the subordinate clause.

1. The polar bear, which lives in the Arctic regions, sometimes reaches temperate latitudes.

This is a complex sentence. The main clause is *the polar bear sometimes reaches temperate latitudes;* the subordinate clause is *which lives in the Arctic regions.* The complete subject of the sentence is *the polar bear, which lives in the Arctic regions;* the complete predicate is *sometimes reaches temperate latitudes.* The simple subject is *bear,* which is modified by the adjectives *the* and *polar* and by the adjective clause *which lives in the Arctic regions.* The simple predicate is *reaches,* which is modified by the adverb *sometimes* and completed by the direct object *latitudes.* This complement, *latitudes,* is modified by the adjective *temperate.* The subordinate clause is introduced by the relative pronoun *which.* [Then analyze the subordinate clause.]

2. The polar bear reaches temperate latitudes when the ice drifts southward.

This is a complex sentence. The main clause is *the polar bear reaches temperate latitudes;* the subordinate clause is *when the ice drifts southward.* The complete subject of the sentence is *the polar bear;* the complete predicate is *reaches temperate latitudes when the ice drifts southward.* The simple subject is *bear,* which is modified by the adjectives *the* and *polar.* The simple predicate is *reaches,* which is modified by the adverbial clause *when the ice drifts southward,* and completed by the noun *latitudes* (the direct object of *reaches*). The complement *latitudes* is modified by the adjective *temperate.* The subordinate clause is introduced by the relative adverb *when.* [Then analyze the subordinate clause.]

3. The polar bear, which lives in the Arctic regions when it is at home, sometimes reaches temperate latitudes.

This is a complex sentence. The main clause is *the polar bear sometimes reaches temperate latitudes;* the subordinate clause is *which lives in the Arctic regions when it is at home,* which is complex, since it contains the adverbial clause *when it is at home,* modifying the verb *lives.*

4. He says that the polar bear lives in the Arctic regions.

This is a complex sentence. The main clause is *he says;* the subordinate clause is *that the polar bear lives in the Arctic regions.* The subject of the sentence is *he,* the complete predicate is *says that the polar bear lives in the Arctic regions.* The simple predicate is *says,* which is completed by its direct object, the noun clause *that . . . regions,* introduced by the conjunction *that.* [Then analyze the subordinate clause.]

5. That the polar bear sometimes reaches temperate latitudes is a familiar fact.

This is a complex sentence. The main clause (*is a familiar fact*) appears as a predicate only, since the subordinate clause (*that the polar bear sometimes reaches temperate latitudes*) is a noun clause used as the complete subject of the sentence. The simple predicate is *is,* which is completed by the predicate nominative *fact.* This complement is modified by the adjectives *a* and *familiar.* The subordinate clause, which is used as the complete subject, is introduced by the conjunction *that.* [Then analyze this clause.]

## COMPOUND COMPLEX SENTENCES

**461.** In analyzing a **compound complex** sentence, we first divide it into the **independent clauses** (simple or complex) of which it consists, and then analyze each of these as if it were a sentence by itself.

See the examples in §§ 456, 457.

# CHAPTER III

## MODIFIERS

**462.** The various kinds of modifiers and complements have all been studied in preceding chapters, — each in connection with the construction which it illustrates. For purposes of analysis, however, it is necessary to consider modifiers as such and complements as such.

The topics will be taken up in the following order : — (1) modifiers, — of the subject, of the predicate ; (2) complements ; (3) modifiers of complements ; (4) modifiers of modifiers.

**463.** A word or group of words that changes or modifies the meaning of another word is called a modifier (§ 19).

Men
*Able* men  } can always find employment.
Men *of ability*

Walls
*Battlemented* walls  } usually enclosed mediæval cities.
Walls *with battlements*

Cottages
*English* cottages  } are often thatched.
Cottages *in England*

The boy listened { *eagerly.*
{ *with eagerness.*

I coughed { *purposely.*
{ *on purpose.*

The bullet passed { *harmlessly.*
{ *without doing harm.*

**464.** Modifiers may be attached not only to substantives and verbs, but also to adjectives and adverbs.

All modifiers of substantives are called **adjective modifiers** ; all modifiers of verbs, adjectives, and adverbs are called **adverbial modifiers**.

NOTE. The terms **adjective modifier** and **adjective** are not synonymous. All adjectives are adjective modifiers, but all adjective modifiers are not adjectives. Thus, in "Henry's skates are rusty," the possessive noun *Henry's* is an adjective modifier, since it limits the noun *skates* as an adjective might do.

**465.** A group of words used as a modifier may be either a phrase or a clause (§§ 40–46).

$$\left.\begin{array}{l}\text{\textit{Able} men}\\ \text{Men \textit{of ability}}\\ \text{Men \textit{who have ability}}\end{array}\right\rbrace \text{can always find employment.}$$

$$\text{I spoke}\left\lbrace\begin{array}{l}\textit{thoughtlessly.}\\ \textit{without thinking.}\\ \textit{before I thought.}\end{array}\right.$$

A phrase or a clause used as an adjective modifier is called an **adjective phrase or clause.**

A phrase or a clause used as an adverbial modifier is called an **adverbial phrase or clause.**

Adjective and adverbial clauses are always **subordinate,** because they are used as parts of speech (§ 46).

## MODIFIERS OF THE SUBJECT

**466.** Any substantive in the sentence may take an adjective modifier, but **modifiers of the subject** are particularly important.

The simple subject may be modified by (1) an **adjective,** an **adjective phrase,** or an **adjective clause**; (2) a **participle**; (3) an **infinitive**; (4) a **possessive**; (5) an **appositive.**

### I. ADJECTIVES, ADJECTIVE PHRASES, ADJECTIVE CLAUSES

**467.** The simple subject may be modified by an **adjective,** an **adjective phrase,** or an **adjective clause.**

$$\left.\begin{array}{l}\textit{Ivory} \text{ trinkets}\\ \text{Trinkets \textit{of ivory}}\\ \text{Trinkets \textit{which were carved from ivory}}\end{array}\right\rbrace \text{lay scattered about.}$$

$$\left.\begin{array}{l}\textit{Treeless} \text{ spots}\\ \text{Spots \textit{without trees}}\\ \text{Spots \textit{where no trees grew}}\end{array}\right\rbrace \text{were plainly visible.}$$

In each of these groups of sentences, the subject of the first sentence is modified by an **adjective**, that of the second by an **adjective phrase**, that of the third by an **adjective clause**.

Most adjective phrases are **prepositional** (§ 42), as in the examples.

**468.** An **adjective clause** may be introduced by a **relative pronoun** or a **relative adverb.** For lists, see § 377.

### I. Relative Pronouns

The architect *who designed this church* was a man of genius.

The painter *whom Ruskin oftenest mentions* is Turner.

A piece of amber *which is rubbed briskly* will attract bits of paper.

The day *that I dreaded* came at last.

The plain *through which this river flows* is marvelously fertile.

The book *from which I got this information* is always regarded as authoritative.

A friend *in whom one can trust* is a treasure beyond price.

The boys *with whom he associates* do him no good.

### II. Relative Adverbs

The spot *where the Old Guard made their last stand* is marked by a bronze eagle.

The morning *when I arrived in Rome* is one of my pleasantest memories.

The year *after Ashton left home* brought fresh disaster.

The land *whence Scyld drifted in his magic boat* will never be known.

Note. A preposition and a relative pronoun may often replace a relative adverb. Thus, in the second example, *on which* might be substituted for *when.*

### II. PARTICIPLES

**469.** The subject may be modified by a **participle** (with or without modifier or complement).

1. *Smiling*, the child shook his head.
2. My aunt, *reassured*, took up her book again.
3. The prisoner sank back *exhausted*.
4. *Exasperated* beyond endurance, the captain cut the rope.
5. John, *obeying* a sudden impulse, took to his heels.

6. *Having broken* one oar, Robert had to scull.
7. The natives, *fearing* captivity above all things, leaped into the river.
8. Albert left the room, *looking* rather sullen.

In the fourth example the participle is modified by an adverbial phrase; in the fifth and sixth, it has an object; in the seventh, it has both an object and a modifier; in the eighth, it is followed by the predicate adjective *sullen*. In analysis, the whole participial phrase (consisting of the participle and accompanying words) may be treated as an adjective phrase modifying the subject; but it is simpler to regard the participle as the modifier, and then to enumerate its modifiers, etc., separately.

Thus, in the seventh example, the simple subject *natives* is modified by the participle *fearing*, which has for a complement *captivity* (the direct object) and is modified by the adverbial phrase *above all things*.

NOTE. A participle, though a modifier of the subject, has at the same time a peculiar relation to the predicate, because it may take the place of an adverbial clause. Thus, in the seventh example, *fearing* is practically equivalent to the clause *because they feared*, which, if substituted for the participle, would of course modify the predicate verb *leaped*. This dual office of the participle comes from its twofold nature as (1) an adjective and (2) a verb. In analyzing, we treat the participle as an adjective modifier of the noun to which it belongs; but its function as a substitute for an adverbial clause is an important means of securing variety in style.

### III. INFINITIVES

**470.** The subject may be modified by an **infinitive.**

Eagerness *to learn* was young Lincoln's strongest passion.
Desire *to travel* made Taylor restless.
The wish *to succeed* prompted him to do his best.
Ability *to write rapidly* is a valuable accomplishment.
Howard's unwillingness *to desert a friend* cost him his life.

In the fourth example, the infinitive has an adverbial modifier (*rapidly*); and in the fifth, it has a complement, its object (*friend*). In such instances, two methods of analysis are allowable, as in the case of participial phrases (§ 469).

### IV. POSSESSIVES

**471.** The subject may be modified by a substantive in the **possessive case.**

Such a substantive may be called a **possessive modifier.**

> *Napoleon's* tomb is in Paris.
> A *man's* house is his castle.
> *One's* taste in reading changes as one grows older.
> A *moment's* thought would have saved me.
> The *squirrel's* teeth grow rapidly.
> The *Indians'* camp was near the river.
> *His* name is Alfred.
> *Your* carriage has arrived.

In each of these examples, a substantive in the possessive case modifies the subject by limiting its meaning precisely as an adjective would do.

NOTE. An adjective phrase may often be substituted for a possessive. Thus, in the first example, instead of "*Napoleon's* tomb" one may say "the tomb *of Napoleon*" (§ 93).

### V. APPOSITIVES

**472.** The subject may be modified by a **substantive in apposition** (§ 88, 5).

Meredith the *carpenter* lives in that house.

Herbert, our *captain*, has broken his leg.

The idol of the Aztecs, a grotesque *image*, was thrown down by the Spaniards.

Many books, both *pamphlets* and bound *volumes*, littered the table. [Here the subject (*books*) is modified by two appositives.]

Appositives often have modifiers of their own.

Thus *carpenter* is modified by the adjective *the*, *captain* by the possessive *our*, *image* by the adjectives *a* and *grotesque*.

In analyzing, the whole appositive phrase (consisting of the appositive and attached words) may be regarded as modifying the subject. It is as well, however, to treat the appositive as the modifier and then to enumerate the adjectives, etc., by which the appositive itself is modified.

**473**. A **noun clause** may be used as an appositive, and so may be an adjective modifier (§ 386).

The question *whether Antonio was a citizen* was settled in the affirmative. [Here the italicized clause is used as a noun in apposition with *question*.]

The statement *that water freezes* seems absurd to a native of the torrid zone. [The clause *that water freezes* is in apposition with *statement*.]

An adjective in the appositive position is often called an **appositive adjective** (§ 172). "A sword, *keen* and *bright*, flashed from the soldier's scabbard."

## MODIFIERS OF THE PREDICATE

**474**. The **simple predicate**, being a verb or verb-phrase, can have only **adverbial modifiers**.

The simple predicate may be modified by (1) an **adverb**, an **adverbial phrase**, or an **adverbial clause**, (2) an **infinitive**, (3) an **adverbial objective**, (4) a **nominative absolute**, (5) an **indirect object**, (6) a **cognate object**.

### I. ADVERB, ADVERBIAL PHRASE, ADVERBIAL CLAUSE

**475**. The simple predicate may be modified by an **adverb**, an **adverbial phrase**, or an **adverbial clause**.

The landlord collects his rents
$\begin{cases} \textit{monthly.} \\ \textit{on the first of every month.} \\ \textit{when the first of the month comes.} \end{cases}$

The old schoolhouse stands
$\begin{cases} \textit{there.} \\ \textit{at the cross-roads.} \\ \textit{where the roads meet.} \end{cases}$

We left the hall
$\begin{cases} \textit{early.} \\ \textit{before the last speech.} \\ \textit{while the last speech was being delivered.} \end{cases}$

In each of these groups, the simple predicate of the first sentence is modified by an adverb, that of the second by an adverbial phrase, and that of the third by an adverbial clause.

Most adverbial phrases are **prepositional** (§ 42).

| ADVERB | ADVERBIAL PHRASE | ADVERB | ADVERBIAL PHRASE |
|--------|------------------|--------|------------------|
| speedily | with speed | rapidly | at a rapid rate |
| furiously | with fury | skilfully | { in a skilful manner<br>{ with skill |
| lately | of late | promptly | on the instant |
| instantly | in an instant | to-morrow | on the morrow |
| there | in that place | unwillingly | against my will |

Peculiar adverbial phrases are : —

to and fro, now and then, up and down, again and again, first and last, full speed, full tilt, hit or miss, more or less, head first, upside down, inside out, sink or swim, cash down.

**476.** An adverbial clause that modifies a verb may be introduced by (1) a **relative adverb**, or (2) a **subordinate conjunction**.

### I. RELATIVE ADVERBS

Our colonel was always found *where the fighting was fiercest.*
*When I give the signal,* press the button.
*Whenever I call,* you refuse to see me.
Miller arrived *after the play had begun.*
Everybody listened *while the vagrant told his story.*
My uncle laughed *until the tears came.*
The prisoner has not been seen *since he made his escape.*

### II. SUBORDINATE CONJUNCTIONS

Archer resigned *because his health failed.*
I will give the address *if you will let me choose my subject.*
Brandon insisted on walking, *although the roads were dangerous.*
The child ran with all her might *lest she should be too late.*
I gave you a front seat *in order that you might hear.*
The town lies at the base of a lofty cliff *so that it is sheltered from the north wind.*

### II. INFINITIVE

**477.** The simple predicate may be modified by an **infinitive** (§ 323).

He lay down *to rest.*
I stopped *to listen.*
The fire continued *to burn.*

> The wind began *to subside.*
> Jack worked hard *to fell* the tree.
> Will did his best *to win* the prize.
> Kate began *to weep* bitterly.
> That draughtsman seems *to be* remarkably skilful.

The infinitive may have a complement or a modifier, as in the last four examples.

### III. ADVERBIAL OBJECTIVE

**478.** The simple predicate may be modified by an **adverbial objective** (§ 109).

> I have waited *ages.*
> We have walked *miles.*
> Arthur practised *weeks.*

The addition of modifiers to the adverbial objective makes an adverbial phrase.

> Walter ran *the entire distance.*
> He stayed *a whole day.*
> I will forgive you *this time.*
> He came at me *full tilt.*
> The wind blew *all night.*
> Come with me *a little way.*

In the first sentence, the adverbial phrase *the entire distance* modifies the verb *ran* as an adverb would do. This phrase consists of the noun *distance* with its adjective modifiers, *the* and *entire.*

### IV. NOMINATIVE ABSOLUTE

**479.** The simple predicate may be modified by a **nominative absolute** (§ 345).

A substantive in the **absolute construction** makes with its modifiers an adverbial phrase.

*The ship having arrived,* we all embarked.
We shall sail on Tuesday, *weather permitting.*
*That done,* repair to Pompey's theatre.
*The bridge across the chasm being only a single tree trunk,* we hesitated to attempt the passage.

In the first sentence, the adverbial absolute phrase, *the ship having arrived*, is equivalent to the adverbial prepositional phrase, *on the arrival of the ship*, and defines the time of the action expressed by the verb *embarked*.

### V. INDIRECT OBJECT

**480.** The simple predicate may be modified by an **indirect object** (§ 105).

> He gave *me* a watch.  [ = He gave a watch *to me*.]
> Tom told *me* the whole story.  [ = Tom told the whole story *to me*.]

In these sentences, the indirect object *me*, being equivalent to a prepositional phrase, is an adverbial modifier.

The objective of service (§ 106) is also an adverbial modifier.

### VI. COGNATE OBJECT

**481.** The simple predicate may be modified by a **cognate object** or by a phrase containing such an object (§ 108).

> The officer looked *daggers* at me [ = looked at me angrily].
> The shepherd sang a merry *song* [ = sang merrily].
> The skipper laughed a scornful *laugh* [ = laughed scornfully].

In the first sentence, the cognate object (*daggers*) modifies the predicate verb (*looked*) as the adverb *angrily* would do. It is therefore an adverbial modifier. In the second and third sentences the modifier of the predicate verb (*sang, laughed*) is an adverbial phrase consisting of a cognate object (*song, laugh*) with its adjective modifiers (*a merry, a scornful*).

# CHAPTER IV

## COMPLEMENTS

**482.** 1. Some verbs have a meaning that is **complete in itself.** Such a verb needs only a subject. When this has been supplied, we have a sentence, for the mere verb, without any additional word or words, is capable of being a predicate.

| | |
|---|---|
| Birds *fly*. | The man *scowled*. |
| Fishes *swim*. | The girl *laughed*. |
| The sun *shines*. | The owls *hooted*. |
| The moon *rose*. | The clock *ticked*. |

Verbs of this kind are sometimes called **complete verbs, or verbs of complete predication.**

2. Other verbs are not, by themselves, capable of serving as predicates. Thus, —

| | |
|---|---|
| The Indians killed ——. | Tom is ——. |
| Mr. Harris makes ——. | The man seemed ——. |

These are not sentences, for the predicate of each is unfinished. The verb requires the addition of a substantive or an adjective to complete its sense.

| | |
|---|---|
| The Indians killed *deer*. | Tom is *captain*. |
| Mr. Harris makes *shoes*. | The man seemed *sorry*. |

Verbs of this kind are often called **incomplete verbs, or verbs of incomplete predication.**

NOTE. The meaning of the verb determines to which of these classes it belongs. Accordingly, the same verb may belong to the first class in some of its senses and to the second in others (§§ 212–215).

**483.** A substantive or adjective added to the predicate verb to complete its meaning is called a complement.

Complements are of four kinds, — the direct object, the predicate objective, the predicate nominative, and the predicate adjective.

In the examples in § 482, *deer* and *shoes* are **direct objects,** — the former denoting the **receiver** of the action, the latter denoting the **product**; *captain* is a **predicate nominative,** denoting the same person as the subject *Tom* (§ 88, 2); *sorry* is a predicate adjective describing the subject *man.*

Complements may, of course, be modified. If they are substantives, they may take adjective modifiers; if adjectives, they may take adverbial modifiers (§§ 464, 494).

**484.** For convenience, the definitions of the four kinds of complements are here repeated, with examples.

## 1. THE DIRECT OBJECT

**485.** Some verbs may be followed by a substantive denoting that which receives the action or is produced by it. These are called transitive verbs. All other verbs are called intransitive.

A substantive that completes the meaning of a transitive verb is called its direct object (§ 100).

The direct object is often called the object complement, or merely the object of the verb.

> Alfred has broken his *arm.*
> Morse invented the electric *telegraph.*
> Black foxes command a high *price.*
> You have accomplished a *task* of great difficulty.
> Have you lost the *dog* which your uncle gave you?
> He asked *me* the *news.* [Two direct objects (§ 103).]

Most of these objects are modified, — *arm* by the possessive *his;* *telegraph* by *the* and *electric;* *price* by *a* and *high;* *task* by the adjective phrase *of great difficulty;* *dog* by *the* and by the adjective clause *which your uncle gave you.*

**486.** A noun clause may be used as the direct object of a verb (§ 386).

> You promised *that my coat should be ready to-day.*
> The mayor ordered *that the street should be closed for three hours.*
> I begged *that my passport might be returned to me.*

For further examples, see §§ 407, 432, 439, 441.

## 2. THE PREDICATE OBJECTIVE

**487.** Verbs of *choosing, calling, naming, making,* and *thinking* may take two objects referring to the same person or thing.

The first of these is the direct object, and the second, which completes the sense of the predicate, is called a predicate objective (§ 104).

The predicate objective is often called the complementary object or the objective attribute.

> The people have elected Chamberlain *governor*.
> Peter calls Richard my *shadow*.
> The court has appointed you the child's *guardian*.
> John thinks himself a *hero*.

**488.** An adjective may serve as a predicate objective. Thus, —

> I thought your decision *hasty*
> I call that answer *impertinent*.
> The jury found the prisoner *guilty*.
> Your letter made him *joyful*.

Care should be taken not to confuse adverbs with adjectives in *-ly* serving as predicate objectives.

> You called him *sickly*. [Adjective.]
> You called him *early*. [Adverb.]

After the passive, a predicate objective becomes a **predicate nominative** (§ 489).

## 3. THE PREDICATE NOMINATIVE

**489.** A substantive standing in the predicate, but describing or defining the subject, agrees with the subject in case and is called a predicate nominative (§ 88, 2).

A predicate nominative is often called a subject complement or an attribute.

The predicate nominative is common after *is* and other copulative verbs, and after certain transitive verbs in the passive voice.

> Chemistry is a useful *science*.
> Boston is the *capital* of Massachusetts.
> Jefferson became *President*.

> This bird is called a *flamingo*.
> Mr. Hale was appointed *secretary*.
> Albert has been chosen *captain* of the crew.
> You are a *friend* upon whom I can rely.

In most of the examples, the predicate nominative has one or more modifiers. In the first sentence, *science* is modified by the two adjectives *a* and *useful ;* in the second, *capital* is modified by the adjective phrase *of Massachusetts ;* in the last, *friend* is modified by the adjective clause *upon whom I can rely.*

For the distinction between the **predicate nominative** and the **direct object**, see § 102.

**490.** A **noun clause** may be used as a predicate nominative (§ 386).

> My plan is *that the well should be dug to-morrow.*
> His intention was *that you should remain here.*
> The result is *that he is bankrupt.*
> Ruth's fear was *that the door might be locked.*

**491.** An **infinitive** may be used as a predicate nominative.

> To hear is *to obey.*
> My hope was *to reach* the summit before dark.
> Their plan was *to undermine* the tower.
> My habit is *to rise* early.

The infinitive may have a complement or modifiers. In the second and third examples, it takes an object; in the fourth it is modified by an adverb.

#### 4. THE PREDICATE ADJECTIVE

**492.** An adjective in the predicate belonging to a noun or pronoun in the subject is called a predicate adjective.

A predicate adjective completes the meaning of the predicate verb and is therefore a complement (§ 172, 3.)

Like the predicate nominative, the predicate adjective is common after copulative verbs and after certain transitive verbs in the passive voice (§§ 172, 3; 252).

> John was *angry*.
> My knife is growing *dull*.
> The task seemed very *easy*.
> The report proved *false* in every particular.
> The boat was thought *unsafe*.
> The cover was made perfectly *tight*.

In some of these examples, the predicate adjective has a modifier. In the third, *easy* is modified by the adverb *very ;* in the fourth, *false* is modified by the adverbial phrase *in every particular ;* in the last, *tight* is modified by *perfectly*.

**493.** An **adjective phrase** may be used as a predicate adjective. Thus, —

> Richard was *out of health*. [Compare : Richard was *ill*.]
> Rachel seemed *in a passion*. [Compare : seemed *angry*.]
> This act is *against my interests*. [Compare : is *harmful* to me.]

The adjective phrase may consist of an infinitive with or without the preposition *about* (§ 319).

> I was *about to speak*.
> This house is *to let*.
> I am *to sail* to-morrow.

# CHAPTER V

## MODIFIERS OF COMPLEMENTS AND OF MODIFIERS

### COMPLEMENTS MODIFIED

**494.** Complements, being either substantives or adjectives, may be modified in various ways, most of which have been noted in Chapter III.

1. A **substantive** used as a **complement** may have the same kinds of modifiers that are used with the **subject** (§ 466).

2. An **adjective complement** admits only **adverbial modifiers**.

**495.** The following sentences illustrate the modifiers of substantive complements : —

Herbert lost *a gold* watch. [The direct object (*watch*) is modified by the adjectives *a* and *gold*.]

The duke built towers *of marble*. [The direct object (*towers*) is modified by the adjective phrase *of marble*.]

My father built *the* house *in which I was born*. [The direct object (*house*) is modified by the adjective *the* and the adjective clause *in which I was born*.]

I saw *a* man *running* across the field. [The direct object (*man*) is modified by the adjective *a* and the participle *running*.]

You have forfeited *your* right *to vote*. [The direct object (*right*) is modified by the possessive pronoun *your* and the infinitive *to vote*.]

I have seen *Henry's* brother. [The direct object (*brother*) is modified by the possessive noun *Henry's*.]

I must ask *my* brother, the *mayor*. [The direct object (*brother*) is modified by the possessive pronoun *my* and the appositive *mayor*.]

The guild has elected Walter *honorary* president. [The predicate object (*president*) is modified by the adjective *honorary*.]

Her husband is *an old* soldier. [The predicate nominative (*soldier*) is modified by the adjectives *an* and *old*.]

Her sons are veterans *of the Franco-Prussian war*. [The predicate nominative (*veterans*) is modified by the adjective phrase *of the Franco-Prussian war*.]

They are rivals *in business*. [The predicate nominative (*rivals*) is modified by the adjective phrase *in business*.]

The author is Will Jewell, *who was formerly editor of " The Pioneer."* [The predicate nominative (*Will Jewell*) is modified by the adjective clause *who was formerly editor,* etc.]

Baldwin is *the* man *standing* under the tree. [The predicate nominative (*man*) is modified by the adjective *the* and the participle *standing.*]

Your chief fault is *your* inclination *to procrastinate.* [The predicate nominative (*inclination*) is modified by the possessive pronoun *your* and the infinitive *to procrastinate.*]

This man is *Gretchen's* brother. [The predicate nominative (*brother*) is modified by the possessive noun *Gretchen's.*]

The first to fall was *the* bugler, *John Wilson.* [The predicate nominative (*bugler*) is modified by the adjective *the* and the appositive *John Wilson.*]

**496.** **Adjective clauses** are very common as modifiers of substantive complements (cf. § 468).

Have you lost the watch *that your cousin gave you?*

This is the very spot *where the temple of Saturn stood.*

The general issued an order *that all non-combatants should be treated well.*

We have abundant proof *that during his stay on the Continent, Bacon did not neglect literary and scientific pursuits.*

**497.** An **adjective** used as a complement may be modified by an **adverb**, an **adverbial phrase**, or an **adverbial clause**.

I am *very* sorry *for you.* [*Sorry* is modified by the adverb *very* and the adverbial phrase *for you.*]

Charles seems $\left\{\begin{array}{l}\textit{rather}\\\textit{very}\\\textit{extremely}\end{array}\right\}$ angry.

The road is rough $\left\{\begin{array}{l}\textit{in places.}\\\textit{where they are repairing it.}\end{array}\right.$

The whole tribe appeared eager *for war.*

He grew envious *of his successful rival.*

Be zealous *in every righteous cause.*

The chief's face looked dark *with passion.*

He was selfish *beyond belief.* [The predicate adjective (*selfish*) is modified by the adverbial phrase *beyond belief.*]

Ellen seemed desirous *that her friends should admire her.*

The secretary appeared unwilling *to resign.* [See § 321, note.]

## MODIFIERS OF OTHER MODIFIERS

**498.** Modifiers may themselves be modified.

The chief varieties of such modification are illustrated in the following sentences.

I. **Adjectives** or **adjective phrases** may be modified by **adverbs** or by words or groups of words used adverbially.

A *very* old man came to the door.
An *exceedingly* dangerous curve lay beyond the bridge.
This *rather* odd proposal interested us.
The quay is *miles* long. [Adverbial objective (§ 109).]
*At least* five different amendments have been offered. [*Five* is modified by the adverbial phrase *at least*.]
The general, *wholly* in the dark as to the enemy's intentions, ordered an advance. [The adjective phrase *in the dark* is modified by *wholly*.]
*Quite* at his ease, John began to speak. [*At his ease* is modified by *quite*.]
Her smile, pathetic *in its weariness*, quickly faded. [The adverbial phrase modifies *pathetic*.]
This sleeve is *a good two inches* short. [The phrase modifies *short*.]

II. **Possessive nouns** may be modified by adjectives or by possessives.

*The poor* man's days are numbered.
*Honest* Tom's face shone with delight.
*The faithful* animal's head drooped.
*My* uncle's barn is on fire.
*John's* brother's name is Reginald.

III. **Appositives** may be modified by adjectives or by groups of words used as adjectives.

Joe, *the old* butler, met me at the station.
Sam, *the cunning* rascal, had stolen the oars.
Her mother, a woman *of fashion*, sadly neglected her.
The other, the man *at the table*, laughed rudely.
Ferdinand Oliver, the engineer *who had charge of the construction*, proved incompetent.
Two Englishmen, friends *whom I visited last summer*, are coming to New York in December.

IV. **Adverbs** or **adverbial phrases** may be modified by adverbs or by words or groups of words used adverbially.

> Jane plays *very* well.
> Robert spoke *almost* hopefully.
> She answered *quite* at random.
> I write to him *at least* once *a year*.

**499.** An adjective may be modified by an **infinitive** (§ 321).

Unable *to move*, I suffered torments of anxiety.

The sailors, eager *to reach* the island, plunged into the sea.

Reluctant *to act*, but unwilling *to stand* idle, Burwell was in a pitiful state of indecision.

**500.** Adjective and adverbial clauses are very common as modifiers of modifiers (cf. § 496).

Geronimo, an old chief *who bore the scars of many battles*, led the attack. [The adjective clause modifies the appositive *chief*.]

The servant, angry *because he had been rebuked*, slammed the door as he went out.

The hunter, confident *that the deer had not heard him*, took deliberate aim.

The fugitive, in a panic *lest he should be overtaken*, made frantic efforts to scale the cliff. [The adverbial clause modifies the adjective phrase *in a panic*.]

# CHAPTER VI

## INDEPENDENT ELEMENTS

**501.** A word or group of words that has no grammatical connection with the sentence in which it stands is called an independent element.

Independent elements are of four kinds, — interjections, vocatives (or nominatives by direct address), exclamatory nominatives, and parenthetical expressions.

> *Ah!* why did I undertake this task?
> Help arrived, *alas!* too late.
> You are a strange man, *Arthur.*
> *Mary,* come here!
> Poor *Charles!* I am sorry for him.
> *Clothes! clothes!* you are always wanting clothes.
> Lucky *she!* we are all envious of her prospects.

The first two sentences contain **interjections** (§ 372); the second two, **vocatives** (or nominatives by direct address) (§88, 3); the last three, **exclamatory nominatives** (§ 88, 4).

When the independent word has a **modifier** (as in the fifth and seventh examples), the whole phrase may be treated as an independent element.

**502.** A word or group of words attached to or inserted in a sentence as a mere comment, without belonging either to the subject or the predicate, is said to be parenthetical.

> The market, *indeed*, was already closed.
> Peter, *to be sure*, was not very trustworthy.
> The house, *at all events*, is safe.
> The road is, *I admit*, very hilly.
> Luttrell's method, *it must be confessed*, was a little disappointing.
> Richard was not a bad fellow, *after all.*

**503.** In analysis, an independent element is mentioned by itself, and not as a part of the complete subject or the complete predicate.

## CHAPTER VII

### COMBINATIONS OF CLAUSES

**504.** The use of subordinate clauses as complements and modifiers, and as modifiers of complements and of modifiers, may produce sentences of great length and complicated structure.

Such sentences, if skilfully composed, are not hard to follow. Their analysis requires merely the intelligent application of a few simple principles, which have already been explained and illustrated.

**505.** These principles may be summed up as follows : —

I. All clauses are either **independent** or **subordinate**. A clause is subordinate if it is used as a part of speech (noun, adjective, or adverb) ; otherwise, it is independent (§ 46).

II. **Coördinate** means "of the same rank" in the sentence (§ 46).

1. Two or more **independent clauses** in the same sentence are manifestly coördinate.

> *The fire blazed* and *the wood crackled.* [Two declarative clauses.]
> *What is your name,* and *where were you born?* [Interrogative clauses.]
> *Sit down* and *tell me your story.* [Imperative clauses.]

2. Two or more **subordinate clauses** are coördinate *with each other* when they are used together in the same construction, — as nouns, adjectives, or adverbs.

Such a group may be regarded as forming one **compound subordinate clause.**

> The truth is, *that I have no money* and *that my friends have forsaken me.* [Noun clauses.]
> The Indians, *who were armed with long lances,* and *who showed great skill in using them,* made a furious attack on the cavalry. [Adjective clauses.]
> *When he had spoken,* but *before a vote had been taken,* a strange tumult was heard in the outer room [Adverbial clauses.]

In the first example, we have a **compound noun clause**; in the second, a **compound adjective clause**; in the third, a **compound adverbial clause**.

3. Coördinate clauses are either joined by coördinate conjunctions (*and, or, but,* etc.), or such conjunctions may be supplied without changing the sense (§ 362).

The good-natured old gentleman, *who was friendly to both parties,* [AND] *who did not lack courage,* AND *who hated a quarrel,* spoke his mind with complete frankness.

III. A subordinate clause may depend on another subordinate clause.

The horse shied *when he saw the locomotive.* [The subordinate clause depends upon the independent (main) clause.]

The horse shied when he saw the locomotive, *which was puffing violently.* [The second subordinate clause depends upon the first, being an adjective modifier of *locomotive.*]

In such cases, the whole group of subordinate clauses may be taken together as forming one **complex subordinate clause.**

Thus, in the second example, *when he saw the locomotive, which was puffing violently* may be regarded as a complex adverbial clause modifying *shied,* and containing an adjective clause (*which was puffing violently*).

**506.** From the principles summarized in § 505, it appears that —

**Clauses (like sentences) may be simple, compound, or complex.**

1. A **simple clause** contains but one subject and one predicate, either or both of which may be compound (§ 451).

2. A **compound clause** consists of two or more coördinate clauses (§ 454).

3. A **complex clause** consists of at least two clauses, one of which is subordinate to the other.

**507.** The **unit** in all combinations of clauses is clearly the **simple sentence**, which, when used as a part of a more complicated sentence, becomes a **simple clause.**

The processes used in such combinations, as we have seen, are really but two in number, — coördination and subordination.

Coördination of clauses produces compound sentences or compound clauses; subordination of one clause to another produces complex sentences or complex clauses.

**508.** Every sentence, however long and complicated, belongs (in structure) to one of the three classes, — simple, compound, and complex.

## SIMPLE SENTENCES

**509.** A simple sentence may have a compound subject or predicate (or both), and may also include a number of modifiers and complements.

Obviously, then, a simple sentence need not be short. It remains simple in structure so long as it contains but one simple or compound subject and one simple or compound predicate. Thus, —

1. You leave Glasgow in a steamboat, go down the Clyde fourteen miles, and then come to Dumbarton Castle, a huge rock five or six hundred feet high, not connected with any other high land, and with a fortress at the top. — WEBSTER.

The length of this sentence is due partly to its compound predicate, partly to the modifier (and modifiers of the modifier) attached to the noun *Dumbarton Castle.*

2. He was little disposed to exchange his lordly repose for the insecure and agitated life of a conspirator, to be in the power of accomplices, to live in constant dread of warrants and king's messengers, nay, perhaps, to end his days on a scaffold, or to live on alms in some back street of the Hague. — MACAULAY.

This sentence is lengthened by means of a series of infinitives used as adverbial modifiers of the complement *disposed* (a participle used as an adjective). Each of these infinitives takes a complement or a modifier (or both).

3. The arbitrary measures of Charles I, the bold schemes of Strafford, and the intolerant bigotry of Laud, precipitated a collision between the opposite principles of government, and divided the whole country into Cavaliers and Roundheads. — MAY.

Both the subject and the predicate are compound. Each of the three nouns in the compound subject has modifiers. The two verbs in the compound predicate have each a complement, and the second has an adverbial modifier (a phrase).

**4.** Twenty of the savages now got on board and proceeded to ramble over every part of the deck and scramble about among the rigging, making themselves much at home and examining every article with great inquisitiveness. — Poe.

The predicate is compound. The sentence is extended by the use of participles (*making* and *examining*), which modify the simple subject *twenty*.

**5.** She was tumbled early, by accident or design, into a spacious closet of good old English reading, without much selection or prohibition, and browsed at will upon that fair and wholesome pasturage. — Lamb.

**6.** The mermaid was still seen to glide along the waters, and mingling her voice with the sighing breeze, was often heard to sing of subterranean wonders, or to chant prophecies of future events. — Scott.

**7.** With early dawn, they were under arms, and, without waiting for the movement of the Spaniards, poured into the city and attacked them in their own quarters. — Prescott.

**8.** Arming a desperate troop of slaves and gladiators, he overpowered the feeble guard of the domestic tranquillity of Rome, received the homage of the Senate, and, assuming the title of Augustus, precariously reigned during a tumult of twenty-eight days. — Gibbon.

Note. A simple sentence with compound predicate often differs very slightly from a compound sentence. Thus in examples 4–7 the insertion of a single pronoun (*they*, *she*) to serve as a subject for the second verb (*proceeded*, *browsed*, etc.) will make the sentence compound.

## COMPOUND AND COMPLEX SENTENCES

**510.** Every sentence that is not simple must be either compound or complex.

A sentence is **compound** if it consists of two or more independent clauses; **complex,** if it consists of one independent (main) clause and one or more subordinate clauses.

**511.** An ordinary **compound sentence** consists of two or more coördinate simple clauses.

Such a sentence may be of great length (as in the last example below), but its structure is usually transparent.

A cricket chirps on the hearth, | and | we are reminded of Christmas gambols long ago. — HAZLITT.

The moments were numbered ; | the strife was finished ; | the vision was closed. — DE QUINCEY.

The old king had retired to his couch that night in one of the strongest towers of the Alhambra, | but | his restless anxiety kept him from repose. — IRVING.

The clock has just struck two ; | the expiring taper rises and sinks in the socket ; | the watchman forgets his hour in slumber ; | the laborious and the happy are at rest ; | and | nothing wakes but meditation, guilt, revelry, and despair. — GOLDSMITH.

The present, indeed, is not a contest for distant or contingent objects ; | it is not a contest for acquisition of territory ; | it is not a contest for power and glory ; | as little is it carried on merely for any commercial advantage, or any particular form of government ; | but | it is a contest for the security, the tranquillity, and the very existence of Great Britain, connected with that of every established government and every country in Europe. — PITT.

**512.** A **complex sentence,** in its most elementary form, consists of one simple independent (main) clause and one simple subordinate clause.

The gas exploded when I struck a match.
Though he is idle, he is not lazy.
The carpenter who fell from the roof has recovered from his injuries.

Their eyes were so fatigued with the eternal dazzle and whiteness, that they lay down on their backs upon deck to relieve their sight on the blue sky. — KEATS.

The shouts of thousands, their menacing gestures, the fierce clashing of their arms, astonished and subdued the courage of Vetranio, who stood, amidst the defection of his followers, in anxious and silent suspense. — GIBBON.

**513.** Both compound sentences and complex sentences admit of much variety in structure, according to the nature and the relations of the clauses that compose them.

## COMPOUND COMPLEX SENTENCES

**514.** Any or all of the coördinate clauses that make up a compound sentence may be complex. In that case, the sentence is called a compound complex sentence.

NOTE. Compound complex sentences form a special class or subdivision under the general head of compound sentences.[1]

Old Uncle Venner was just coming out of his door, with a wood-horse and saw on his shoulder ; and, trudging along the street, he scrupled not to keep company with Phœbe, so far as their paths lay together ; nor, in spite of his patched coat and rusty beaver, and the curious fashion of his tow-cloth trousers, could she find it in her heart to outwalk him.

HAWTHORNE.

This sentence consists of **three coördinate clauses**, each independent of the others. These are joined by the coördinate conjunctions *and, nor*. The first and the third clause are **simple**, but the second clause is **complex**. Hence the whole forms one **compound complex sentence**.

The complex clause consists of two clauses, the second of which is subordinate to the first. Taken as a whole, however, this complex clause is manifestly coördinate with the two simple clauses, since the three form a series joined by coördinate conjunctions.

**515.** Further examples of **compound complex sentences** are : —

**1.** The people drove out King Athamas, because he had killed his child ; and he roamed about in his misery, till he came to the Oracle in Delphi. — KINGSLEY.

**2.** Society is the stage on which manners are shown ; novels are their literature. — EMERSON.

**3.** We keep no bees, but if I lived in a hive I should scarcely have more of their music. — COWPER.

**4.** The same river ran on as it had run on before, but the cheerful faces that had once been reflected in its stream had passed away. — FROUDE.

**5.** There are some laws and customs in this empire very peculiar ; and if they were not so directly contrary to those of my own dear country, I should be tempted to say a little in their justification. — SWIFT.

**6.** Here they arrived about noon, and Joseph proposed to Adams that they should rest awhile in this delightful place. — FIELDING.

**7.** I never saw a busier person than she seemed to be; yet it was difficult to say what she did. — C. BRONTË.

---

[1] Instead of **compound complex**, the term **complex compound** is often used. The terms are synonymous, both meaning " compound in general structure, but complex in one or more members."

8. Malaga possessed a brave and numerous garrison, and the common people were active, hardy, and resolute; but the city was rich and commercial, and under the habitual control of opulent merchants, who dreaded the ruinous consequences of a siege. — IRVING.

9. The Spaniards were not to be taken by surprise; and, before the barbarian horde had come within their lines, they opened such a deadly fire from their heavy guns, supported by the musketry and crossbows, that the assailants were compelled to fall back slowly, but fearfully mangled, to their former position. — PRESCOTT.

10. Her cheeks were as pale as marble, but of a cold, unhealthy, ashen white; and my heart ached to think that they had been bleached, most probably, by bitter and continual tears. — HOOD.

11. The hawk, having in spiral motion achieved the upper flight, fell like a thunderbolt on the raven, stunned him with the blow, clutched him in his talons, folded him in his wings, and, the hawk undermost, they tumbled down like a black ball, till within a short distance from the earth. — TRELAWNY.

In this sentence *they were* is understood after *till*.

## VARIETIES OF THE COMPLEX SENTENCE

**516.** A complex sentence may be expanded either by compounding the main clause, or by increasing the number of subordinate clauses. Both methods may be used in the same sentence.

**517. The independent (main) clause of a complex sentence may be compound.**

When they saw the ship, *they shouted for joy and some of them burst into tears.*

As they turned down from the knoll to rejoin their comrades, *the sun dipped and disappeared, and the woods fell instantly into the gravity and grayness of the early night.* — STEVENSON.

*The eye of the young monarch kindled and his dark cheek flushed with sudden anger,* as he listened to proposals so humiliating. — PRESCOTT.

*Sharpe was so hated in Scotland during his life, and his death won him so many friends, or pitying observers,* that it is not easy to write of him without prejudice or favor. — A. LANG.

As has been the case with many another good fellow of his nation, *his life was tracked and his substance wasted by crowds of hungry beggars and lazy dependents.* — THACKERAY.

Note that the subordinate clause depends on the compound main clause, not upon either of its members.

Thus, in the first example, the subordinate clause (*when they saw the ship*) depends upon the compound main clause, *they shouted for joy and some of them burst into tears.* It is an adverbial modifier of both *shouted* and *burst.*

**518.** Though a complex sentence can have but one (simple or compound) main clause, there is, in theory, no limit to the number of subordinate clauses.

**519.** Subordinate clauses may be attached to the main clause (1) as **separate modifiers or complements** ; (2) in a **coördinate series of clauses,** all in the same construction, and forming one **compound clause** ; (3) in a series of **successively subordinate clauses,** forming one **complex clause.**

**520. Two or more subordinate clauses may be attached to the main clause separately, each as a distinct modifier or complement.**

The bridge, *which had been weakened by the ice*, fell with a crash *while the locomotive was crossing it.* [The first subordinate clause is an adjective modifier of *bridge ;* the second is an adverbial modifier of *fell.*]

The architect *who drew the plans* says *that the house will cost ten thousand dollars.* [The first subordinate clause is an adjective modifier of *architect ;* the second is a complement, being the object of *says.*]

Isabella, *whom every incident was sufficient to dismay*, hesitated *whether she should proceed.* — H. WALPOLE.

As the boat drew nearer to the city, the coast which the traveller had just left sank behind him into one long, low, sad-colored line. — RUSKIN.

Those dangers which, in the vigor of youth, we had learned to despise, assume new terrors as we grow old. — GOLDSMITH.

When Farmer Oak smiled, the corners of his mouth spread till they were within an unimportant distance of his ears. — HARDY.

As Florian Deleal walked, one hot afternoon, he overtook by the wayside a poor aged man, and, as he seemed weary with the road, helped him on with the burden which he carried, a certain distance. — PATER.

While Joe was absent on this errand, the elder Willet and his three companions continued to smoke with profound gravity and in a deep silence, each having his eyes fixed on a huge copper boiler that was suspended over the fire. — DICKENS.

**521.** Two or more subordinate clauses in the same construction, forming one compound clause, may be attached to the main clause as a modifier or complement.

1. The truth was *that Leonard had overslept, that he had missed the train, and that he had failed to keep his appointment.*

2. The guide told us *that the road was impassable, that the river was in flood, and that the bridge had been swept away.*

3. Ellis, *whose pockets were empty and whose courage was at a low ebb,* stared dismally at the passing crowd.

4. *Before the battle was over and while the result was still in doubt,* the general ordered a retreat.

5. *After we had arrived at the hotel, but before we had engaged our rooms,* we received an invitation to stay at the castle.

6. My first thought was, *that all was lost, and that my only chance for executing a retreat was to sacrifice my baggage.* — DE QUINCEY.

7. The author fully convinced his readers *that they were a race of cowards and scoundrels, that nothing could save them, that they were on the point of being enslaved by their enemies, and that they richly deserved their fate.* — MACAULAY.

In the first and second examples, three coördinate noun clauses are joined to make one compound clause, which is used as a complement, — as a predicate nominative in the first sentence, as the direct object of *told* in the second.

In the third example, a compound adjective clause modifies *Ellis.* In the fourth and fifth, a compound adverbial clause modifies the predicate verb (*ordered, received*). In the seventh, four *that*-clauses unite in one compound clause.

**522.** Two or more successively subordinate clauses, forming one complex clause, may be joined to the main clause as a modifier or complement.

In such a series, the first subordinate clause is attached directly to the main clause, the second is subordinate to the first, the third to the second, and so on in succession.

In the course of my travels, I met a good-natured old gentleman, (*a*) *who was born in the village* (*b*) *where my parents lived* (*c*) *before they came to America.*

Here *gentleman* (a complement in the main clause) is modified by the adjective clause *who was born in the village* (*a*). *Village*, in clause *a*, is modified by the adjective clause *where my parents lived* (*b*). *Lived*, the predicate verb of clause *b*, is modified by the adverbial clause *before they came to America* (*c*).

Thus it appears that *a* is subordinate to the main clause, and that *b*, in turn, is subordinate to *a*, and *c* to *b*. In other words, the three clauses (*a, b, c*) are united to make one complex clause, — *who was born in the village where my parents lived before they came to America.* This clause, taken as a whole, serves as an adjective modifier describing *gentleman*.

**523.** Further examples of the **successive subordination** of one clause to another may be seen in the following sentences : —

I have passed my latter years in this city, *where I am frequently seen in public places, though there are not above half-a-dozen of my select friends that know me.* — ADDISON.

In this manner they advanced by moonlight *till they came within view of the two towering rocks that form a kind of portal to the valley, at the extremity of which rose the vast ruins of Istakar.* — BECKFORD.

The young fellow uttered this with an accent and a look so perfectly in tune to a feeling heart, *that I instantly made a vow I would give him a four-and-twenty sous piece, when I got to Marseilles.* — STERNE. [The conjunction *that* is omitted before *I would* (§ 388).]

Three years had scarcely elapsed *before the sons of Constantine seemed impatient to convince mankind that they were incapable of contenting themselves with the dominions which they were unqualified to govern.* — GIBBON.

Mr. Lewis sent me an account of Dr. Arbuthnot's illness, *which is a very sensible affliction to me, who, by living so long out of the world, have lost that hardness of heart contracted by years and general conversation.* — SWIFT.

NOTE. The method of forming complex clauses by **successive subordination**, if overworked, produces long, straggling, shapeless sentences, as in the following example from Borrow : — "I scouted the idea that Slingsby would have stolen this blacksmith's gear ; for I had the highest opinion of his honesty, *which* opinion I still retain at the present day, *which* is upwards of twenty years from the time of *which* I am speaking, during the whole of *which* period I have neither seen the poor fellow nor received any intelligence of him." A famous instance of the use of this structure for comic effect is "The House that Jack Built."

## SPECIAL COMPLICATIONS

**524**. The processes of coördination and subordination (§§ 514–523) may be so utilized in one and the same sentence as to produce a very complicated structure.

Examples of such sentences are given below, for reference (§§ 525–526). Their structure, however elaborate, is always either **complex** or **compound complex**.

### I. IN COMPLEX SENTENCES

**525**. The following sentences are complex. They contain either compound or complex clauses, or both.

**1**. They preferred the silver with which they were familiar, and which they were constantly passing about from hand to hand, to the gold which they had never before seen, and with the value of which they were unacquainted. — MACAULAY.

The main clause of this **complex sentence** is *they preferred the silver to the gold*. To this are separately attached (§ 520) two adjective clauses, both **compound**: (1) *with which . . . hand*, modifying *silver ;* (2) *which they had . . . unacquainted*, modifying *gold*.

**2**. All London crowded to shout and laugh round the gibbet where hung the rotting remains of a prince who had made England the dread of the world, who had been the chief founder of her maritime greatness and of her colonial empire, who had conquered Scotland and Ireland, who had humbled Holland and Spain. — MACAULAY.

The sentence is **complex**. The main clause is *all London crowded to shout and laugh round the gibbet*. The rest of the sentence (*where . . . Spain*) forms one long complex adjective clause, modifying *gibbet*. In this complex clause, the first clause (*where . . . prince*) has dependent on it a compound adjective clause (modifying *prince*), made up of four coördinate clauses, each beginning with *who*. The subordination of this compound clause to that which precedes (*where . . . prince*) produces the long complex subordinate clause *where . . . Spain*.

**3**. As we cannot at present get Mr. Joseph out of the inn, we shall leave him in it, and carry our reader on after Parson Adams, who, his mind being perfectly at ease, fell into a contemplation on a passage in Æschylus, which entertained him for three miles together, without suffering him once to reflect on his fellow-traveller. — FIELDING.

**In** this complex sentence, two subordinate clauses are separately attached to the main clause: (1) the adverbial clause *as . . . inn;* (2) the adjective clause *who . . . fellow-traveller.* This latter clause is complex, since it contains the adjective clause *which . . . fellow-traveller,* dependent on *who . . . Æschylus,* and modifying *passage.*

**4.** As I sit by my window this summer afternoon, hawks are circling about my clearing ; the tantivy of wild pigeons, flying by twos and threes athwart my view, or perching restlessly on the white pine boughs behind my house, gives a voice to the air ; a fishhawk dimples the glassy surface of the pond and brings up a fish ; a mink steals out of the marsh before my door and seizes a frog by the shore; the sedge is bending under the weight of the reed-birds flitting hither and hither ; and for the last half hour I have heard the rattle of railroad cars, now dying away and then reviving like the beat of a partridge, conveying travellers from Boston to the country. — THOREAU.

This sentence is **complex.** Its main clause is compound, consisting of a series of six coördinate simple clauses. The whole of this long compound main clause is modified by the adverbial clause with which the sentence begins (*as . . . afternoon*).

**5.** That they had sprung from obscurity, that they had acquired great wealth, that they exhibited it insolently, that they spent it extravagantly, that they raised the price of everything in their neighborhood, from fresh eggs to rotten boroughs ; that their liveries outshone those of dukes, that their coaches were finer than that of the Lord Mayor, that the examples of their large and ill-governed households corrupted half the servants in the country ; that some of them, with all their magnificence, could not catch the tone of good society, but in spite of the stud and the crowd of menials, of the plate and the Dresden china, of the venison and the Burgundy, were still low men, — these were things which excited, both in the class from which they had sprung, and in that into which they attempted to force themselves, that bitter aversion which is the effect of mingled envy and contempt. — MACAULAY.

This **complex sentence,** though very long, is perfectly easy to follow. It begins with a long compound noun clause (consisting of nine coördinate *that-*clauses). This would be the subject of the main predicate verb *were,* but for the fact that the pronoun *these* is inserted to act as the subject (referring back to the compound noun clause and summing it up in a single word). To the complement *things* is attached the adjective clause *which excited . . . contempt.* This clause is complex, for it contains three adjective clauses, (1) *from which they had sprung* (modifying *class*), (2) *into which . . . themselves* (modifying *that*), and (3) *which is . . . contempt* (modifying *aversion*). All three are separately attached to the clause on which they depend, *which excited that bitter aversion.* Thus all that portion of the sentence which follows *things* forms one complex clause, modifying that noun.

6. That I may avoid the imputation of throwing out, even privately, any loose, random imputations against the public conduct of a gentleman for whom I once entertained a very warm affection, and whose abilities I regard with the greatest admiration, I will put down, distinctly and articulately, some of the matters of objection which I feel to his late doctrines and proceedings, trusting that I shall be able to demonstrate to the friends whose good opinion I would still cultivate, that not levity, nor caprice, nor less defensible motives, but that very grave reasons, influence my judgment. — BURKE.

This is a fine example of a long, but well-constructed complex sentence. The main clause is *I will put down, distinctly and articulately, some of the matters of objection.* Upon this simple clause, everything else in the sentence depends in one way or another.

## II. IN COMPOUND COMPLEX SENTENCES

**526.** Any complex sentence, however elaborate, may be used as one of the coördinate complex clauses that make up a compound complex sentence.

1. While the king was treated at this rude rate, Cromwell, with his army, was in Scotland, obstructing the motions that were making in his favor; but on the approach of the Scots, who were much superior in number, he was forced to retire towards Dunbar, where his ships and provisions lay. — BURNET.

In this compound complex sentence, both coördinate clauses are complex. In each, the main clause has two subordinate clauses attached to it separately (§ 520).

2. They had seen me cut the cables, and thought my design was only to let the ships run adrift, or fall foul on each other; but when they perceived the whole fleet moving in order, and saw me pulling at the end, they set up such a scream of grief and despair as it is almost impossible to describe or conceive. — SWIFT.

In this compound complex sentence, both of the two coördinate clauses are complex. The first contains the noun clause [*that*] *my design . . . each other*, used as the object of *thought*. The second contains two subordinate clauses, separately attached to the main clause (*they set . . . despair*). For the infinitive *cut*, see § 322. The infinitive *to let* is used as a predicate nominative (§ 491); it has as its object the infinitive clause *the ships . . . each other*, containing two infinitives, *run* and *fall* (§ 325).

3. While things went on quietly, while there was no opposition, while everything was given by the favor of a small ruling junto, Fox had a

decided advantage over Pitt; but when dangerous times came, when Europe was convulsed with war, when Parliament was broken up into factions, when the public mind was violently excited, the favorite of the people rose to supreme power. — MACAULAY.

This compound complex sentence consists of two complex clauses, joined by the coördinate conjunction *but*. In each of these, the subordinate clause is compound (§ 521), consisting of several coördinate adverbial clauses introduced by relative adverbs (*while* in the first, *when* in the second).

**4.** The clear and agreeable language of his despatches had early attracted the notice of his employers; and before the Peace of Breda he had, at the request of Arlington, published a pamphlet on the war, of which nothing is now known, except that it had some vogue at the time, and that Charles, not a contemptible judge, pronounced it to be very well written. — MACAULAY.

In this compound complex sentence, the first coördinate clause is simple, the second is complex. In the second, the adjective clause *of which nothing is known* has dependent on it the group of words *except . . . well written*, consisting of the preposition *except* and its object (the compound noun clause, *that . . . time, and that . . . well written*). This group serves as an adjective modifier of the noun *nothing*. The whole passage *of which . . . well written* forms a complex adjective clause, modifying *pamphlet*. *It to be very well written* is a complement, being an infinitive clause used as the object of *pronounced* (§ 325).

# CHAPTER VIII

## ELLIPTICAL SENTENCES

**527.** Good usage does not demand that all sentences shall be absolutely complete. It often allows (and sometimes requires) the omission of words that, though necessary to the construction, are so easily supplied by the mind that it would be mere waste of time to utter them.

**528.** The omission of a word or words necessary to the grammatical completeness of a clause or sentence is called ellipsis.

A clause or sentence that shows ellipsis is said to be elliptical.

Ellipsis is a Greek word meaning "omission."

In the following examples the omitted words are supplied in brackets.

[I] thank you.
[I] pray do not [you] move.
[You] pass me that book.
Her hair is light, her eyes [are] dark blue.
Some of the strangers spoke French, others [spoke] Spanish.
Some of the patriots were armed with old flintlocks, others [were armed] with swords, still others [were armed] with pitchforks.
When [he was] a youth, he travelled in the East.
Though [he is] timid, he is no coward.
They were amused, though [they were] somewhat vexed.
While [we were] drifting downstream, we grounded on a sand bar.
If [it is] possible, send me word to-night.
You shall have the money this week, if [it is] necessary.
They marched slowly as if [they were] worn out.
Why [are] these tears ?
Why [are you] so dejected ?
He was ten years of age, his brother [was] eight [years of age].
I have more confidence in James than [I have] in Edmund.
Mary is younger than George [is young].
Tom likes you better than [he likes] me.
You like him better than I do [like him].

I like him better than Charles does [like him].
This racket is not so heavy as that [is heavy].
You are not so old as I [am old].
Peace [be] to his memory !
This is the only pencil [that] I have.
Is that the boy [whom] you hired yesterday ?
They say [that] you are going to Europe soon.

**529.** The examples in § 528 show that most cases of ellipsis fall under two heads :

**1.** To avoid repetition, words are often omitted in one part of the sentence when they occur in another part.

**2.** Pronouns, the conjunction *that*, and some forms of the verb *is*, are often omitted when they are readily supplied.

Under the second head come (1) the ellipsis of the subject (*thou* or *you*) in imperative sentences (§ 268), (2) that of relative pronouns in the objective case (§ 151), (3) that of *is, are,* etc. (with the subject pronoun) in subordinate clauses introduced by *when, though, if,* and the like (§§ 397, 399, 417).

Note. The so-called "telegraphic style" omits *I* with any verb or with all verbs. It should be confined to telegrams, where space is money.

**530.** Adverbs indicating direction (like *forward, back*) are often used without a verb in imperative sentences.

> *Forward*, brave companions !
> *Down* on your knees !
> *Up*, guards, and at them !

Note. In older English, the omission of the verb of motion was common, even in sentences not imperative, as in the following examples from *Julius Cæsar:* — "We 'll along ourselves, and meet them "; "Shall we on, and not depend on you ? "

**531.** The ellipsis of the subordinate conjunction *that* is very common, especially in indirect discourse (§§ 388, 433).

> I know [*that*] you are my friend.
> Jack said [*that*] the boat had sunk.
> He told me [*that*] he was sorry.

**532.** Many constructions, originally elliptical, have become established idioms in which no ellipsis is felt. In such cases it is usually better to take the sentence as it stands, and not to supply the omitted words.

Thus, in " He eats *as if he were famished*" the italicized words are properly treated as a subordinate clause modifying *eats* and introduced by the compound conjunction *as if*. Yet in strictness this construction is an ellipsis for " He eats as [*he would eat*] if he were famished."

**533.** Various ellipses are illustrated in the following sentences : —

1. Although in a friendly country, they marched always as if in a land of enemies.
2. The aspect of the country was as wild and dreary as the climate.
3. Do not serious and earnest men discuss Hamlet as they would Cromwell or Lincoln ? — LOWELL.
4. Not so with the others.
5. Though rather shy and distrustful of this new acquaintance, Rip complied with his usual alacrity.
6. Arras was famed for its rich tapestries, Brussels for its carpets, Cambrai for its fine cambric, Lisle for its thread and the fabrics woven from it.
7. Every day brings its task, which, if neglected, is doubled on the morrow.
8. It is not easy to recover an art when once lost.
9. I wish you would go down with me to Newstead.
10. The men are all soldiers, and war and the chase their sole occupation.
11. While in this state of irresolution, she was startled by a low knock.
12. The house was tall, the skylight small and dirty, the day blind with fog.
13. I little thought you would have deserted me.
14. He is the best Oriental scholar I know.
15. Cromwell was evidently laying, though in an irregular manner, the foundations of an admirable system.
16. He was a foot taller than I.
17. This concerns you rather than me.
18. My father loved Sir Rowland as his soul.

# EXERCISES

1. Tell whether each of the following sentences is declarative, interrogative, imperative, or exclamatory. If a sentence is both declarative and exclamatory, mention the fact. Mention the subject and the predicate of each sentence. Note all instances of the inverted order (§ 5).

1. You need not answer this letter. 2. Many surmises of evil alarm the hearts of the people. — LONGFELLOW. 3. Here I am again in the land of old Bunyan. 4. Me this uncharter'd freedom tires. — WORDSWORTH. 5. Twilight's soft dews steal o'er the village green. — ROGERS. 6. Were there many robbers in the band ? 7. How will posterity the deed proclaim ! — BYRON. 8. At dawn the towers of Stirling rang. — SCOTT. 9. You cannot recall the spoken word. — EMERSON. 10. The boughs over my head seemed shadowy with solemn thoughts as well as with rustling leaves. — HAWTHORNE. 11. So you don't like Raphael ! 12. All around lay a frightful wilderness. 13. Why does the sea moan evermore ? — ROSSETTI. 14. What lonely straggler looks along the wave ? — BYRON. 15. Off went his wig ! 16. For some minutes he continued to scrutinize the drawing minutely. 17. Our strength grows out of our weakness.— EMERSON. 18. Rudely carved was the porch. 19. What hopes the prince to gain by Lacy's death ? 20. Trust thyself.

21. The rest of the men were morose and silent. 22. Here are the ruins of the emperor's palace. 23. Now rumbles along the carriage of some magnate of the city. 24. Wild was the life we led. 25. How poor, and dull, and sleepy, and squalid it seemed ! 26. Built are the house and the barn. 27. With what tenderness he sings ! 28. Marked ye the younger stranger's eye ? 29. One or two idlers, of forbidding aspect, hung about in the murky gaslight. 30. Several mountains crowned with snow shone brilliantly in the distance. 31. Follow me through this passage. 32. Stop me not at your peril. 33. Carry thou this scroll to the castle.

2. Write ten interrogative sentences concerning each topic Reply in declarative sentences.

(1) The American Revolution ; (2) the Pilgrim Fathers ; (3) the history of your own state ; (4) the government of the United States ; (5) hygiene ; (6) the manufactures (or other industries) of your town or city.

3. Write ten imperative sentences, each giving an order concerning —

(1) the playing of a game ; (2) the building or sailing of a boat ; (3) the care of the health ; (4) the manufacture of some article of common use ; (5) the writing of a business letter.

4. Write ten exclamatory sentences. Tell whether each is declarative, interrogative, or imperative.

### EXERCISE 2

#### (§§ 6–25, pp. 3–11)

1. Tell the parts of speech (including verb-phrases).

1. The rain pattered upon the roof and the sky gloomed through the dusty garret windows. — HAWTHORNE. 2. Make yourself necessary to somebody. — EMERSON. 3. I have a regard for every man on board that ship, from the captain down to the crew. 4. "An artist," said Michael Angelo, "must have his measuring tools not in the hand, but in the eye." — EMERSON. 5. Time had wintered o'er his locks. 6. Must we in all things look for the how, and the why, and the wherefore ? 7. Power dwells with cheerfulness. — EMERSON. 8. What hurrahs rang out ! 9. He sneaked about with a gallows air. 10. So ! you see things go on as when you were with us.

11. Rigby and his brother hirelings frightened them with hideous fables and ugly words. — DISRAELI. 12. These are prize peaches. 13. Ha ha ! how vilely doth this cynic rhyme ! 14. O Antony, beg not your death of us. 15. Wordsworth was praised to me in Westmoreland because he afforded to his country neighbors an example of a modest household where comfort and culture were secured without display.

16. Shake hands with this knot of good fellows. 17. He had been deserted by the Moderates. 18. The moderate Liberals held a meeting very early in the struggle. 19. After a dreadful night of anxiety, perplexity, and peril, the darkness, which I thought had lasted an eternity, slowly disappeared. — TRELAWNY.

**2.** Use the following words in sentences of your own: —

Sleep (*noun, verb*); dry (*adjective, verb, noun*); very (*adverb, adjective*); express (*noun, verb, adjective*); bellow (*verb, noun*); American (*adjective, noun*); future (*adjective, noun*); to-morrow (*noun, adverb*); flower (*noun, verb*); sovereign (*noun, adjective*); summer (*noun, verb, adjective*); double (*adjective, adverb, verb*); well (*adjective, adverb*); fast (*adjective, adverb, noun, verb*); content (*noun, adjective, verb*); last (*adjective, adverb, verb, noun*); down (*adverb, preposition*); for (*preposition, conjunction*); downright (*adjective, adverb*); home (*noun, adjective, adverb*); lower (*adjective, adverb, verb*); iron (*noun, adjective, verb*); off (*adverb, preposition, adjective*); up (*adverb, preposition*); high (*adjective, adverb, noun*); except (*verb, preposition*); inside (*adjective, adverb, preposition, noun*); past (*noun, adjective, preposition*); what (*adjective, pronoun, interjection*); round (*noun, adjective, verb, preposition, adverb*); sound (*noun, verb, adjective, adverb*); black (*noun, verb, adjective*); all (*noun, adjective, adverb*); open (*noun, adjective, verb*); while (*noun, verb*).

### EXERCISE 3

#### (§§ 26–33, pp. 11–13)

Point out the infinitives and the participles. Tell when they occur in verb-phrases. Use them in sentences.

**1.** I did wrong to smile. **2.** Luttrell adjured me with mock pathos to spare his blushes. **3.** I begged my friend Sir Roger to go with me into her hovel. **4.** I was wonderfully pleased to see the workings of instinct in a hen followed by a brood of ducks. **5.** A man's first care should be to avoid the reproaches of his own heart. — ADDISON. **6.** I was highly entertained to see the gentlemen of the county gathering about my old friend, and striving who should compliment him most. **7.** He was le' loose among the woods as soon as he was able to ride on horseback. **8.** Plutarch says very finely that a man should not allow himself to hate even his enemies. **9.** It gives me a serious concern to see such a spirit of dissension in the country.

**10.** It was his intention to remain there for two or three days. **11.** Every part of every carriage had been cleaned, every horse had been groomed. **12.** Liberated from the embarrassments of the city, and issuing into the broad uncrowded avenues of the northern suburbs, we soon begin to enter upon our natural pace of ten miles an hour. **13.** The beggar, rearing himself against the wall, forgets his lameness. **14.** Three miles beyond Barnet, we see approaching another private carriage. **15.** We saw many lights moving about as we drew near.

## EXERCISE 4

### (§§ 34–39, pp. 13–15)

1. Mention the simple subject and the simple predicate of each sentence in Exercise 1 (p. 227). Tell whether the simple subject is a noun or a pronoun, and whether the simple predicate is a verb or a verb-phrase.

2. Study in the same way your own sentences in Exercise 1.

3. Divide each sentence into the complete subject and the complete predicate. If the sentence has a compound subject, mention the substantives that compose it; if the sentence has a compound predicate, mention the verbs (or verb-phrases).

1. The Queen and Prince Albert came to London from Windsor on Saturday morning. 2. You and Lockhart must not abandon the good cause. 3. I saw that he was weak, and took advantage of a pause to remind him not to forget his drive. 4. Two or three of my English biographies have something of the same historical character. 5. Lord Grey, Clanricarde, Labouchere, Vernon Smith, and Seymour will fill up the places. 6. Every change of season, every change of weather, indeed, every hour of the day, produces some change in the magical hues and shapes of these mountains. — IRVING. 7. He looked round, and could see nothing but a crow winging its solitary flight across the mountain. 8. They suddenly desisted from their play and stared at him. 9. The sea flashes along the pebbly margin of its silver beach, forming a thousand little bays and inlets, or comes tumbling in among the cliffs of a rock-bound coast, and beats against its massive barriers with a distant, hollow, continual roar. — LONGFELLOW.

10. A wide gateway ushered the traveller into the interior of the building, and conducted him to a low-roofed apartment, paved with round stones. 11. The strange visitant gruffly saluted me, and, after making several ineffectual efforts to urge his horse in at the door, dismounted and followed me into the room. — WHITTIER. 12. The foolish and the dead alone never change their opinion. — LOWELL. 13. They will slink into their kennels in disgrace, or perchance run wild and strike a league with the wolf and the fox. — THOREAU. 14. Strong will and keen perception overpower old manners and create new. — EMERSON. 15. Neither Aristotle, nor Leibnitz, nor Junius, nor Champollion has set down the grammar-rules of this dialect. 16. His mantle and hood were of the best Flanders cloth, and fell in ample and not ungraceful folds. 17. A deep fosse or ditch was drawn round the whole building.

## EXERCISE 5

(§§ 40–42, p. 16)

**1.** Point out the noun-phrases, verb-phrases, adjective phrases, and adverbial phrases. Which of these phrases are prepositional?

1. Sometimes he spent hours together in the great libraries of Paris. 2. He assumed the garb of a common sailor, and in this disguise reached the Dutch coast in safety. 3. Some of the frigate's men were still endeavoring to escape. 4. Was Milton rich or at his ease when he composed "Paradise Lost"? 5. It was a cold-blooded exhibition of marksmanship. 6. He then continued on to the place of rendezvous at Speedwell's Iron Works on Troublesome Creek. — IRVING. 7. The gates of Amsterdam had been barred against him. 8. They heard his confession with suspicion and disdain. 9. The stagecoach always drew up before the door of the cottage. 10. The wind moaned through the silent streets. 11. The clouds are scudding across the moon. 12. Steele had known Addison from childhood. 13. A broad ray of light fell into the garret. — DICKENS. 14. The fate of his insulted and broken-hearted brother still rankled in his mind. 15. All day with fruitless strife they toiled. — SCOTT.

**2.** Fill each blank with a single word. Substitute for the word a phrase with the same meaning. Mention in each instance (1) the part of speech, (2) the kind of phrase.

1. He spoke to me ——.
2. The grounds were shut in by a high —— wall.
3. The fire engine —— past.
4. The three girls were laughing ——.
5. The poor child looked —— at the toys.
6. Harold —— the bunch of grapes.
7. The proprietor is a —— man.
8. The archbishop placed upon the king's head a —— crown.
9. The book which I hold in my hand is ——.
10. The —— ordered the *Conqueror* to open fire.
11. The enemy retreated ——.
12. The rain —— heavily all day.
13. The rain came down —— all day.
14. The —— is in his office.
15. A —— boy came to the door.
16. My brother is president of ——.

## EXERCISE 6

### (§§ 43–51, pp. 16–21)

1. Tell whether each sentence is simple, compound, or complex. If the sentence is compound, divide it into its independent clauses, and mention the simple subject (noun or pronoun) and the simple predicate (verb or verb-phrase) of each clause.

If the sentence is complex, divide it into the main (independent) and the subordinate clause, and tell whether the latter is used as an adjective or as an adverb.

1. The great gate slowly opened, and a steward and several serving-men appeared. 2. The victors set fire to the wigwams and the fort; the whole was soon in a blaze; many of the old men, the women, and the children perished in the flames. 3. Night closed in, but still no guest arrived. 4. The black waves rolled by them, and the light at the horizon began to fade, and the stars were coming out one by one. — WILLIAM BLACK. 5. Mr. Nickleby closed an account book which lay on his desk. 6. By ceaseless action all that is subsists. — COWPER. 7. When the morning broke, the Moorish army had vanished. 8. At midnight, when the town was hushed in sleep, they all went quietly on board. 9. Fortune had cast him into a cavern, and he was groping darkly round. 10. I paced the deserted chambers where he had composed his poem. 11. I strove to speak; my voice utterly failed me. 12. The only avenue by which the town could be easily approached, was protected by a stone wall more than twenty feet high and of great thickness.

13. The night fell tempestuous and wild, and no vestige of the hapless sloop was ever after seen. 14. The simple majesty of this anecdote can gain nothing from any comment which we might make on it. 15. Raleigh speaks the language of the heart of his country when he urges the English statesmen to colonize Guiana. — FROUDE. 16. Men, in their youth, go to push their fortune in the colony; they succeed; they acquire property there; they return to their native land; they continue to draw the income from their colonial estates. — BROUGHAM. 17. The moonlight glistened upon traces of the gilding which had once covered both rider and steed. 18. While this brief conversation passed, Donatello had once or twice glanced aside with a watchful air. 19. Pray for us, Hilda; we need it.

2. Divide the compound complex sentences into their coördinate clauses. Tell whether each of these clauses, when standing alone, is a simple or a complex sentence.

1. It would be dark before he could reach the village, and he heaved a heavy sigh when he thought of encountering the terrors of Dame Van Winkle.   2. Language gradually varies, and with it fade away the writings of authors who have lived their allotted time.   3. The tallest and handsomest men whom England could produce guarded the passage from the palace gate to the river-side, and all seemed in readiness for the queen's coming forth, although the hour was yet so early.   4. Edward the Confessor died on the fifth of January, 1066, and on the following day an assembly of the thanes and prelates present in London, and of the citizens of the metropolis, declared that Harold should be their king.

### EXERCISE 7

#### (§§ 54–64, pp. 27–30)

1. Point out all the common nouns and all the proper nouns. Mention all the examples of personification.

1. There Guilt his anxious revel kept. — Scott.   2. The first vessel we fell in with was a schooner, which, after a long chase, we made out to be an American.   3. You will be sauntering in St. Peter's perhaps, or standing on the Capitol while the sun sets.   4. I am very deep in my Aristophanes.   5. I saw a most lovely Sir Joshua at Christie's a week ago. — Fitz Gerald.   6. I hear there is scarce a village in England that has not a Moll White in it. — Addison.   7. Such a spirit is Liberty. At times she takes the form of a hateful reptile. She grovels, she hisses, she stings. But woe to those who in disgust shall venture to crush her ! — Macaulay.   8. Rough Wulfstane trimmed his shafts and bow. — Scott.   9. To-day we have been a delightful drive through Ettrick Forest, and to the ruins of Newark — the hall of Newark, where the ladies bent their necks of snow to hear " The Lay of the Last Minstrel." — Maria Edgeworth.

10. The same waves wash the moles of the new-built Californian towns, and lave the faded but still gorgeous skirts of Asiatic lands, older than Abraham ; while all between float milky-ways of coral isles, and low-lying, endless, unknown Archipelagoes and impenetrable Japans. — Melville.   11. The duchess said haughtily that she had done her best for the Esmonds.   12. To see with one's own eyes men and countries is better than reading all the books of travel in the world. — Thackeray.   13. Defeat and mortification had only hardened the king's heart.   14. Earth, Ocean, Air, beloved brotherhood ! — Shelley.   15. The iron tongue of St. Paul's has told twelve.   16. The Indians, brandishing their weapons, answered only with gestures of angry defiance.

2. Point out all the abstract, all the collective, and all the compound nouns.

1. The poet binds together by passion and knowledge the vast empire of human society. — WORDSWORTH. 2. The country is now showing symptoms of greenness and warmth. 3. When the public are gone, we at once put up the great iron shutters. 4. Washington returned to headquarters at Newbury. 5. The Bruce's band moves swiftly on. — SCOTT. 6. He shall with speed to England. — SHAKSPERE. 7. Soon were dismissed the courtly throng. — SCOTT. 8. Sickness, desertion, and the loss sustained at Guilford Courthouse had reduced his little army. 9. A detachment was sent against them. 10. Never before this summer have the kingbirds, handsomest of flycatchers, built in my orchard. 11. The young suddenly disperse on your approach, as if a whirlwind had swept them away. — THOREAU. 12. This lighthouse, known to our mariners as Cape Cod or Highland Light, is one of our "primary seacoast lights." 13. We have some salt of our youth in us. — SHAKSPERE. 14. Thou hast nor youth nor age. — SHAKSPERE.

15. The passion for hunting had revived with Washington on returning to his old hunting grounds. 16. A circle there of merry listeners stand. — BYRON. 17. The act of the Congress of Vienna remains the eternal monument of their diplomatic knowledge and political sagacity. — DISRAELI. 18. Lee undertook the task with alacrity. 19. A row of surfboats and canoes lay along the beach. 20. The situation he had held as aide-de-camp to the commander-in-chief had given him an opportunity of observing the course of affairs. 21. The ground was frozen to a great depth. 22. He was aware of his unpopularity. 23. The stern old war-gods shook their heads. — EMERSON.

24.   Freckled nest eggs thou shalt see
      Hatching in the hawthorn tree. — KEATS.

25.   Fair morn ascends, and sunny June has shed
      Ambrosial odors o'er the garden-bed,
      And wild bees seek the cherry's sweet perfume
      Or cluster round the full-blown apple-bloom. — CAMPBELL.

26.                   For in their looks divine
      The image of their glorious Maker shone,
      Truth, wisdom, sanctitude severe and pure. — MILTON.

27.   Steer, helmsman, till you steer our way
      By stars beyond the line. — CAMPBELL.

28.                   Say I sent thee thither:
      I, that have neither pity, love, nor fear. — SHAKSPERE.

## EXERCISE 8

(§§ 66–84, pp. 31–39)

1. Make a list containing thirty nouns, ten in each of the three genders. Use each of these nouns in a sentence.

2. Write ten sentences, each containing a noun of common gender.

3. Write sentences containing the masculine forms corre-sponding to the feminine forms in this list, and the feminine forms corresponding to the masculine : —

earl, abbess, schoolmaster, porter, hind, mare, ram, sire, witch, sultan, czar, widow, marquis, executor, salesman, tailor, hero, bride, songster, great-uncle, nephew, buck, horseman, bachelor, belle.

4. Mention the gender and the number of each noun. Tell whether the gender is shown by the form, by the meaning, or by both. Whenever it is possible, give the plural of each noun that is singular, and the singular of each noun that is plural.

1. Oft Music changed, but never ceased her tone. — BYRON. 2. Grace Crawley was at this time living with the two Miss Prettymans. — TROLLOPE. 3. The Catos and the Scipios of the village had gathered in front of the hotel. 4. This gunner was an excellent mathematician, a good scholar, and a complete sailor. — DEFOE. 5. I was, in fact, in the chapel of the Knights Templars. — IRVING. 6. The luckless culprit was brought in, forlorn and chapfallen, in the custody of gamekeepers, huntsmen, and whippers-in, and followed by a rabble rout of country clowns. — IRVING. 7. The hare now came still nearer to the place where she was at first started. — BUDGELL. 8. The Fairfaxes were no longer at hand. — IRVING. 9. All the peers and peeresses put on their coronets. 10. Time is no longer slow; his sickle mows quickly in this age. — DISRAELI. 11. Under the humblest roof, the commonest person in plain clothes sits there massive, cheerful, yet formidable, like the Egyptian colossi. — EMERSON.

12. Within forty-eight hours, hundreds of horse and foot came by various roads to the city. 13. The hart and hind wandered in a wilder-ness abounding in ferny coverts and green and stately trees. — DISRAELI. 14. The ship had received a great deal of damage, and it required some time to repair her. — DEFOE. 15. When Mary, the nurse, returns with

the little Miss Smiths from Master Brown's birthday party, she is narrowly questioned as to their behavior. **16.** Of all our fleet, consisting of a hundred and fifty sail, scarce twelve appeared. — SMOLLETT. **17.** Hindoos, Russians, Chinese, Spaniards, Portuguese, Englishmen, Frenchmen, Genoese, Neapolitans, Venetians, Greeks, Turks, descendants from all the builders of Babel, come to trade at Marseilles, sought the shade alike. — DICKENS. **18.** There lies the port; the vessel puffs her sail. — TENNYSON. **19.** I had desire to see the old family seat of the Lucys. — IRVING.

**20.** The Miss Lambs were the belles of little Britain. — IRVING. **21.** Lord Culloden at length appeared with his daughters, Ladies Flora and Grizell. — DISRAELI. **22.** Still his honied wealth Hymettus yields. — BYRON. **23.** Josephine has been made executrix of her father's estate. **24.** Georgette crouched by the fire, reading a wonderful tale of kings, princesses, enchanted castles, knights and ladies, monks and nuns, wizards and witches. **25.** She was a vixen when she went to school. — SHAKSPERE. **26.** Keep a gamester from the dice and a good student from his book. — SHAKSPERE. **27.** They are sheep and calves which seek out assurance in that. — SHAKSPERE. **28.** A score of good ewes may be worth ten pounds. — SHAKSPERE. **29.** Let ay's seem no's and no's seem ay's. — GAY.

> **30.** She clasps a bright child on her upgathered knee;
> It laughs at the lightning, it mocks the mixed thunder
> Of the air and the sea. — SHELLEY.

### EXERCISE 9

#### (§§ 71-84, pp. 34-39)

**1.** Write sentences in which the following words, letters, or figures are used in the plural number: —

German, radius, lens, moose, wharf, index, piano, thesis, 4, 500, p, q, and, syllabus, staff, die, s, t, seraph, hero, stimulus, crisis, elf, heathen, brother-in-law, July, March, spoonful, memorandum, Miss Allen, Master Allen, Mr. Hayes, General Raymond, Knight Templar, head (of cattle), animalcule, potato, valley, formula, penny, curriculum, dwarf, man-child.

**2.** Write sentences in which the following nouns are used in the singular number: —

strata, phenomena, alumnæ, alumni, candelabra, species, cherubim, errata, bacteria, Japanese, beaux, vertebræ, Messrs., theses, oases.

## EXERCISE 10

(§ 88, pp. 41–42)

Mention all the nouns that are in the nominative case, and give the construction (or syntax) of each, — as subject, predicate nominative, vocative (or nominative of direct address), exclamatory nominative, or nominative in apposition.[1]

1. A weary lot is thine, fair maid. — SCOTT. 2. At last, our small acquaintance, Ned Higgins, trudged up the street, on his way to school. — HAWTHORNE. 3. The soil is in general a moist and retentive clay. 4. Rumors alone were their guides through a wild and desolate country. — LONGFELLOW. 5. Young man, have you challenged Charles the wrestler ? — SHAKSPERE. 6. Ralph was an Eton boy, and hence, being robust and shrewd, a swimmer and a cricketer. 7. Here Harold was received a welcome guest. — SCOTT. 8. The tall Highlander remained obdurate. 9. The beams and rafters, roughly hewn and with strips of bark still on them, and the rude masonry of the chimneys, made the garret look wild and uncivilized. 10. Deathlike the silence seemed. 11. Sorrow and silence are strong, and patient endurance is godlike. — LONGFELLOW. 12. Fly, fly, detested thoughts, forever from my view ! — BEATTIE. 13. Time must not be counted by calendars, but by sensation, by thought. — DISRAELI.

14. This is the history of Charlotte Corday. 15. The nabobs soon became a most unpopular class of men. 16. Before him stretched the long, laborious road, dry, empty, and white. — HARDY. 17. With the great mass of mankind, the test of integrity in a public man is consistency. — MACAULAY. 18. These are trifles, Mr. Premium. 19. My thanks are due to you for your trouble and care. 20. Here's my great uncle, Sir Richard Ravelin. 21. Rowley, my old friend, I am sure you congratulate me. 22. David, you are a coward ! 23. Here come other Pyncheons, the whole tribe, in their half-a-dozen generations. 24. Uncle Venner, trundling a wheelbarrow, was the earliest person stirring in the neighborhood. 25. Up the chimney roared the fire, and brightened the room with its broad blaze. 26. Liberty ! freedom ! tyranny is dead !— SHAKSPERE. 27. The hostess's daughter, a plump Flanders lass, with long gold pendants in her ears, was at a side window. — IRVING.

28. Horses ! can these be horses that bound off with the action and gesture of leopards ? — DE QUINCEY. 29. Peace ! silence ! Brutus speaks. 30. The rains, frosts, and tempests splinter the chalk above and the waves gnaw it away below. — GEIKIE.

[1] Or parse the nominatives according to the models in § 112.

### EXERCISE 11

(§§ 89–96, pp. 43–47)

**1.** Point out all the nouns in the possessive case, and parse them according to the model in § 112.

1. James's parliament contained a most unusual proportion of new ministers.   2. I live in general quietly at my brother-in-law's in Norfolk (see § 96).   3. There is a small cottage of my father's close to the lawn gates.   4. We had found, in that day's heap of earth, about fifty pounds' weight of gold dust. — DEFOE.   5. Much the most striking incident in Burns's life is his journey to Edinburgh.   6. As to freaks like this of Miss Brooke's, Mrs. Cadwallader had no patience with them. — GEORGE ELIOT.   7. Homeward they bore him through the dark woods' gloom. — MORRIS.   8. The eye travels down to Oxford's towers. — ARNOLD.   9. I obeyed all my brother's military commands with the utmost docility.   10. Tellson's wanted not elbowroom, Tellson's wanted no light, Tellson's wanted no embellishment.   Noakes & Co.'s might, or Snooks Brothers' might ; but Tellson's — thank heaven ! — DICKENS.

**2.** Examine the nouns in the possessive case in **1** (above), and tell which of the possessives might be replaced by an *of*-phrase. Mention particularly those passages in which the possessive would not be used in modern prose.

**3.** Write sentences containing the possessive singular of —

Henry, James, Thomas, Mr. Fox, child, Charles Price, Mrs. Gibbs, Edward, General Edwards, horse, Hortense, Miss Bellows, father-in-law, Major Ellis, commander-in-chief, Thompson and Howard (*a firm*), Eustis and Morris (*a firm*), Messrs. Cartwright and Robbins, Apollo, Brutus, Ulysses.

**4.** Write sentences containing the possessive plural of —

Englishman, fireman, washerwoman, fox, sheep, horse, ox, child, emperor, empress, robin, Norman, German, hawk, Knight Templar, lady, sailor, heir, heiress, teacher, whale, walrus, critic, poet, vireo.

**5.** In which of the sentences that you have written (under **3** and **4**) would it be possible to substitute an *of*-phrase for the possessive ?   In which of them (if any) would this phrase be preferable ?   Why ?

## EXERCISE 12

(§§ 97–110, pp. 47–53)

Parse the nouns in the objective case, according to the mode in § 112. Tell the particular construction in each instance, — direct object, predicate objective, indirect object, etc.

1. Such was the narrative of Jack Grant, the mate. 2. Rippling waters made a pleasant moan. — BYRON. 3. Swiftly they hurried away to the forge of Basil the blacksmith. — LONGFELLOW. 4. A pale fog hung over London. 5. So like a shattered column lay the king. — TENNYSON 6. Then sing, ye birds, sing, sing a joyous song. — WORDS-WORTH. 7. A blighted spring makes a barren year. — JOHNSON. 8. Dark and neglected locks overshadowed his brow. 9. Imagine the wind howling, the sea roaring, the rain beating. 10. Lay these vain regrets aside. 11. Birds of passage sailed through the leaden air. 12. Authority forgets a dying king. — TENNYSON. 13. Three years she grew in sun and shower. — WORDSWORTH. 14. The sound of horns came floating from the valley, prolonged by the mountain echoes. 15. Hours had passed away like minutes. 16. Your mistrust cannot make me a traitor. — SHAKSPERE.

17. She halted a moment before speaking. 18. The room opened on a terrace adorned with statues and orange trees. 19. The sun is coming down to earth, and the fields and the waters shout to him golden shouts. — MEREDITH. 20. England is unrivalled for two things — sports and politics. — DISRAELI. 21. Thus we lived several years in a state of much happiness. 22. The old gentleman's whole countenance beamed with a serene look of indwelling delight. 23. I am reading Selwyn's "Correspondence," a remarkable book. 24. I have lived my life. — TENNYSON. 25. My heart is like a singing bird. — CHRISTINA ROSSETTI. 26. How like a winter hath my absence been. — SHAKSPERE. 27. Three weeks we westward bore. — LONGFELLOW. 28. It rains pitchforks. — FITZ GERALD. 29. The sublimer and more passionate poets I still read, by snatches and occasionally. — DE QUINCEY. 30. Coningsby slept the deep sleep of youth and health. — DISRAELI.

31. Thou mightst call him a goodly person. 32. My father named me Autolycus. 33. A country fellow brought him a huge fish. 34. I'll make you the queen of Naples. 35. You call honorable boldness impudent sauciness. — SHAKSPERE. 36. Sir Roger generally goes two or three miles from his house before he beats about in search of a hare or partridge. 37. This misconception caused Washington some embarrassment. 38. I now thank you for Beattie, the most agreeable and amiable writer I ever met with. — COWPER.

## EXERCISE 13

(§§ 97–110, pp. 47–53)

**1.** Write fifteen sentences, each containing a transitive verb and its direct object (§§ 99–100).

**2.** Substitute a pronoun for each noun in the objective case.

**3.** Write ten sentences containing both a direct object and a predicate objective (§ 104).

**4.** Use in sentences fifteen of the verbs in the list in § 105, each with both a direct and an indirect object.

**5.** For each indirect object, substitute *to* with an object. Change the order, if necessary.

**6** Write ten sentences, each containing a cognate object (§ 108).

**7.** Write ten sentences, each containing an adverbial objective (§ 109).

**8.** Write ten sentences, each containing a noun in apposition with a noun in the objective case (§ 110).

## EXERCISE 14

(§§ 54–112, pp. 27–54)

Parse every noun, according to the models in § 112.

**1.** Pennon and banner wave no more. **2.** They soon gained the utmost verge of the forest, and entered the country inhabited by men without vice. — GOLDSMITH. **3.** Our avenue is strewn with the whole crop of autumn's withered leaves. — HAWTHORNE. **4.** He is the rich man who can avail himself of all men's faculties. — EMERSON. **5.** Like an awakened conscience, the sea was moaning and tossing. — LONGFELLOW. **6.** He again called and whistled after his dog. **7.** She wrote and addressed a hurried note. **8.** The light and warmth of that long-vanished day live with me still. **9.** Violet and primrose girls, and organ boys with military monkeys, and systematic bands very determined in tone if not in tune, filled the atmosphere. — MEREDITH. **10.** The blood left Wilfrid's ashen cheek. **11.** Give us manners, virtue, freedom, power ! — WORDSWORTH. **12.** A great deal of shrubbery clusters along the base of the stone wall, and takes away the hardness of its outline.

**13.** I travelled the whole four hundred miles between this and Madras on men's shoulders. **14.** Here we set up twelve little huts like soldiers' tents. **15.** Swiftly they glided away, like the shade of a cloud on the prairie. **16.** Athens, even long after the decline of the Roman empire, still continued the seat of learning, politeness, and wisdom. — GOLDSMITH. **17.** Four times the sun had risen and set. **18.** Speak! speak! thou fearful guest! **19.** The oak rose before me like a pillar of darkness. **20.** Another long blast filled the old courts of the castle with its echoes, and was answered by the warder from the walls. **21.** Sound, sound the clarion, fill the fife! — SCOTT. **22.** Now, Falstaff, where have you been all this while? **23.** Sounds of a horn they heard, and the distant lowing of cattle. **24.** Homer was always his companion now. **25.** Forgive me these injurious suspicions. **26.** O, pride! pride! it deceives me with the subtlety of a serpent. **27.** I made Mr. Wright's gardener a present of fifty sorts of plant seeds. **28.** Your mother and I last week made a trip to Gayhurst, the seat of Mr. Wright, about four miles off. **29.** Beneath the shelter of one hut, in the bright blaze of the same fire, sat this varied group of adventurers. **30.** The cares of to-day are seldom the cares of to-morrow. — COWPER.

## EXERCISE 15

(§§ 115–129, pp. 55–62)

**1.** Parse the personal pronouns, using the models in § 168.

**1.** She peeped from the window into the garden. **2.** The little marquis immediately threw himself into the attitude of a man about to tell a long story. **3.** It pours and it thunders, it lightens amain. — SCOTT. **4.** Master, master, look about you! **5.** Leontine, with his own and his wife's fortune, bought a farm of three hundred a year. — ADDISON. **6.** The Tories carry it among the new members six to one. — SWIFT. **7.** I wrote to him, but could tell him nothing. **8.** On the next morning after breakfast the major went out for a walk by himself. **9.** Their hearts quaked within them, at the idea of taking one step farther. **10.** Mrs. Forrester's surprise was equal to ours. **11.** It's twenty years since he went away from home. **12.** I seated myself in a recess of a large bow window. **13.** At the last moment his heart failed him, and he looked round him for some mode of escape. **14.** A friend of mine has been spending some time at Sir Walter Scott's.

**15.** Send me a letter directed to me at Mr. Watcham's. **16.** I have lately received from my bookseller a copy of my subscribers' names. **17.** We came in our first morning's march to very good springs of fresh water. **18.** We are both of us inclined to be a little too positive. **19.** Heyne's best teacher was himself. — CARLYLE.

**20.** Aspasia, you have lived but few years in the world, and with only one philosopher — yourself. **21.** I got to the side in time to see a huge liner's dim shape slide by like a street at night; she would have been invisible but for her row of lights. **22.** The cataracts blow their trumpets from the steep. — WORDSWORTH. **23.** I am he they call Old Care. — PEACOCK. **24.** The sharp and peevish tinkle of the shop-bell made itself audible. **25.** The heroes themselves say, as often as not, that fame is their object. **26.** He seems to himself to touch things with muffled hands. **27.** She took counsel with herself what must be done. **28.** The head of the Pyncheons found himself involved in serious financial difficulties. **29.** Ha! here is Hepzibah herself!

**2.** Write sentences in which the personal pronoun of the first person is used as direct object, as indirect object, as predicate nominative; in the possessive singular with a noun; in the possessive singular without a noun.

**3.** Fill the blanks with personal pronouns of the first or the third person.

1. He thought the burglars were ——.
2. He mistook the burglars for ——.
3. William is better at his lessons than ——.
4. It is ——.
5. These are ——.
6. Nobody volunteered except Edward and ——.
7. —— boys have formed a debating club.
8. Mr. Jones is going to give —— boys a baseball field.
9. Who is there? ——.
10. Between you and ——, I am not sorry that he has resigned.
11. If I were —— I would study art.
12. Arthur likes you better than ——.
13. Behind Ruth and —— came the guest of honor.
14. Automobiles are not for such as ——.
15. It was —— that Joseph meant.
16. —— two are always together.
17. Richard dislikes everybody, —— most of all.

**4.** Write sentences in which *myself, yourself, ourselves, himself, herself, themselves* are used (1) intensively, (2) reflexively as direct object, (3) reflexively as indirect object.

## EXERCISE 16

(§§ 131–142, pp. 62–65)

**1.** Parse the demonstratives and the indefinites. In parsing the word, tell whether it is used as a pronoun or as an adjective. If it is used as a pronoun, tell the number and the case and give the reason for the case. If it is used as an adjective, mention the substantive which it modifies.

**1.** What is the meaning of all this? **2.** On either side extended a ruinous wooden fence. **3.** You have seen that picture, then! **4.** This very Judge Pyncheon was the original of the miniature. **5.** Twenty years ago this man was equally capable of crime or heroism; now he is fit for neither. — STEVENSON. **6.** None are all evil. **7.** Solitude has many a dreary hour. **8.** Every science has its hitherto undiscovered mysteries. — GOLDSMITH. **9.** The same day we visited the shores of the isle in the ship's boats. **10.** None but picked recruits were enlisted. **11.** A longing for the brightness and silence of fallen snow seizes him at such times. **12.** Such were Addison's talents for conversation. **13.** Nicholas Vedder! why, he is dead and gone these eighteen years! **14.** What a lamentable situation was that of the poor baron! **15.** Several houses were pillaged and destroyed.

**16.** Each warrior was a chosen man. **17.** See how yond justice rails upon yond simple thief! — SHAKSPERE. **18.** Our naval annals owe some of their interest to the fantastic and beautiful appearance of old warships. — STEVENSON. **19.** Some are too indolent to read anything till its reputation is established. — JOHNSON. **20.** In both sexes, occasionally, this lifelong croak, accompanying each word of joy or sorrow, is one of the symptoms of settled melancholy. — HAWTHORNE. **21.** Such voices have put on mourning for dead hopes. **22.** Another phenomenon was a package of lucifer matches. **23.** How few appear in those streets which but some few hours ago were crowded! **24.** This was a very different camp from that of the night before.

**25.** Alternations of wild hope and cold despair succeeded each other. **26.** The poor know best how to console each other's sorrows. **27.** Everybody has his own interpretation for that picture. **28.** I strove with none, for none was worth my strife. — LANDOR. **29.** Scarcely any of the items in the above-drawn parallel occurred to Phœbe. **30.** He went about moping. None spake to him. No one would play with him. — LAMB. **31.** Ah, that good Kent! He said it would be thus. **32.** How easy is the explanation to those who know! **33.** There has been a quarrel between him and Hepzibah this many a day.

2. Fill each blank with a personal pronoun (§ 141).

1. Each of us should do —— best.
2. Everybody thinks —— own way is wise.
3. If anybody has a better plan, now is the time for —— to speak.
4. It was an old-fashioned picnic, every person furnishing —— share of the provisions.
5. When anybody is talking, it is bad manners to interrupt ——.

### EXERCISE 17

#### (§§ 143–156, pp. 66–71)

1. Parse the relative pronouns, using the models in § 168.

1. The lights in the shops could hardly struggle through the heavy mist, which thickened every moment. 2. I shall not budge from the position that I have taken up. 3. The land of literature is a fairy land to those who view it at a distance. — IRVING. 4. I hate people who meet Time half-way. — LAMB. 5. The weather, which had been stormy and unsettled, moderated toward the evening. 6. He that once indulges idle fears will never be at rest. — JOHNSON. 7. The only ford by which the travellers could cross was guarded by a party of militia. 8. One dark unruly night she issued secretly out of a small postern gate of the castle, which the enemy had neglected to guard. 9. I paused to contemplate a tomb on which lay the effigy of a knight in complete armor. 10. He who loves the sea loves also the ship's routine. — CONRAD. 11. There were two or three indefatigable men among them, by whose courage and industry all the rest were upheld. — DEFOE. 12. Thou hadst a voice whose sound was like the sea. — WORDSWORTH. 13. They slander thee sorely who say thy vows are frail. — MOORE. 14. The first great poet whose works have come down to us, sang of war long before war became a science or a trade. — MACAULAY. 15. The gusts that drove against the high house seemed ready to tear it from its foothold of rock. 16. At its western side is a deep ravine or valley, through which a small stream rushes. 17. A weak mother, who perpetually threatens and never performs, is laying up miseries both for herself and for her children. — SPENCER. 18. As they approached, a raven, who sat upon the topmost stone, black against the bright blue sky, flapped lazily away. — KINGSLEY. 19. To such of her neighbors as needed other attention, she would give her time, her assistance, her skill. 20. It was such a battle-axe as Rustum may have wielded in fight upon the banks of Oxus. 21. I may neither choose whom I would, nor refuse whom I dislike.

2. Point out the descriptive and the restrictive relatives in 1 (above).

3. Write ten sentences, each containing a descriptive relative; ten sentences, each containing a restrictive relative.

4. Fill the blanks with relatives. In the first eight sentences, at least, use *who* or *whom*.

1. This is the boy —— I recommended.
2. The boy —— I recommended is a Swede.
3. The boy —— brought the letter is not the one —— I recommended.
4. I told Anna, —— I knew would keep my secret.
5. I told Anna, —— I knew I could trust.
6. I told Anna, —— I knew to be trustworthy.
7. I told Anna, —— I knew intimately.
8. No one —— you know lives in this street.
9. All —— I can say is, I am sorry.
10. Give me the same horse —— I had yesterday.
11. A dog, —— showed his teeth and growled, blocked the way.
12. Choose the partner —— you like best.
13. The policeman was leading a little child —— had lost its mother.
14. Take such measures —— you deem necessary.
15. Take —— measures seem necessary.
16. Take the measures —— seem to you necessary.
17. My hat is of the same size —— yours.
18. This is the picture —— I am so proud of.
19. This is the picture of —— I am so proud.
20. The man —— is talking to Henry is the one —— owns this house

5. Supply the relatives that are " understood " (§ 151).

1. It was a bold step she had taken.
2. I am not altogether unqualified for the business I have in hand.
3. His taste of books is a little too just for the age he lives in.
4. Censure is the tax a man pays to the public for being eminent
5. Who is the wittiest man you know ?
6. Morton was the only friend I had.
7. That sonata was the first piece I learned.
8. Ten dollars is the price he asks.
9. Are you the man I bought the coat of ?
10. This is the book we are reading evenings.
11. Take any seat you like.
12. " Faust " is the only opera I care for.
13. I have done all I can.

(§§ 157–162, pp. 71–73)

Parse the relatives.

1. Whatever wisdom and energy could do William did. 2. Whatever is done skilfully appears to be done with ease. 3. We must suspect what we see, distrust what we hear, and doubt even what we feel!— Miss Burney. 4. Whoever has been in a state of nervous agitation, must know that the longer it continues the more uncontrollable it grows. — Irving. 5. Time hath reft whate'er my soul enjoyed. — Byron. 6. The gallant major showed no hesitation whatever. 7. Whoever has made a voyage up the Hudson must remember the Kaatskill Mountains. 8. A recollection of what I had seen and felt the preceding night still haunted my mind. 9. Hard work was what he needed now. 10. Whatever regrets Mrs. Thorverton might indulge in secret, she had had the strength of mind to hide them. 11. Like all weak men, they had recourse to what they called strong measures. 12. We see in him a freer, purer development of whatever is noblest in ourselves. 13. Sir Roger was what you call a fine gentleman. 14. Sweet princes, what I did, I did in honor. — Shakspere. 15. He was really interested in what Coningsby had seen and what he had felt. 16. What was to be seen at Naples, Addison saw.

(§§ 163–168, pp. 73–74)

Parse the interrogative pronouns, mentioning gender, number, person, and case. If the interrogative word is an adjective, tell what noun it limits.

1. Who would not sing for Lycidas? 2. What that sigh meant I cannot say. 3. Columns, arches, pyramids, what are they but heaps of sand? 4. Which of the two was daughter to the duke? 5. Whom next shall we summon from the dusty dead? — Lamb. 6. Why! Peggy, what have you brought us? 7. What's fame? A fancied life in others' breath. — Pope. 8. To what shall I compare it? 9. And what art thou, O melancholy voice? — Shelley. 10. Proud sufferer, who art thou? 11. What were Swigby's former pursuits I can't tell. What need we care? Had n't he five hundred a year? Ay, that he had. — Thackeray. 12. What does it matter? 13. Which way have you looked for Master Caius? 14. What business had they in Prussia?

### EXERCISE 20

(§§ 163-168, pp. 73-74)

Fill each blank with *who* or *whom*, as the construction may require.

1. He asked me —— was elected.
2. From —— did she hear this news?
3. To —— did you apply for assistance?
4. —— do you regard as the better scholar of the two?
5. —— shall I ask for the key?
6. —— did you see when you called?
7. —— do you think is the best physician in town?
8. —— can I trust in such an emergency?
9. With —— have you discussed this affair?
10. —— do you suppose this letter is from?
11. —— do you suppose I am?
12. —— do you suppose I saw?
13. —— do you think will help us?

### EXERCISE 21

(§§ 113-168, pp. 55-74)

Point out each pronoun; tell to what class it belongs, and give its construction.

1. His mind now misgave him. 2. Under the dark and haunted garret were attic chambers which themselves had histories. 3. Passion itself is very figurative, and often bursts out into metaphors. — GOLD-SMITH. 4. He had a wiry, well-trained, elastic figure, a stiff military throw-back of his head, and a springing step, which made him appear much younger than he was. 5. It was the owl that shrieked. 6. Slowly, slowly, slowly the days succeeded each other. 7. Say nothing to the men, but have all your wits about you. 8. He saw that it would be dark long before he could reach the village. 9. I must do myself the justice to open the work with my own history. 10. Economy in our affairs has the same effect upon our fortunes which good breeding has upon our conversations. — STEELE. 11. It was a cloudy night, with frequent showers of rain. 12. "Fair sirs," said Arthur, "wherefore sit ye here?" 13. Who would be free, themselves must strike the blow. — BYRON. 14. This is my son, mine own Telemachus. — TENNYSON.

15. Richard bade them adieu. 16. Ye men of Kent, 't is victory or death! — WORDSWORTH. 17. We dined yesterday with your friend and

mine, the most companionable and domestic Mr. C. **18.** Great is the power of the man who has nothing to lose. — DOYLE. **19.** Each hamlet started at the sound. **20.** Look on me with thine own calm look. **21.** Mr. Rigby was not a man who ever confessed himself at fault. **22.** They were conversing with much earnestness among themselves. **23.** He heard the deep behind him, and a cry before. **24.** When Deerslayer reached the fire, he found himself surrounded by no less than eight grim savages. **25.** Mine hostess, indeed, gave me a long history how the goblet had been handed down from generation to generation. **26.** The uncle and nephew looked at each other for some seconds without speaking. **27.** We had yet seen no wild beasts, or, at least, none that came very near us. — DEFOE. **28.** We envy you your sea-breezes. **29.** Which is he that killed the deer? **30.** There was the choice, and it was still open to him to take which side he pleased. **31.** There is always something to worry you. It comes as regularly as sunrise.

### EXERCISE 22

(§§ 169–188, pp. 75–82)

**1.** Point out every adjective. Tell whether it is descriptive or definitive (§§ 169–171), and mention the substantive to which it belongs. If the adjective can be compared, give its three degrees of comparison.[1]

**1.** The old, unpainted shingles of the house were black with moisture. **2.** "My very dog," sighed poor Rip, "has forgotten me!" **3.** Loud was the lightsome tumult on the shore. — BYRON. **4.** Sweet are the shy recesses of the woodland. **5.** Rows of pewter and earthen dishes glittered along the dresser. **6.** The major spoke in a matter-of-fact way. **7.** The sheep and the cow have no cutting teeth, but only a hard pad in the upper jaw. — HUXLEY. **8.** The faint, foggy daylight glimmered dimly on the bare floor and stairs. **9.** He wiped his serious, perplexed face on a red bandanna handkerchief, a shade lighter than his complexion. **10.** The yellow moonlight sleeps on all the hills. — BEATTIE. **11.** The young hostess seemed to perform her office with a certain degree of desperate determination. **12.** This warning is meant in a friendly spirit.

**13.** The house remained untenanted for three years. **14.** Numberless torrents, with ceaseless sound, descend to the ocean. **15.** The contest between the two branches of the legislature lasted some days longer.

[1] For exercises in the use of the comparative and the superlative, see pp. 249–250, 252.

**2.** Write five sentences containing descriptive adjectives; five containing definitive adjectives.

**3.** Write sentences containing demonstrative, indefinite, relative, and interrogative adjectives.

**4.** Write sentences in which the indefinite article is directly followed by —

honorable, youthful, yew, ewe, euphonious, historical, history, hymn, humble, hilarious, university, express, horticultural, oratorio, automatic, heritage, harmonious.

### EXERCISE 23

#### (§§ 181–187, pp. 79–82)

Point out the comparatives and the superlatives. Mention any superlatives used for emphasis (§ 200).

**1.** The Governor-General is the frankest and best-natured of men.
**2.** The company grew merrier and louder as their jokes grew duller.
**3.** A knock alarmed the outer gate.   **4.** At once there came the politest and friendliest reply.   **5.** Many a poet has been poorer than Burns, but no one was ever prouder. — CARLYLE.   **6.** The last tyrant ever proves the worst. — POPE.   **7.** The profoundest secrecy was observed in the whole transaction.   **8.** Earth has not anything to show more fair.
**9.** The natural principle of war is to do the most harm to our enemy with the least harm to ourselves. — IRVING.   **10.** During the rest of the journey, Rose was in the strangest state of mind.   **11.** There's not a nobler man in Rome than Antony.   **12.** Little he ate, and less he spake.
**13.** Our journey hither was through the most beautiful part of the finest country in the world.   **14.** Meanwhile the throng without was constantly becoming more numerous and more savage.   **15.** Vain are his weapons, vainer is his force.   **16.** She might have been more lenient.
**17.** You'll have to be more practical.   **18.** How does a love of gain transform the gravest of mankind into the most contemptible and ridiculous! — GOLDSMITH.   **19.** Most authors speak of their fame as if it were quite a priceless matter.

**20.**  Loveliest and best! thou little know'st
     The rank, the honor, thou hast lost! — SCOTT.

**21.**  Of two such lessons, why forget
     The nobler and the manlier one? — BYRON.

### EXERCISE 24

(§§ 189–198, pp. 83–87)

1. Parse each adverb by telling whether it is an adverb of manner, time, place, or degree, and by mentioning the verb, adjective, or adverb which it modifies. Compare the adverbs which are capable of comparison.

1. A great part of the island is rather level. 2. They had worked very hard and very cheerfully. 3. When spake I such a word? 4. We can ill spare the commanding social benefits of cities. — EMERSON. 5. She looked up and met his eyes, and thereupon both became very grave. 6. The silence of the prairie at night was well-nigh terrible. 7. Far in the West there lies a desert land. 8. The whistling ploughman stalks afield. 9. Swiftly they glided along. 10. He has only just arrived in England. 11. Fast the white rocks faded from his view. 12. Whole ranks instantly laid down their pikes and muskets. 13. Thick clouds of dust afar appeared. 14. Bitter sobs came thick and fast. 15. How long are you going to be in Paris? 16. To-morrow I intend to hunt again. 17. Answer made King Arthur, breathing hard. 18. Some of us laughed heartily. 19. They had spoken simply and openly about that from the very start.

2. Form an adverb of manner from each of the following adjectives. Use each adverb in a sentence. Tell what it modifies.

Proud, careless, vehement, tender, vigorous, dainty, brave, formal, courteous, blunt, sharp, keen, weary, heavy, true, skilful, legible.

3. Fill each blank with an adverb of degree modifying the adjective or the adverb.

1. Ogilvie was —— lucky that day.
2. They were thought to be —— fashionable people.
3. She made her objections —— delicately as she could.
4. July has been —— hot.
5. Carlyle was —— dainty about his food.
6. Jack did not come early —— to find a seat.
7. The tide runs —— fast round this point.
8. The balloon soared —— high that it disappeared.
9. The fugitive reached the pier —— late to take the steamer.
10. The bear growled —— savagely that the dogs were frightened.
11. You write —— more legibly than I.

## EXERCISE 25

(§§ 194-196, p. 86)

**1.** Point out the relative adverbs, and mention the subordinate clause introduced by each. Tell whether each adverb expresses time, place, or manner.

1. Just as the sun went down, they heard a murmur of voices. **2.** On waking, he found himself on the green knoll whence he had first seen the old man of the glen. **3.** There is no place of general resort wherein I do not often make my appearance. **4.** Wherever he determines to sleep, there he prepares himself a sort of nest. **5.** I hastened to the spot whence I had come. **6.** Where rolled the ocean, thereon was his home. — BYRON. **7.** Where shineth thy spirit, there liberty shineth too! — MOORE. **8.** He will look on the world, wheresoever he can catch a glimpse of it, with eager curiosity. **9.** Until Lady Glenmore came to call next day, we heard of nothing unusual. **10.** When she and Miss Pole left us, we endeavored to subside into calmness. **11.** Small service is true service while it lasts. **12.** Long before we saw the sea, its spray was on our lips. **13.** As they ascended, Rip every now and then heard long rolling peals, like distant thunder. **14.** The village clock struck five as Mr. Millbank and his guests entered the gardens of the mansion. **15.** When only a small space was left between the armies, the Highlanders suddenly drew their broadswords and rushed forward with a fearful yell. — MACAULAY. **16.** When he rejoined his companions, he said something to them in Welsh.

**2.** Point out the interrogative adverbs, and tell what each modifies.

1. Why look'st thou so? **2.** Whence came ye, jolly satyrs? whence came ye? — KEATS. **3.** Where now shall I go, poor, forsaken, and blind? — CAMPBELL. **4.** Why weep ye by the tide? — SCOTT. **5.** See how the world its veterans rewards! — POPE. **6.** How wildly will ambition steer! — DRYDEN. **7.** Where have you been these twenty long years? **8.** Here was a Cæsar! When comes such another? — SHAKSPERE. **9.** When shall we three meet again? **10.** History is clarified experience, and yet how little do men profit by it! Nay, how should we expect it of those who so seldom are taught anything by their own? — LOWELL. **11.** Why did you not bring what I asked for?

**3.** Write ten sentences containing relative adverbs; ten containing interrogative adverbs.

1. Point out the comparatives and superlatives. Tell whether each is an adjective or an adverb.

1. I thought it the most prudent method to lie still. 2. When the people observed I was quiet, they discharged no more arrows. 3. You know your own feelings best. 4. He was taller than any of the other three who attended him. 5. The song and the laugh grew less and less frequent. 6. The harder I try to forget it, the more it comes into my mind. 7. The night grew darker and darker ; the stars seemed to sink deeper in the sky. 8. I answered in a few words, but in a most submissive manner. 9. Their sight is much more acute than ours. 10. The natives came by degrees to be less apprehensive of any danger from me. 11. Whoever performs his part with the most agility, and holds out longest in leaping, is rewarded with the blue-colored silk. 12. It received less damage than I expected. 13. Long live the most puissant king of Lilliput ! 14. Fast are the flying moments, faster are the hoofs of our horses. 15. Nigh come the strangers and more nigh. — SCOTT.

2. Write sentences containing either the comparative or the superlative of the following words : —

merry, uncomfortable, ill, joyfully, northern, old (*both forms*), far, in, out, early, little (*adjective*), little (*adverb*), badly, often, worthy, wonderful, accurate, far, nigh, top, much, severe.

3. Write six sentences containing adverbs which are incapable of comparison; six containing adjectives which are incapable of comparison.

1. Write five sentences in which cardinal numerals are adjectives, five in which they are nouns. Use the same numerals in the ordinal form as adjectives, as nouns.

2. Write five sentences, each containing a numeral adverb; five containing an adverbial phrase that includes a numeral.

## EXERCISE 28

(§§ 209–215, pp. 91–93)

**1.** Point out all the verbs and verb-phrases. Tell whether each is transitive or intransitive. Tell which are copulative; which are auxiliary. Mention any examples of the copula.

1. Little tasks make large return. 2. We must now return to the fortress of Tillietudlem and its inhabitants. 3. Though I look old, yet I am strong and lusty. 4. The sunshine might now be seen stealing down the front of the opposite house. 5. He sat apart from them all, and looked at them with a melancholy, haughty countenance ; while the rest hallooed and sang and laughed, and the room rang. 6. You cannot relieve me, but you may add to the torments I suffer. 7. One gains nothing by attempting to shut out the sprites of the weather. They come in at the keyhole ; they peer through the dripping panes ; they insinuate themselves through the crevices of the casement, or plump themselves down chimney astride of the raindrops. — WHITTIER. 8. A large lamp threw a strong mass of light upon the group. 9. The baron pardoned the young couple on the spot. 10. Every now and then he would turn his head slowly round.

11. The river sleeps along its course and dreams of the sky and of the clustering foliage. 12. A severe gale compelled him to seek shelter. 13. Miss Betsy Barker dried her eyes and thanked the Captain heartily. 14. Pray you, look not sad. 15. I am ! yet what I am who cares, or knows ? — CLARE. 16. After all, it is a glorious pastime to find oneself in a real gale of wind, in a big ship, with not a rock to run against within a thousand miles. — KINGSLEY. 17. We will talk over all this another time. 18. What is progress ? Movement. But what if it be movement in the wrong direction ? — DISRAELI. 19. They say you are a melancholy fellow. 20. The valiant Clifford is no more. 21. The wreck had evidently drifted about for many months ; clusters of shellfish had fastened about it, and long seaweed flaunted at its sides. — IRVING. 22. Times grew worse and worse with Rip Van Winkle as years of matrimony rolled on.

**2.** Frame twenty sentences, each containing a verb-phrase. Use the auxiliaries mentioned in § 210. Let some of the sentences be interrogative.

**3.** Make a list of twenty verbs that are transitive in one sense, intransitive in another (§ 212). Use these verbs in sentences.

4. Illustrate the absolute use of transitive verbs by framing ten sentences (§ 213).

5. Make a list of six copulative verbs (§ 214). Use them in sentences. Frame sentences in which the same verbs are not copulative (§ 215).

6. Use the copula (§ 214) in twenty sentences, several of which shall illustrate its use in verb-phrases.

### EXERCISE 29

#### (§§ 217-225, pp. 94-99)

1. Write ten sentences in each of which a weak (or regular) verb is used in the past tense; ten, in each of which a strong (or irregular) verb is used in the past tense.

2. Construct sentences in which the past tense of each of the following verbs is used : *drink, lie, sow, get, wake, dwell, sing, pay, bid, light, bereave, build, ride, hang, swim, lay, split, shrink, slay, wring, weave, thrive, spin, tread, shake, burst, slink, dive, flee, fly, swing, wet, fling, kneel, let, chide.*

3. Point out all the verbs (except the copula and auxiliaries) in Exercise 28, 1, and conjugate them in the present and the past tense. Tell which are weak (regular) and which are strong (irregular). Account for the person and number.

### EXERCISE 30

#### (§§ 226-232, pp. 100-102)

1. Fill each blank with *am, is,* or *are.*

1. England and the United States —— at peace.
2. Neither Arthur nor John —— right.
3. Either a saw or an axe - — necessary.
4. Either you or Dorothy - — going.
5. You and I —— going.
6. You and he —— going.
7. Is it Mr. Allen or is it his children who —— going ?
8. Either he —— going or you ——.

9. Either you —— going or I ——.

10. The sum and substance of the article —— this.

11 Half the sheep —— missing.

12. A number of Italians —— present.

13. The number of Italians in this town —— small.

14. Mathematics —— my most difficult study.

15. The number of applicants —— not sufficient.

16. A number of reasons —— alleged.

17. The jury —— in agreement.

18. The jury —— being charged by the judge.

19. The committee —— composed of five members.

20. The committee —— always wrangling with one another.

21. I, who —— only a beginner, cannot compete with Richards, who —— an expert.

22. He is one of those men who —— always out of work.

23. I am not a man who —— easily frightened.

24. Walter is one of the best fellows there —— in this town.

25. Is it the king and queen who —— coming?

26. Is it the king or the queen who —— coming?

27. They made me, who —— the shyest of mortals, respond to a toast.

28. A gift of four hundred books, eighteen maps, and ten plaster casts —— to be made to our school.

29. Vocal and instrumental music —— taught here.

30. Neither vocal nor instrumental music —— taught here.

31. Neither elementary nor advanced physics —— taught here.

32. Neither organic nor inorganic chemists —— trained here.

33. One or two pages —— missing.

34. Physics, together with algebra and Latin, —— taught the first year.

35. Stevenson's "Memories and Portraits" —— lying on the table.

36. The insurgent general with ten of his followers —— said to have surrendered.

37. James, as well as his sisters, —— coming.

38. Six months —— a long time to wait.

39. A series of lectures —— given here every winter.

2. Make a list of ten collective nouns. Use them in sentences (1) with a singular verb, (2) with a plural verb. Explain the difference in meaning.

3. Use the relative *who* in ten sentences in which the antecedent is in the first or the second person.

### EXERCISE 31

(§§ 233-241, pp. 102-105)

**1.** Explain the use of *will* and *shall* in the following sentences.

**1.** We shall never forget what you have done for us. **2.** "You ought to know my military secretary," said the general, as Lothair entered, "and therefore I will introduce you." **3.** I am very patient; I will wait. **4.** If I do return, I will vote against them. But I will not return. I have made up my mind to that. **5.** I will send you Jennings's poem, if you like. **6.** You will of course make a drawing and an estimate, and send them to me (§ 240). **7.** Do congratulate her for me, will you? **8.** Another Athens shall arise. — SHELLEY. **9.** "I won't allow it!" cried Lady Niton, "he sha'n't go!" **10.** Shall I find you at home if I call some day soon, between five and six o'clock? **11.** You must be convinced, and on reflection you will be convinced. **12.** Before my journey to Rochdale, you shall have due notice where to address me. **13.** I consider myself a first-rate shot, and you shall practise with me. **14.** Shall I ever forget that party? **15.** Shall you hunt to-morrow, Mr. Deronda? **16.** When shall you be at Cambridge?

**17.** Lady St. Jerome is a little indisposed — a cold caught at one of her bazaars. She will hold them, and they say that no one ever sells so much. — DISRAELI. **18.** Will you be good enough to keep an account of all the manuscripts you receive, for fear of omission? **19.** O rest ye, brother mariners, we will not wander more. — TENNYSON. **20.** Will you forward the inclosed immediately to Corbet, whose address I do not exactly remember? **21.** Byron was no common man : yet if we examine his poetry with this view, we shall find it far enough from faultless. — CARLYLE. **22.** I shall be in town by Sunday next, and will call and have some conversation on the subject of Westall's proposed design. **23.** Will you go down, dear? I will follow you in a moment. **24.** Will not your trip to Bath afford you an opportunity to take a peep at Weston? **25.** Never, as long as I live, will I speak to you again, nor shall Harry, whom you have humiliated!

**26.** Yet he for whom I grieve shall never know it. **27.** Shall you let him go to Italy? **28.** Prone to the dust Oppression shall be hurled. — CAMPBELL. **29.** You sha'n't go on with this affair, I tell you, Harry. **30.** I shall probably return this evening, but I will see you before I go. — TROLLOPE. **31.** In the interim I shall leave town ; on Sunday I shall set out for Herefordshire, from whence, when wanted, I will return. **32.** If my father does not return with me in the spring, it shall not be for want of urging on my part. — COOPER.

**2.** Fill each blank with *will* or *shall*.

1. I —— be glad to see you.
2. We —— be obliged to go home early.
3. I —— help you whenever you wish.
4. I promise that he —— not trouble you again.
5. You —— be kind enough to take your seat.
6. We —— miss our train, I fear.
7. I must hurry or I —— be late.
8. Robert —— have as much as is good for him.
9. Arthur —— disobey me in spite of all I can do.
10. Arthur —— obey you, I am sure.
11. Arthur —— obey me, or I —— punish him.
12. If we reject these offers, we —— regret it.
13. I —— no longer endure his insolence.
14. —— they return in season for dinner?
15. I —— have to excuse you this time, I suppose.
16. I —— gladly see you at any time.
17. You —— not leave this room until you have confessed.
18. He —— give you the money, I feel confident.
19. He —— give you the money, or I —— have no more to do with him.
20. —— we allow them to do as they please?

**3.** Write declarative sentences, using *will or shall* in the first person (singular or plural) to express a threat, a promise, resolution, consent, desire, determination, simple futurity.

**4.** Fill the blanks in the following questions with *will* or *shall*. Write sentences (using *will* or *shall*) in answer.

1. —— you promise to do better?
2. —— you make any promises if he insists?
3. —— we miss our train?
4. —— we go? Just ask us!
5. —— I go now? I fear I am wearying you.
6. —— I tell you what I really think?
7. —— you call a cab for me, if you please?
8. —— you be glad to see him?
9. —— you see me if I call at one o'clock?
10. —— we see you this evening?
11. —— you be kind enough to open that door, or —— I?
12. —— you miss your brother?
13. —— we wait here, or —— you relent and let us go with you?
14. —— we allow this evil to continue?
15. —— you forgive me?

### EXERCISE 32

(§§ 242–245, pp. 106–107)

**1.** Name all the complete (or compound) tenses and explain their formation.

**1.** Four long years in the times of the war had he languished a captive. — Longfellow.  **2.** The adventurer has subsequently returned to his native country.  **3.** Spiders had built their webs in the angles of the walls and ceilings.  **4.** Whole fleets had been cast away. Large mansions had been blown down.  **5.** I am just returned from staying three days at a delightful inn by the river Ouse, where we always go to fish (§ 242, 1, note). — Fitz Gerald.  **6.** In the evening we reached a village where I had determined to pass the night.  **7.** I have sent by the Gisbornes a copy of the " Elegy on Keats."  **8.** I have really done my best.  **9.** Our visits to the islands have been more like dreams than realities.  **10.** We are here arrived at the crisis of Burns's life.  **11.** The chills of a long winter had suddenly given way ; the north wind had spent its last gasp ; and a mild air came stealing from the west.  **12.** The officer at last turned away, having satisfied himself that the room was empty.  **13.** Carson will have reached shelter long before this.

**2.** Construct ten sentences in which the verbs in Exercise 29, 2 are used in the perfect tense.

**3.** Turn the verbs in these sentences into the pluperfect tense ; into the future perfect tense. Write sentences in which the same verbs are used as perfect participles ; as perfect infinitives.

### EXERCISE 33

(§§ 246–254, pp. 107–112)

**1.** Tell whether each verb is in the active or the passive voice.

**2.** If the verb is active, change it to the passive, and make such other changes as may be necessary. If the verb is active, change it to the passive.

**3.** Conjugate each verb in the tense in which it occurs.

**1.** The customs of mankind are influenced in many ways by climate. **2.** The door, which was slightly ajar, was suddenly pushed open. **3.** The landlord handed the stranger the newspaper. **4.** After a short pause, my host resumed his narration. **5.** During the greater part of that night my slumbers were disturbed by strange dreams. **6.** Not a word was spoken, not a sound was made. **7.** The great willow tree had caught and retained among its leaves a whole cataract of water. **8.** Early in the morning I was awakened by the voices of Peter and his wife. **9.** He that is loudly praised will be clamorously censured.—JOHNSON. **10.** Out of this story he formed a tragedy. **11.** The assailants were repulsed in their first attack, and several of their bravest officers were shot down in the act of storming the fortress sword in hand. **12.** This fatal question has disturbed the quiet of many other minds. **13.** No genius was ever blasted by the breath of critics.—JOHNSON. **14.** The jury then heard the opinion of the judge.

**15.** What cruel maxims are we taught by a knowledge of the world! — MISS BURNEY. **16.** Their departure made another material change at Mansfield. **17.** The appearance of a housemaid prevented any further conversation. **18.** Each word of this leave-taking was overheard by Kezia. **19.** Before nine o'clock next morning the two canoes were installed on a light country cart. **20.** An old harper was summoned from the servants' hall. **21.** He had been wounded at Waterloo. **22.** This advice struck the disputants dumb. **23.** Through the night were heard the mysterious sounds of the desert. **24.** A violent storm of rain obliged them to take shelter in an inn. **25.** Far was heard the fox's yell.—SCOTT. **26.** Adams highly commended the doctor's opinion.

**4.** Rewrite the following sentences, changing the form of the verbs from active to passive, or from passive to active. Notice the effect upon subjects and objects.

**1.** I was brought up by my uncle. **2.** I have found them. **3.** We were delayed by the storm. **4.** They were warned by the pilot. **5.** She saw us. **6.** That winter will never be forgotten by any of us. **7.** You surprise me. **8.** Will you meet me? **9.** Was he struck by a bullet? **10.** Have you forgotten me? **11.** How the crowd cheered him! **12.** Tom, the blacksmith, makes horseshoes. **13.** The schooner was run down by the steamship. **14.** The old man has opened a little shop. **15.** Mary has invited Ellen. **16.** Mary might have invited Ellen. **17.** Mary will invite Ellen. **18.** The storm has made great havoc along the coast. **19.** The children have been called home by their nurse. **20.** He vexes me. **21.** The tower was struck by lightning yesterday. **22.** A policeman helped her over the crossing. **23.** I was amused by your letter.

5. Use each of the following verbs in both the active and the passive of the past, the future, and the perfect (or present perfect): — *send, bring, teach, drink, get, set, lay, leave, find, forget.*

6. Use each of the verbs in § 105 in the active voice of the past tense with both a direct and an indirect object. Change to the passive.

### EXERCISE 34

(§§ 255-261, pp. 113-114)

1. Point out all the progressive and all the emphatic verb phrases. Mention the tense and voice of each. Note any instances where *do* and *did* are not emphatic.

1. Thus did the long sad years glide on. 2. Now pray do settle in England. 3. Meanwhile, I go about in my little ship, where I do think I have two honest fellows to deal with. 4. I remember. I do indeed remember — too well! 5. Not until it was broad daylight did I quit the haunted house. 6. Do but look on her eyes. 7. Roland reached the boat just as the gang plank was being hauled in. 8. We are being entertained by the Archers. 9. The man at our wheel was spinning his spokes desperately to avoid banging into vessels we could not see, but whose bells were ringing everywhere about us. 10. Wild weeds are gathering on the wall. 11. I did actually pick up a French crown piece, worth about a dollar and six cents, near high-water mark. 12. I was loitering about the old gray cloisters of Westminster Abbey. 13. The friends of Coningsby were now hourly arriving. 14. My eyes have been leaving me in the lurch again.

15. They had been for some time passing through narrow gorges of the mountains, along the edges of a tumbling stream. 16. We are just sitting down to dinner with a pleasant party. 17. The large Newfoundland house-dog was standing by the door. 18. "Do thou," said Bertram, "lead the way." — Scott. 19. Music in his ears his beating heart did make. 20. Over the hillsides the wild knell is tolling. — Holmes.

2. Write sentences in which the verb *teach* is used in the present progressive, past progressive, future progressive, perfect progressive, pluperfect progressive, and future perfect progressive tenses of the active voice.

3. Write ten questions containing some form of *do* (or *did*).

## EXERCISE 35

(§§ 262–286, pp. 115–123)

Point out all the verbs in the imperative or the subjunctive mood. Tell the subjects of the imperatives and explain the forms and uses of the subjunctives.

1. And now dispatch we toward the court, my lords. — SHAKSPERE. 2. I think you had better speak to Lady Corisande yourself (§ 285). 3. My dear boy, God bless thee a thousand times over ! 4. O that the desert were my dwelling place ! 5. "Rest we here," Matilda said. — SCOTT. 6. Go where thy destiny calls thee. 7. Now Hesper guide my feet. — AKENSIDE. 8. O that such hills upheld a freeborn race ! — BYRON. 9. Perish those riches which are acquired at the expense of my honor or my humanity ! — GOLDSMITH. 10. Would all were well ! but that will never be. — SHAKSPERE. 11. The distaff were more fitting for you. 12. Robert hesitated, as if he were inclined to refuse. 13. Do what they might, the hook was in their gills. — GEORGE MEREDITH. 14. Fare you well, fair gentlemen. — SHAKSPERE. 15. Suffice it to say, the robbers were defeated. 16. Disclose thy treachery, or die ! 17. Let us not be influenced by any angry feelings. 18. Be that as it may, Kidd never returned to recover his wealth.

19. I would to God my heart were flint, like Edward's. — SHAKSPERE. 20. Move we on. — SCOTT. 21. Mark that the signal-gun be duly fired. — BYRON. 22. The hull drives on, though mast and sail be torn. 23. I am glad that you liked my song, and, if I liked the others myself so well as that I sent you, I would transcribe them for you also. — COWPER. 24. I beseech you, punish me not with your hard thoughts. — SHAKSPERE. 25. If there be change, no change I see. — LANDOR. 26. Be it as thou wilt. 27. Weep you no more, sad fountains. 28. If thou leave thy father, he will die. — WORDSWORTH. 29. Come thou no more for ransom, gentle herald. — SHAKSPERE. 30. Learn thou his purpose. 31. Come, go we in procession to the village. — SHAKSPERE. 32. The destruction of property which took place within a few weeks would be incredible, if it were not attested by witnesses unconnected with each other and attached to very different interests.

33. I wish I were as I have been,
Hunting the hart in forest green. — SCOTT.

34. Come what come may,
Time and the hour runs through the roughest day. — SHAKSPERE

35. Buried be all that has been done,
Or say that naught is done amiss. — CRABBE.

## EXERCISE 36

(§§ 272–286, pp. 118–123)

Fill each blank with a verb in the appropriate form.

1. O that he —— here !
2. Would that I —— there !
3. If he —— a little older, I should take him into partnership.
4. —— you asked me to go, I should have refused.
5. —— you to ask me, I should refuse.
6. If you —— there, I should have seen you.
7. I am glad I saw the play, even if I —— a little disappointed.
8. I should have been glad to see the play, even if I —— a little disappointed.
9. I should be glad to see the play, even if I —— a little disappointed.
10. I shall be glad to see the play, even if I —— a little disappointed.
11. Though he —— to increase my salary, I should not remain in his employ. [Use the copula.]
12. Unless he —— to increase my salary, I should not remain in his employ. [Use the copula.]
13. When Tom saw you, you looked as if you —— angry. [Use the copula.]
14. When Tom sees you, I suppose you will look as if you —— angry.
15. I must remind him to post this letter, lest he —— it.

## EXERCISE 37

(§§ 287–295, pp. 124–127)

Explain the meaning of each potential verb-phrase, and parse the phrase. In parsing such a phrase, describe it merely as a potential verb-phrase and tell the tense, voice, person, and number, without assigning it to any mood.

1. Enough ! You may depart. 2. Men should travel. 3. What must be shall be. That's a certain text. — SHAKSPERE. 4. At times, with a strong effort, he would glance at the open door which still seemed to repel his eyes. 5. Nothing can bring you peace but yourself. — EMERSON. 6. It was sometimes sad enough to watch him as he sat alone. He would have a book near him, and for a while would keep it in his hands. — TROLLOPE. 7. O, my friend ! may I believe you ? May I speak to you ? 8. Presently he faced Adrian, crying, "And I might have stopped it !" 9. Nothing is impossible to the man who can will. — EMERSON. 10. A

scholar may be a well-bred man, or he may not. — EMERSON. **11.** "I trust we're at liberty to enter," said the elder lady with urbanity. "We were told that we might come at any time." **12.** I sent for you that I might have your counsel and assistance. **13.** I could no longer doubt the doom prepared for me.

**14.** I am as well as I can expect to be under the excitement which I suffer. **15.** I can become a party to no such absurd proceeding. **16.** I could scarcely refrain from tears. **17.** Come ! we must go back. **18.** We must be strangers to each other in future. **19.** As my horse must now have eaten his provender, I must needs thank you for your good cheer, and pray you to show me this man's residence, that I may have the means of proceeding on my journey.

### EXERCISE 38

(§§ 289–291, pp. 125–126)

1. Fill each blank with *can* or *may*.

**1.** —— I borrow your pen ?

**2.** Yes, you ——.

**3.** No, you —— not.

**4.** I —— swim across this river some day, for I know well enough that I ——.

**5.** I shall ask my father if I —— swim across this river. I know well enough that I —— .

**6.** My father is confident that I —— swim across the river safely.

**7.** My father says that I —— swim across the river if I will wait until he —— go with me.

**8.** —— I trouble you to give me that tennis racket ?

**9.** It —— be that you will regret this.

**10.** It —— not be that you will regret this.

**11.** —— you take a vacation this year, or is permission still refused ?

**12.** Why not ask if you —— take a vacation ?

**13.** You —— take your vacation after I have taken mine.

**14.** The weather man says we —— hope for sunshine to-morrow.

**15.** He —— be thankful that he escaped so easily.

**16.** When you are twenty-one, you —— have your own way.

2. Write sentences asking permission in the first, second, and third persons. Write sentences (1) granting these requests; (2) refusing them.

## EXERCISE 39

(§§ 297–308, pp. 127–132)

**1.** Justify the use of the auxiliary (*should* or *would*). In some of the sentences, *should* might be substituted for *would*. Which are they?

**1.** If I were you, I would not dwell too much on this fancy of yours. **2.** I have neither servants nor clothes, and, if it had not been for these good people, I should not have had food. **3.** I should delight in having her for a sister-in-law. **4.** I should hardly wish to go out before Friday. **5.** I should n't wonder if this made him set his teeth. **6.** Well, that's over! and I 'm sure neither Oliver nor I would go through it again for a million of money. **7.** If I were you, I would turn it over in my mind. **8.** I should be afraid to express myself in this manner, if the matter were not clear and indisputable. — BURKE. **9.** I should like to remain where I am for another week or ten days. **10.** Would you do me the favor to look at a few specimens of my portrait-painting? — DICKENS. **11.** "Would you come?" she said, with a serious, searching glance, and in a kind of coaxing manner. — "I should be an intruder, my dear lady," said Theodore, declining the suggestion. — DISRAELI.

**12.** I should not like to be out of my seat were the House in session.— W. J. LOCKE. **13.** If I were you I would not tempt Fate by remaining here a day longer.— W. E. NORRIS. **14.** Candidates would rather, I suppose, climb in at a window than be absolutely excluded. — COWPER. **15.** Impey would not hear of mercy or delay. **16.** I should not be surprised if he were here immediately. **17.** There 's a plantation of sugar-canes at the foot of that rock : should you like to look? — GEORGE ELIOT.

**2.** Explain the use of the auxiliary (*shall, should,* or *will, would*) in each subordinate clause.

**1.** With this purpose in view, he sent a skilful architect to build him such a palace as should be fit for a man of his vast wealth to live in. **2.** Their majesties commanded me to submit to whatever Bobadilla should order in their name. **3.** Should you find yourself able to push on to Braemar, your visit will be most welcome. **4.** It 's a simple affair enough, if you 'll just leave it as it stands. **5.** Fearing to awaken Joseph a second time, lest he should again hazard all by his thoughtlessness, he crept softly out of the wigwam. **6.** I watched the grapes from day to day till they should have secreted sugar enough from the sunbeams. **7.** If an old prophecy should come to pass, we may see a man, some time or other, with exactly such a face as that. **8.** He kept his heart continually open, and thus was sure to catch the blessing from on high, when it should come. — HAWTHORNE. **9.** This law provided that the presidency of Bengal should exercise a control over the other possessions of the Company. **10.** It is time that we should proceed.

**11.** It is necessary that he should have some work to do. **12.** I shall be thankful if you will condescend to enlighten my ignorance. **13.** It was natural that the leading authors should affect a style of levity and derision. — JEFFREY. **14.** I will take care that you shall not be troubled by him again. **15.** That the Duke of Wellington should cordially approve is singular enough. **16.** "Boys," interrupted Wilder, "it is now proper that you should know something of my future movements." — COOPER. **17.** We all stood ready to succor them if there should be occasion. — DEFOE. **18.** You are so well qualified for the task yourself that it is impossible you should need any assistance ; at least, it is hardly possible that I should afford you any. — COWPER. **19.** The brave sufferer refused to purchase liberty, though liberty to him would have been life, by recognizing the authority which had confined him. **20.** I meant that he should walk off, but he did not choose to understand me. **21.** When time shall serve, you shall have the fruit of my labors. — COWPER.

**22.** I shall be so glad if you will tell me what to read.— GEORGE ELIOT. **23.** I protest against such a combat, until the king of England shall have repaid the fifty thousand bezants.— SCOTT. **24.** Unless something should go wrong, I flatter myself that the performance will elicit your generous approbation. **25.** A seat in the cabinet was offered to him, on condition that he would give efficient support to the ministry in Parliament. **26.** The proposition which he made was, that Fox should be Secretary of State.

**27.** That night he put forth a proclamation, directing that the posts should be stopped, and that no person should, at his peril, venture to harbor the accused members. — MACAULAY. **28.** Hyde interfered, and proposed that the question should be divided. **29.** I am sorry that you should be bothered in this way. **30.** I am sorry that Murray should groan on my account.— BYRON. **31.** There are old brass andirons, waiting until time shall revenge them on their paltry substitutes. **32.** Should he be acquitted, that, I imagine, should end the matter. **33.** A rumor was circulated that some new pageant was about to be exhibited, which should put a fitting close to the splendid festivities. **34.** If this new purpose of conquest shall be abandoned, Richard may yet become King of Jerusalem by compact. — SCOTT. **35.** Saladin desires no converts save those whom the holy prophet shall dispose to submit themselves to his law. **36.** Pride now came to Montezuma's aid, and, since he must go, he preferred that it should appear to be with his own free will. **37.** God forbid that I should regret those gifts !

(§§ 309-323, pp. 132-137)

**1.** Point out each infinitive and explain its construction as noun, as complementary infinitive, as infinitive of purpose, as modifier of a noun or an adjective, or as part of a verb-phrase (with an auxiliary).

**2.** Point out any modifiers or objects of infinitives.

**1.** To advance toward London would have been madness. **2.** To trace the exact boundary between rightful and wrongful resistance is impossible.— MACAULAY. **3.** I was too young to keep any journal of this voyage. **4.** The baron hastened to receive his future son-in-law. **5.** It was her habit to go over to the deanery (§ 318). **6.** He could not consent to turn his back upon a party of helpless travellers. **7.** The fixed purpose of these men was to break the foreign yoke. **8.** Here rise no cliffs the vale to shade. **9.** They saw the gleaming river seaward flow (§ 322). **10.** She perceived one of the eyes of the portrait move. **11.** His first scheme was to seize Bristol. **12.** The first business of the Commons was to elect a Speaker. **13.** The old man frequently stretched his eyes ahead to gaze over the tract that he had yet to traverse. **14.** When other things sank brooding to sleep, the heath appeared slowly to awake and listen.— HARDY. **15.** All were anxious to hear the story of the mysterious picture. **16.** I see the lights of the village gleam through the rain and the mist. **17.** Then the bishop rose from his chair to speak.

**18.** To dismiss him from his high post was to emancipate him from all restraint. **19.** This is not a time to hesitate. **20.** Burghers hastened to man the wall. **21.** I felt Leslie's hand tremble on my arm. **22.** He heard a mighty bowstring twang.— MORRIS. **23.** Mr. Ralph Nickleby sat in his private office one morning, ready dressed to walk abroad. **24.** I put down the letters, and began to muse over their contents. **25.** Waves of clear sea are, indeed, lovely to watch. **26.** Halifax had now nothing to give. **27.** The neighborhood seemed to breathe a tranquil prosperity. **28.** It is always perilous to adopt expediency as a guide. **29.** Soldiers were drawn up to keep the passage clear.

**3.** Write sentences containing an infinitive used as subject, as predicate nominative, as appositive, as the object of a preposition, as an adjective; a complementary infinitive; an infinitive of purpose; an infinitive used with *shall*, with *will*, with *must*.

**4.** Note any modifiers or objects that you have used with the infinitives.

**EXERCISE 41**

(§§ 324–328, pp. 137–139)

1. Point out each infinitive clause. Mention the verb of which it is the object. Find the subject of each infinitive. When it is possible, substitute a *that*-clause for the infinitive clause.

**1.** It might seem irreverent to make the gray cathedral and the tall time-worn palaces echo back the exuberant vociferation of the market. **2.** We have made you wait. **3.** We then went to Pembroke College, and waited on his old friend Dr. Adams, the master of it, whom I found to be a most polite, pleasing, communicative man. — BOSWELL. **4.** The doctor expects Captain Starbuck to recover. **5.** For a good sailor to foul the first buoy was ludicrous enough. **6.** Will you ask Annie to feed the parrot? **7.** I believe it to be a speaking likeness. **8.** I suppose them to be utterly ignorant of their own condition.

**9.** Hepzibah bade her young guest sit down. **10.** Calamity and peril often force men to combine. **11.** He knew himself to be a liar whom nobody trusted. **12.** I must not ask the reader to suppose that he was cheerful. **13.** I felt this melancholy to be infectious. **14.** No one on seeing Mr. Crawley took him to be a happy man, or a weak man, or an ignorant man, or a wise man. — TROLLOPE. **15.** Humanity impelled him to rescue the poor wretch.

2. Write sentences containing infinitive clauses used after verbs of *wishing, commanding, believing, declaring, perceiving*

3. Fill each blank with a personal pronoun.

**1.** He believes the author to be ——. [First person.]
**2.** He believes that the author is ——. [First person.]
**3.** I knew the thief to be ——. [Third person.]
**4.** I thought that the thief was ——. [Third person.]
**5.** We thought the strangers to be ——. [Third person.]
**6.** We thought that the strangers were ——. [Third person.]

4. Fill each blank with *who* or *whom*.

**1.** The man —— I believe to be responsible for this accident is the engineer.
**2.** I believe that the man —— is responsible for this accident is the engineer.
**3.** My knock was answered by a lad —— I believed to be a lodger.
**4.** You are not the person —— I believed you to be.

## EXERCISE 42

(§§ 329–343, pp. 140–143)

**1.** Point out all the participles, present and past, and tell what substantive each modifies. Mention such as are used as pure adjectives. Mention any modifiers or objects of participles.

**1.** The ship is anchored safe and sound, its voyage closed and done. — WHITMAN. **2.** Even the tight windows and the heavy silken curtains drawn close could not shut out the sound of the driving sleet. **3.** Godolphin was not a reading man. **4.** Mr. Sikes, dragging Oliver after him, elbowed his way through the thickest of the crowd. **5.** Betrayed, deserted, disorganized, unprovided with resources, begirt with enemies, the noble city was still no easy conquest. **6.** Thus regretted and cautioned on all hands, Mordaunt took leave of the hospitable household. **7.** Far away, an angry white stain undulating on the surface of steely-gray waters, shot with gleams of green, diminished swiftly, without a hiss, like a patch of pure snow melting in the sun. — CONRAD. **8.** I set her on my pacing steed. — KEATS.

**9.** But the poor traveller paused here barely for a minute, and then went on, stumbling through the mud, striking his ill-covered feet against the rough stones in the dark, sweating in his weakness, almost tottering at times, and calculating whether his remaining strength would serve to carry him home.— TROLLOPE. **10.** His teeth are set, his hand is clenched. **11.** Passing through the ravine, they came to a hollow, like a small amphitheatre. **12.** He found the house gone to decay — the roof fallen in, the windows shattered, and the doors off the hinges. **13.** And now, sir, when you next go to the British Museum, look for a poet named Vaughan. **14.** A heavy sea struck us on our starboard quarter, almost throwing us on our beam-ends. **15.** He stood chuckling and rubbing his hands, and scarcely hearing a word the parson said. **16.** The light struggles dimly through windows darkened by dust. **17.** We sailed merrily forward for several days, meeting with nothing to interrupt us.

**2.** Write sentences containing the past participles of six weak verbs; of six strong verbs.

**3.** Write sentences containing a participle used as a pure adjective; a participle used as a predicate adjective; a participle modified adverbially; a participle taking an object.

**4.** Write ten sentences each containing a perfect participle. Substitute for each a clause introduced by *when*.

## EXERCISE 43

(§§ 344–346, p. 144)

Explain all examples of the nominative absolute. Substitute a modifying clause in each sentence.

**1.** A carriage, drawn by half a dozen horses, came driving at a furious rate, the postilions smacking their whips like mad. **2.** As far as the eye could reach, the sea in every direction was of a deep blue color, the waves running high and fresh, and sparkling in the light. **3.** For some years past there had been a difficulty about the rent, things not having gone at the Dragon of Wantly as smoothly as they had used to go. **4.** He began to talk rapidly, all diffidence subdued. **5.** Noon coming, and the Doctor not returning, Mr. Lorry advised with Lucie. **6.** The second mate falling ill during the passage, I was promoted to officer of the watch. **7.** The dog now roused himself and sat on his haunches, his ears moving quickly backward and forward. **8.** This done, Mazeppa spread his cloak. **9.** She was seated alone, her arms on the table, her head bent down. **10.** There being some time upon his hands, he left his luggage at the cloak-room, and went on foot along Bedford Street to the church.

## EXERCISE 44

(§§ 347–353, pp. 145–147)

**1.** Point out the present participles, and also the verbal nouns in -*ing* (participial nouns). Show the difference. Mention any modifiers or complements used with either.

**1.** The consternation was extreme. Some were for closing the gates and resisting; some for submitting; some for temporizing. **2.** A troop of strange children ran at his heels, hooting after him, and pointing at his gray head. **3.** The wicket opened on a stone staircase leading upward. **4.** Watching and toil were to me pleasure, for my body was strong, and my spirits winged. **5.** The lingerings of decent pride were visible in her appearance. **6.** His deep bass voice had a quavering in it, his eyes looked dim, and the lines on his face were deep. **7.** There were several French privateers hovering on the coast. **8.** He does not like talking of these matters to strangers. **9.** Miss Matty cared much more for the circumstance of her being a very good card-player. **10.** His discourse was broken off by his man's telling him he had called a coach. **11.** Swallows and martens skimmed twittering about the eaves. **12.** I have loved, lived with, and left the sea without ever seeing a ship's tall fabric of sticks, cobwebs, and gossamer go by the board. — CONRAD.

**13.** The sexton was a meek, acquiescing little man, of a bowing, lowly habit; yet he had a pleasant twinkling in his eye. **14.** The rain always made a point of setting in just as he had some outdoor work to do. **15.** I have been employed this morning in composing a Latin motto for the king's clock. **16.** Two more of the boats were lost by being stove and swamped alongside. **17.** I heard the ripple washing in the reeds. **18.** After wandering through two or three streets, I found my way to Shakspere's birthplace. **19.** Rip's heart died away at hearing of these sad changes in his home and friends. **20.** The fish did not bite freely, and we frequently changed our fishing ground without bettering our luck. **21.** Lady Niton sat blinking and speechless. **22.** I cannot help hearing things, and reading things, and observing things, and they fill me with disquietude. **23.** Here was circumstance after circumstance goading me onward. **24.** I sat staring at a book of my own making. **25.** That thought actually drove out of my head the more pressing danger.

**2.** Write sentences in which (1) a verbal noun and (2) a present participle are formed from —

run, hunt, leap, swim, strike, find, speak, sing, shout, play, skate, blow, spend, listen, eat, move, translate, recite, murmur, whisper, read, talk, complain, paint, build, give, breathe, teach, flow, shine.

**3.** Whenever it is possible, substitute either a noun or an infinitive for each verbal noun in your sentences.

**4.** Select three of these verbal nouns, and write other sentences in which each is used (1) as a subject, (2) with a direct and an indirect object, (3) with an adjective modifier, (4) with an adverbial modifier.

### EXERCISE 45

(§§ 354–371, pp. 148–154)

**1.** Point out and parse the prepositions and conjunctions.

In parsing a preposition, tell (1) the object, and (2) the word to which the preposition shows the relation of the object.

In parsing a conjunction, indicate the words or groups of words which it connects, tell whether it is coördinate or subordinate, and mention its correlative (§ 369) if it has one.

**1.** Neither witch nor warlock crossed Mordaunt's path. **2.** But I will be bolder, and do not doubt to make it good, though a paradox, that one great reason why prose is not to be used in serious plays, is, because it is too near the nature of converse. — DRYDEN. **3.** All down that immense vista of gloomy arches there was one blaze of scarlet and gold. **4.** No doubt, something of Shakspere's punning must be attributed to his age, in which direct and formal combats of wit were a favorite pastime of the courtly and accomplished. — COLERIDGE. **5.** Bodily labor is of two kinds : either that which a man submits to for his livelihood, or that which he undergoes for his pleasure. — ADDISON. **6.** Early upon the morrow the march was resumed. **7.** The camp was broken up, and the troops were sent to quarters in different parts of the country. **8.** My attention was called off for a moment by the cries of birds and the bleatings of sheep. **9.** This is well to be weighed, that boldness is ever blind, for it seeth not dangers and inconveniences. — BACON. **10.** At a little distance from Sir Roger's house, among the ruins of an old abbey, there is a long walk of aged elms. **11.** Then I sent you the Greek instead of the Persian whom you asked for ? — FITZ GERALD. **12.** Rowland's allowance at college was barely sufficient to maintain him decently, and, his degree nevertheless achieved, he was taken into his father's counting-house to do small drudgery on a proportionate stipend.

**13.** Though this lady never expressed an idea, Richard was not mistaken in her cleverness. **14.** If I am tired, your letter will refresh me. **15.** The young ladies however, and Mr. Pecksniff likewise, remained in the very best of spirits in spite of these severe trials, though with something of a mysterious understanding among themselves. **16.** He went along almost gaily, nor felt the fatigue of the road.

2. Write sentences in which the following words are used as indicated : —

for (*preposition, conjunction*), then (*conjunction, adverb*), notwithstanding (*preposition, conjunction*), since (*preposition, adverb, relative adverb*), until (*preposition, relative adverb*), as (*conjunction, relative pronoun, relative adverb*), that (*conjunction, relative pronoun, demonstrative adjective, demonstrative pronoun*), but (*preposition, conjunction*).

3. Construct sentences containing *either* and *or*, *neither* and *nor*, *whether* and *or*, *not only* and *but also*, *both* and *and*, *though*, *if*, *because*.

4. Construct six sentences containing coördinate conjunctions ; six containing subordinate conjunctions ; six containing relative adverbs.

### EXERCISE 46

(§§ 372–375, pp. 155–156)

Point out all interjections, all other parts of speech used here in exclamation, and all exclamatory phrases.

1. Ring the alarum-bell ! Murder and treason ! — SHAKSPERE. 2. Kipling is by far the most promising young man who has appeared since — ahem — I appeared. — STEVENSON. 3. O, to be in England ! 4. "Courage !" he said, and pointed toward the land. —TENNYSON. 5. Ah ! my lord Arthur, whither shall I go ? 6. Alas for my credulous fancy ! 7. Tut, man ! we must take things as they come. 8. O day, the last of all my bliss on earth ! — MARLOWE. 9. Adieu, fair Cadiz ! yea, a long adieu ! — BYRON. 10. Peace, sister, peace ! 11. Fie, fie, my brother ! 12. How now, Thersites ? what, lost in the labyrinth of thy fury ? 13. Farewell for the present, my dear sir. 14. O Jupiter ! how weary are my spirits ! — SHAKSPERE. 15. Guilty, my lord, guilty ! I confess, I confess ! 16. Hence, you long-legg'd spinners, hence ! 17. O monstrous ! O strange ! we are haunted ! 18. Faith, he is gone unto the taming school. 19. But, soft ! whom have we here ?
20. A Tory ! a Tory ! a spy ! a refugee ! hustle him ! away with him ! 21. What ! this gentleman will outtalk us all. 22. Up, up, Glentarkin ! rouse thee, ho ! — SCOTT. 23. And now good-bye, my dear fellow. 24. Ahem ! you remember, friend ? Grand triumphs those, eh ?

### EXERCISE 47

(§§ 376–392, pp. 157–162)

1. Construct ten sentences in which the simple subject (noun or pronoun) is modified by an adjective clause ; ten in which the simple predicate is modified by an adverbial clause.

2. Tell the construction (as subject, predicate nominative, object, etc.) of each noun clause in § 392. Mention the simple subject and predicate of each clause.

### EXERCISE 48

(§§ 395–402, pp. 163–165)

1. Tell whether each of the subordinate clauses expresses place, time, cause, or concession. Is the clause adjective or adverbial ? What introduces it ? What does it modify ?

**1.** Though often misled by prejudice and passion, he was emphatically an honest man. **2.** When a prisoner first leaves his cell, he cannot bear the light of day. **3.** As I walked through the wilderness of this world, I lighted on a certain place where was a den. — BUNYAN. **4.** He postponed his final decision till after the Parliament should have reassembled. **5.** They gave a dismal croak or two, and hopped aside into the darkest corner, since it was not yet their hour to flap duskily abroad. **6.** Calmly and sadly she waited, until the procession approached her. **7.** Half the task was not done when the sun went down. **8.** However I might be disposed to trust his probity, I dare not trust his prejudices. **9.** After a little more conversation we strolled to the stable, where my horse was standing. **10.** As we approached the house, we heard the sound of music, and now and then a burst of laughter. **11.** His face was not cruel, though it was desperate.

**12.** We again set out for the hut, at which we deposited our golden burdens. **13.** It will be midnight before we arrive at our inn. **14.** Though I was not particularly well supplied with money, I had enough for the expenses of my journey. **15.** The day, though it began brightly, had long been overcast. **16.** As there were no men in the company, the girls danced with each other. **17.** Although without fear, I did not neglect to use all proper precautions. **18.** When I return, I shall find things settled. **19.** Clifford, as the company partook of their little banquet, grew to be the gayest of them all. **20.** The mill where Will lived with his adopted parents stood in a falling valley between pinewoods and great mountains. **21.** As Ichabod approached this fearful tree, he began to whistle. **22.** Infected be the air whereon they ride ! — SHAKSPERE. **23.** So they were forced to go, because he was stronger than they.

**24.** Since you will not help me, I must trust to myself. **25.** When they beheld his face, they recognized Basil the blacksmith. **26.** This is the third day since we came to Rome. **27.** Amsterdam was the place where the leading Scotch and English assembled. **28.** These considerations might well have made William uneasy, even if all the military means of the United Provinces had been at his absolute disposal. **29.** Although the breeze had now utterly ceased, we had made a great deal of way during the night.

2. Illustrate clauses of place, time, cause, and concession, by constructing twenty sentences, five for each.

3. Tell whether the clauses are adjective or adverbial. What does each modify ?

4. See if you can replace your clauses of time by participles or adverbial phrases.

**1.** Point out the clauses of purpose and those of result.

**1.** The weather was so bad I could not embark that night. **2.** She opened the casement that the cool air might blow upon her throbbing temples. **3.** So intent were the servants upon their sports, that we had to ring repeatedly before we could make ourselves heard. **4.** The consequence was that, according to the rules of the House, the amendment was lost. **5.** Therefore I am going this way, as I told you, that I may be rid of my burden. **6.** Tess's friends lived so far off that none could conveniently have been present at the ceremony. **7.** Sometimes I was afraid lest I should be charged with ingratitude. **8.** There is such an echo among the old ruins and vaults that, if you stamp but a little louder than ordinary, you hear the sound repeated. — ADDISON. **9.** They durst not speak without premeditation, lest they should be convicted of discontent or sorrow. **10.** My purpose was, to admit no testimony of living authors, that I might not be misled by partiality, and that none of my contemporaries might have reason to complain. — JOHNSON. **11.** It is King Richard's pleasure that you die undegraded.

**2.** Write five sentences containing each a clause of purpose; of result; an infinitive clause expressing purpose.

**3.** Write ten sentences in which the infinitive (without a subject) expresses purpose.

**4.** Review Exercise 40.

**1.** Tell whether the conditional clauses in the following sentences are non-committal or contrary to fact, and whether they represent present, past, or future condition.

**1.** Should Hayley be with you, tell him I have given my friend Mr. Rose an introductory letter to him. **2.** If the judgment against him was illegal, it ought to have been reversed. If it was legal, there was no ground for remitting any part of it. **3.** If I ever saw horror in the human face, it was there. **4.** His affliction would have been insupportable, had not he been comforted by the daily visits and conversations of his friend. **5.** We perish if they hear a shot. — SCOTT. **6.** Can Freedom breathe if Ignorance reign? — HOLMES. **7.** If power be in the hands of men, it will sometimes be abused. **8.** If hopes were dupes, fears may be liars. — CLOUGH. **9.** If you write to Moore, will you tell him that I shall answer his letter the moment I can muster time and spirits? **10.** If you have any good news to tell, it will not be unwelcome; if any bad, you need not be afraid. **11.** I feel quite as much bored with this foolery as it deserves, and more than I should be, if I had not a headache. **12.** Will you let me offer you this little book? If I had anything better, it should be yours.

**13.** I shall hope, if we can agree as to dates, to come to you sometime in May. **14.** If I could only get to work, we could live here with comfort. **15.** If he had been left to himself, he would have whistled life away in perfect contentment. **16.** If this frolic should lay me up with a fit of rheumatism, I shall have a blessed time with Dame Van Winkle. **17.** I know that two and two make four, and should be glad to prove it, if I could, — though, I must say, if by any sort of process I could convert two and two into five, it would give me much greater pleasure.— BYRON. **18.** I would not say this if I could help it. **19.** If you are disposed to write — write; and if not, I shall forgive your silence, and you will not quarrel with mine. **20.** Had not exercise been absolutely necessary for our well-being, nature would not have made the body so proper for it.— ADDISON. **21.** Nothing will ever be attempted, if all possible objections must first be overcome.— JOHNSON. **22.** If fashion gives the word, every distinction of beauty, complexion, or stature ceases.— GOLDSMITH.

**2.** Write twenty sentences, each containing a conditional clause. Tell whether each condition refers to present, past, or future time. Which of them are contrary to fact?

### EXERCISE 51

(§§ 428-429, p. 173)

**1.** Point out the clauses of comparison and explain such forms of verbs or pronouns as may require comment.

**1.** Dull as a flower without the sun, he sat down upon a stone. **2.** He sighed as if he would break his heart. **3.** The modern steamship advances upon a still and overshadowed sea with a pulsating tremor of her frame, an occasional clang in her depths, as if she had an iron heart in her iron body. — CONRAD. **4.** It would have been as difficult, however, to follow up the stream of Donatello's ancestry to its dim source, as travellers have found it to reach the mysterious fountains of the Nile. **5.** I will become as liberal as you. **6.** The triumph was as destructive to the victorious as to the vanquished. **7.** The public conduct of Milton must be approved or condemned, according as the resistance of the people to Charles the First shall appear to be justifiable or criminal. **8.** There was no one in all Clavering who read so many novels as Madame Fribsby. **9.** No kind of power is more formidable than the power of making men ridiculous. — MACAULAY.

**10.** The leader of the orchestra was sawing away at his violin as savagely as if he were calling on his company to rush up and seize a battery of guns. — BLACK. **11.** He shouts as if he were trying his voice against a northwest gale of wind. **12.** The playground seemed smaller than when I used to sport about it. **13.** The blood in me ran cold, and I drew in my breath as if I had been struck. **14.** There are few things more formidable than the unwonted anger of a good-natured man. — MILLER. **15.** Nor was Lochiel less distinguished by intellectual than by bodily vigor. **16.** He showed less wisdom than virtue. **17.** He was as courageous an animal as ever scoured the woods. **18.** As fierce a beak and talon as ever struck — as strong a wing as ever beat, belonged to Swift — THACKERAY.

**19.** Homer's description of war had as much truth as poetry requires. — MACAULAY. **20.** Of all the objects I have ever seen, there is none which affects my imagination so much as the sea. — ADDISON. **21.** "Somebody must go," murmured Mrs. Heathcliff, more kindly than I expected. **22.** We do not so often disappoint others as ourselves. — JOHNSON. **23.** The battle raged as fiercely on the lake as on the land. **24.** The young man looked down on me from the corner of his eyes, for all the world as if there were some mortal feud unavenged between us. — E. BRONTË.

**2.** Write ten sentences containing *as if* with a subjunctive
**3.** Insert personal pronouns of the first or third person.

1. You are much stronger than ——.
2. Your anger hurts yourself more than it hurts ——.
3. You are not so studious as ——.
4. He was quite as much to blame as ——.
5. I blame myself rather than ——.
6. You should rather blame yourself than ——.
7. How much older are you than —— ?
8. Is Jack more ambitious than —— ?
9. Do you wish to please yourself more than —— ?
10. Your conduct was less censurable than ——.

## EXERCISE 52

### (§§ 430–436, pp. 173–176)

**1.** Change the direct statements to indirect discourse, prefixing *He said.* Thus, —

> Supper was announced shortly after my arrival.
> He said that supper was announced shortly after his arrival.

Be careful to make the proper changes in person and tense.

**1.** Supper was announced shortly after my arrival. **2.** Misery loves company. **3.** Iron floats in mercury. **4.** The grime and sordidness of the House of the Seven Gables seem to have vanished. **5.** Nothing is to be seen. **6.** Straws show which way the wind blows. **7.** I remained undecided whether or not to follow my servant. **8.** Rest of mind and body seems to have reëstablished my health. **9.** The fortifications consist of a simple wall overgrown with grass and weeds. **10.** Fire is a good servant but a bad master. **11.** Not a cheer was heard ; not a member ventured to second the motion. **12.** The most rigid discipline is maintained. **13.** Without our consent, such an expedition cannot legally be undertaken. **14.** The newspapers will happily save me the trouble of relating minute particulars.

**15.** The ringing of bells is at an end ; the rumbling of the carriages has ceased ; the pattering of feet is heard no more. **16.** My mind has been much disturbed, and too agitated for conversation. **17.** While all this is taking place within the Towers, vast bodies of people are assembling without. **18.** The spelling and handwriting are those of a man imperfectly educated. **19.** I have an unconquerable repugnance to return to my chamber. **20.** I like to see a man know his own mind.

**2.** Change into a direct statement each clause that is in the indirect discourse. Mention the construction of the clause (as subject, object, etc.).

**1.** The booming of a gun told them that the last yacht had rounded the lightship. **2.** All of a sudden she thought she heard something move behind her. **3.** Though they spoke French fluently, I perceived that it was not their native language. **4.** I soon found that, in making the acquaintance of the young man, I had indeed made a valuable acquisition. **5.** I thanked him, but said that Dr. Johnson had come with me from London, and I must return to the inn and drink tea with him ; that my name was Boswell, and I had travelled with him in the Hebrides. **6.** I discovered that he was wonderfully fond of interfering with other people's business.　**7.** I had heard that he had been unhappy, that he had roamed about, a fevered, distempered man, taking pleasure in nothing.　**8.** I had observed that the old woman for some time past had shown much less anxiety about the book.　**9.** I learned that times had gone hard with her.　**10.** I perceived that the objects which had excited my curiosity were not trees, but immense upright stones.

**11.** That no man can legally promise what he cannot legally perform is a self-evident proposition. — MACKINTOSH.　**12.** That there are some duties superior to others will be denied by no one.　**13.** It can hardly be doubted that the highest obligation of a citizen is that of contributing to preserve the community.　**14.** Reports had been brought back that six Christians were lingering in captivity in the interior of the country. **15.** If it be true that, by giving our confidence by halves, we can scarcely hope to make a friend, it is equally true that, by withdrawing it when given, we shall make an enemy. — PRESCOTT.　**16.** He concluded with the assurance that the whole fleet would sail on the following day. **17.** Pen protested that he had not changed in the least.

**3.** Write five sentences in which indirect discourse is expressed by an infinitive clause (§ 435).

### EXERCISE 53

(§ 436, p. 176)

**1.** Change each of the sentences quoted at the end of § 436 into one of the other two passive constructions described in that section.

**2.** Write ten sentences in each of which a clause in the indirect discourse is the subject of a passive verb.

### EXERCISE 54

(§§ 438–439, pp. 177–178)

**1.** Explain the use of *shall*, *should*, *will*, or *would* in each instance. Change the indirect discourse to the direct.

**1.** I believe I should like to live in a small house just outside a pleasant English town all the days of my life. — FITZ GERALD.　**2.** The sultan said he would oblige us with donkeys or anything else if we would only give him a few more pretty cloths.— SPEKE.  3. I think that I should like it to be always summer.  4. He often told his friends afterwards, that unless he had found out this piece of exercise, he verily believed he should have lost his senses. — ADDISON.  5. Do you remember once saying to me that you hoped you should never leave Brentham ?  6. I knew that he would not have accepted office in 1841–1842 if he could have avoided it.  7. Promise you will give him this little book of drawings.  8. I have often thought that there has rarely passed a life of which a judicious and faithful narrative would not be useful.— JOHNSON.  9. She said, very quietly, that she wished to speak to him after breakfast, and that he would find her in her sitting room.  10. Lady Annabel had promised the children that they should some day ride together to Marringhurst.

11. One of them told us that he would make us a canoe.  12. Promise, Marion — pray promise you will not even mention my name to him when you write next.  13. He felt that no argument of his would be of any use.  14. I know very well that I shall sign my own death warrant on the day when I retire from business.  15. She knew very well now that Grandcourt would not go without her ; but if he must tyrannize over her, he should not do it precisely in the way he would choose. She would oblige him to stay in the hotel.  16. They were afraid that they should not long be able to put him off with promises.  17. Bungay replied that he should be happy to have dealings with Mr. Pendennis.

2. Fill the blanks with the proper auxiliary (*shall* or *should*, or *will* or *would*).

1. Your father said that he —— be glad to see me.
2. I told him that I —— be obliged to dismiss him.
3. I wrote that we —— gladly accept his invitation.
4. My friends believed that I —— not be willing to go.
5. Robert thinks that he —— have to work evenings.
6. Robert says that I —— have to work evenings.
7. They say that Robert —— work evenings, although he ought not.
8. I promised that Robert —— not work evenings.
9. I told Mary that I was sure she —— succeed.
10. Mary said she had no doubt that I —— succeed.
11. Mary will say that she has no doubt I —— succeed.
12. I repeat that I have no doubt you —— succeed.
13. He declared that you —— go, even against your will.
14. The report is that we —— dissolve partnership.

3. Change the indirect statements in the sentences which you have just made to direct statements.

## EXERCISE 55

### (§§ 440–445, pp. 179–181)

**1.** Some, but not all, of the following sentences contain in-direct questions. Point out these questions and tell what introduces them (interrogative pronoun, interrogative adverb, subordinate conjunction). Mention the construction of each interrogative clause (as subject, object, etc.).

**2.** Turn each indirect question into a direct question.

**3.** Point out such relative clauses as you find in the sentences. Are they adjective or adverbial modifiers?

**1.** Warrington did not know what his comrade's means were. **2.** He could scarcely tell whether she was imbued with sunshine, or whether it was a glow of happiness that shone out of her. **3.** I started the question whether duelling was consistent with moral duty. — BOSWELL. **4.** The pilgrims then began to inquire if there was no other way to the gate. **5.** He knew not what to make of the letter. **6.** I hardly heard what he said. **7.** Every one knows practically what are the constituents of health or of virtue. — NEWMAN. **8.** Think calmly over what I have written. **9.** Then she asked him whence he was and whither he was going ; and he told her. **10.** What to expect, he knew not. **11.** Theseus wondered what this immense giant could be. **12.** Hack says it was Mrs. Bungay who caused all the mischief. **13.** The question was how best to extricate the army from its perilous position. **14.** Addison was a delightful companion when he was at his ease. **15.** I doubt whether the wisest of us know what our own motives are.

**16.** I puzzled my head for some time to find out which of the two cases was the more applicable. **17.** I returned to the studies which I had neglected. **18.** I cannot tell how I dared to say what I did. **19.** How long he slept he could not say. **20.** Fanny, in dismay at such an unprecedented question, did not know which way to look, or how to be prepared for an answer. — MISS AUSTEN. **21.** What my course of life will be when I return to England is very doubtful. **22.** I cannot tell you how vaingloriously I walked the streets. **23.** Then I told what a tall, upright, graceful person their great-grandmother Field once was. **24.** When the bean-vines began to flower on the poles, there was one particular variety which bore a vivid scarlet blossom. **25.** I know not which way I must look. **26.** Why she submitted, Mrs. Turpin could not have told you. **27.** I began to become conscious what a strange den that sanctum was. **28.** How Ferguson escaped, was, and still is, a mystery. **29.** How far he felt the force of this obligation will appear in the sequel.

**4.** Write sentences containing indirect questions introduced by *who, which, what, when, how, why, whether, if.*

**5.** Fill the blanks with *who* or *whom.* Tell, in each sentence, whether *who* or *whom* is an interrogative or a relative pronoun.

1. I know —— it was that broke the window.
2. I know —— it was that you saw.
3. I know —— you saw.
4. I know the person —— you saw.
5. I asked if the man —— we saw was Douglas.
6. I asked if the boy —— broke the window was Archer.
7. I know —— it was you overheard.
8. Tell me —— it is that I resemble.
9. Tell me —— I resemble.
10. Tell me —— you think I resemble.
11. Tell me if I resemble anybody —— you know.

**6.** Turn all the indirect questions which you have just written into direct questions.

**7.** Construct sentences in which each of the verbs (or verb-phrases) is followed by an indirect question : —

asked, tell, inquire, is learning, see, might discover, had heard, have found, doubt, have perceived, is thinking, wonders, knew, was told, understands, to comprehend, is, could ascertain, has reported, will announce.

### EXERCISE 56

(§ 447, p. 182)

**1.** Turn each indirect question into the direct form. Explain the use of *shall, should, will, would.*

1. "I doubt," said Donatello, "whether they will remember my voice now." 2. I did not know whether to resent his language or pursue my explanations. 3. I clambered to its apex, and then felt much at a loss as to what should be next done. 4. How we shall live I cannot imagine. 5. When I shall get to town I cannot divine, but it will be between this and Christmas. 6. I scarcely know which of us three would be the sorriest. 7. I can feel for you, because I know what I should feel in the same situation. 8. Let us see if she will know you. 9. I wonder how

you will answer me a year hence. **10.** I asked if Georgiana would accompany her. **11.** You must see the carriage, Jane, and tell me if you don't think it will suit Mrs. Rochester exactly, and whether she won't look like Queen Boadicea, leaning back against those purple cushions. — C. Brontë. **12.** Catherine had no idea why her father should be crosser or less patient in his ailing condition than he was in his prime. **13.** Mr. Hindley will have to proceed to extremities, — see if he won't !

**2.** Fill the blanks with the proper auxiliary (*shall, should, will, would*). Then change each indirect question to the direct form.

1. Tom asked me if I —— like to go with him.
2. They inquired whether I —— prefer to go or to stay.
3. She asked me if I —— help her.
4. Tell me whether he —— consent or not.
5. He wishes to know if you —— recommend him.
6. I was in doubt whether I —— succeed or fail.
7. I do not know whether you —— find her at home or at her uncle's.
8. He is in doubt whether or not he —— get the appointment.
9. We think we —— like to sail on the twentieth.
10. He thinks he —— like to be a farmer.

### EXERCISE 57

(§§ 448–453, pp. 183–186)

**1.** Mention the substantives that make up the compound subjects and the verbs that make up the compound predicates in § 450; in Exercise 4.

**2.** See if you can make any of the sentences compound by inserting personal pronouns as subjects.

**3.** Divide each compound sentence in § 452 and in Exercise 6 into the independent coördinate clauses that compose it.

**4.** Make each sentence in § 450 complex by inserting or adding a subordinate clause. Is your clause adjective or adverbial? What does it modify?

**5.** Divide each complex sentence in Exercises 17, 25, 39 (2), 48–51, into the independent (main) clause and the subordinate clause.

## EXERCISE 58

### (§§ 458–461, pp. 188–190)

1. Analyze (according to the directions in §§ 458–461) the simple sentences in Exercise 1. In analyzing, describe each sentence as declarative, interrogative, etc. If the sentence is imperative, supply the subject.

2. Analyze the compound and the complex sentences in Exercises 6, 17, 25, 39 (2), 48–51.

3. Analyze the compound complex sentences in §§ 456–457, 515.

## EXERCISE 59

### (§§ 462–473, pp. 191–196)

1. Point out the adjectives used as modifiers of the subject. Substitute for each an adjective phrase; an adjective clause (§§ 467–468).

1. Standing in the door was a tearful child. 2. A tall Scot shut off my view. 3. An iron mask concealed the prisoner's face. 4. Honorable men pay their debts. 5. A tumble-down shed stood in the hollow. 6. A three-cornered hat was cocked over one of his ears. 7. The American Indians are becoming extinct. 8. An experienced stenographer should spell correctly. 9. A deep fosse or ditch was drawn round the whole building. 10. The royal army was assembled at Salisbury. 11. The midday meal was excellent. 12. The morning mist lies heavy upon yonder chain of islands.

2. Construct sentences, using the following adjective phrases as modifiers of the subject : —

of great height; in a red hat; with black hair; from Cairo; to Indianapolis; from India; with high gables; of brilliant plumage; on the rear platform; in a state of intense agitation; between the two ships; over the mountain; on the summit of the tower.

3. Substitute (if possible) an adjective clause for each adjective phrase in the sentences you have just written.

4. Point out all participles used as modifiers of the simple subject in Exercise 42. Write ten sentences containing such modifiers (§ 469).

5. Construct ten sentences similar to those in § 470 (with infinitives modifying the simple subject).

6. Write ten sentences containing nouns or pronouns in the possessive case used as modifiers of the subject (§ 471).

7. Write ten sentences containing nouns in apposition with the subject (§§ 88, 5; 472); five in which a noun clause is thus used (§§ 386, 473).

### EXERCISE 60

#### (§§ 474–481, pp. 196–199)

1. Point out all the adverbs used to modify the simple predicate. Substitute for each an adverbial phrase or clause.

1. The witness chose his words deliberately. 2. The old man moved slowly down the street. 3. I carefully avoided making that promise. 4. Do not speak so loud. 5. I am eagerly looking forward to your visit. 6. That golf ball must have hit him hard. 7. Allan has played in public twice. 8. I shall call you early. 9. We often see your eccentric friend. 10. The priest shook his head doubtfully. 11. Your father barely escaped drowning. 12. The next morning Chester awoke late. 13. The accident happened here. 14. The captain had gone below. 15. Marion refuses to go by coach unless she can sit outside. 16. Frank left home three years ago, and has not been heard from since. 17. Look yonder and tell us where the path lies.

18. We were then presented to Governor Gore. 19. I have not been there since April. 20. Bruce was afterward ashamed of his discouragement. 21. The sun will soon set. 22. You are expected to arrive in good season hereafter. 23. Alice cannot spell correctly. 24. The Indian suddenly disappeared. 25. The girl laughed carelessly. 26. The moose fell heavily to the earth. 27. He passionately longs to see Italy. 28. All foreigners seem to speak rapidly. 29. Edith listened attentively.

2. Write ten sentences in which the simple predicate is modified by an infinitive (§§ 323, 477); by an adverbial objective or by a phrase containing one (§§ 109, 478); by a nominative absolute (§§ 345, 479); by an indirect object (§§ 105, 480); by a cognate object (§§ 108, 481).

3. Point out the complementary infinitives and the infinitives of purpose in Exercise 40, and tell what verb each modifies.

1. Point out the complements and describe each (as direct object, predicate nominative, etc.). Analyze the sentences.

1. The most amazing wonder of the deep is its unfathomable cruelty. — CONRAD. 2. Music is Love in search of a word. — LANIER. 3. The destination of the fleet was still a matter of conjecture. 4. The reports from the front made Washington anxious. 5. Plato says that the punishment which the wise suffer who refuse to take part in the government, is, to live under the government of worse men. — EMERSON. 6. I thought your book an imposture; I think it an imposture still. — JOHNSON. 7. Moses chose able men out of all Israel and made them heads over the people. 8. The old gray porter raised his torch. 9. This you will call impudence. 10. Firm and irrevocable is my doom. 11. In return for mere board and lodging, Topham became Mr. Starkey's assistant. 12. It was they who attacked us.

13. Serene will be our days and bright. 14. Warwick thought the situation awkward, but he held his peace. 15. If there were not too great a risk of the dispersion of their fleet, I should think their putting to sea a mere manœuvre to deceive. — IRVING. 16. I thought "Aladdin" capital fun. — STEVENSON. 17. The faces of the father and mother had a sober gladness; the children laughed; the eldest daughter was the image of Happiness at seventeen ; and the aged grandmother, who sat knitting in the warmest place, was the image of Happiness grown old. 18. His stories were what frightened people worst of all. 19. The old man was nervous, fidgety, and very pale. 20. I am growing old, the grey hairs thicken upon me, my joints are less supple, and, in mind as well as body, I am less enterprising than in former years. — SOUTHEY. 21. I was uneasy about my letter 22. Confidence is almost everything in war. 23. He thinks me a troublesome fellow.

24. At the end of this strange season, Burns gloomily sums up his gains and losses. 25. Little fire grows great with little wind. — SHAKSPERE. 26. As he rose to walk, he found himself stiff in the joints. 27. Noise had been my native element. 28. I caught tantalizing glimpses of green fields, shut from me by dull lines of high-spiked palings. 29. One house in a back street was bright with the cheerful glare of lights.

2. Write ten simple sentences, each containing the direct object of a verb ; a predicate objective ; a predicate nominative : a predicate adjective. Analyze your sentences.

## EXERCISE 62

### (§§ 494–497, pp. 205–206)

1. Point out any modifiers of complements in the sentences called for in Exercise 61, 2. Introduce other modifiers of complements if you can without injuring the sentences.

2. Write sentences similar to those in § 492, taking care to include in each a complement modified.

3. Write ten sentences, each containing a substantive complement modified by an adjective clause (§ 496); an adjective complement modified by an adverbial clause (§ 497). Analyze your sentences.

4. Point out all modifiers of complements in Exercises 12 and 22.

5. Analyze the sentences in § 495.


## EXERCISE 63

### (§§ 498–500, pp. 207–208)

1. Write ten sentences illustrating adjectives (or adjective phrases) modified either by adverbs or by groups of words used adverbially.

2. Write ten sentences, each containing a possessive noun modified; an appositive modified; an adverbial phrase modified.

3. Write ten sentences illustrating the use of adjective or adverbial clauses as modifiers of modifiers.

4. Analyze the sentences in § 498.


## EXERCISE 64

### (§§ 501–503, p. 209)

Point out the independent elements. Tell whether each is an interjection, a vocative (nominative by direct address), an exclamatory nominative, or a parenthetical expression. Analyze the sentences.

1. The king, Melfort said, was determined to be severe. 2. O Mary, go and call the cattle home. 3. Pardon me, my dear fellow. 4. Between ourselves, I shall not be sorry to have a quiet evening. 5. Knowledge, indeed, and science express purely intellectual ideas. — NEWMAN. 6. Oh ! oh ! pictures don't pay. 7. To make a long story short, the company broke up. 8. True, our friend is already in his teens. 9. To use a ready-made similitude, we might liken universal history to a magic web. — CARLYLE. 10. Poor fellows ! they only did as they were ordered, I suppose. 11. The world, as we said, has been unjust to him. 12. Therefore, good Brutus, be prepared to hear.

13. Peace ! count the clock. 14. Excuse, no doubt, is in readiness for such omission. 15. The lord — for so I understood he was — looked at me with an air of surprise. 16. Lo, Cæsar is afraid. 17. Delay not, Cæsar ; read it instantly. 18. My counsel, I need not say, made full use of this hint. 19. My small services, you remember, were of no use. 20. I knew — one knows everything in dreams — that they had been slain. 21. I knew it, I say, to be a fallacy. 22. Liberty ! freedom ! tyranny is dead ! 23. Stay, ho ! and let us hear Mark Antony.

### EXERCISE 65

#### (§§ 504-523, pp. 210-219)

1. Analyze the simple sentences in § 509; the compound sentences in § 511; the complex sentences in § 512; the compound complex sentences in §§ 514-515.

2. Study the examples in §§ 517-523, and explain their structure orally. Tell whether the various subordinate clauses are simple, compound, or complex, and why. Give the construction of each. Analyze the sentences.

3. Construct five complex sentences on the principle of § 517; of § 520; of § 521; of § 522.

### EXERCISE 66

#### (§§ 524-526, pp. 220-223)

1. Study the sentences in §§ 525-526 until you can explain their structure.

2. Find, in some good English or American author, ten sentences of considerable length and explain their structure.

### EXERCISE 67

(§§ 527–533, pp. 224–226)

**1.** Analyze the sentences in § 528. Explain the ellipsis in each sentence.

**2.** Supply the word or words omitted in each of the elliptical sentences in § 533 (p. 226). Explain the ellipsis in each sentence.

**3.** Analyze the sentences in § 533.

**4.** Write five sentences illustrating each of the following kinds of ellipsis : — (1) the subject of an imperative; (2) a relative pronoun; (3) the conjunction *that;* (4) the copula and its subject with *while, when, though, if;* (5) ellipsis in a clause with *as* or *than.*

### EXERCISE 68

(§§ 448–526, pp. 183–223)

The following compound, complex, and compound complex sentences will give further practice in analysis and in study of the relations of clauses.

**1.** Deerslayer hesitated a single instant ere he plunged into the bushes. **2.** The mind of man is like a clock that is always running down and requires to be as constantly wound up. — HAZLITT. **3.** He became sensible that his life was still in imminent peril. **4.** A young author is apt to run into a confusion of mixed metaphors, which leave the sense disjointed, and distract the imagination. — GOLDSMITH. **5.** Everybody kept his head as best he might and scrambled for whatever he could get. **6.** The dialogue had been held in so very low a whisper that not a word of it had reached the young lady's ears. **7.** The captain screwed his lips up, and drummed on the table, but he did not speak. **8.** Poor Andrew Fern had heard that his townsman's sloop had been captured by a privateer. **9.** Through the grounds we went, and very pretty I thought them. **10.** He sometimes made doleful complaint that there were no stagecoaches, nowadays.

**11.** Lights gleamed in the distance, and people were already astir. **12.** That few men celebrated for theoretic wisdom live with conformity to their precepts, must be readily confessed. — JOHNSON. **13.** Down went Pew with a cry that rang high into the night. **14.** Pluck the dog off, lest he throttle him. **15.** I knew that the worst of men have their good points. **16.** A rumor spread that the enemy was approaching in great force. **17.** Mr. Henry went and walked at the low end of the hall without reply ; for he had an excellent gift of silence. **18.** It is a bright brisk morning, and the loaded wagons are rolling cheerfully past my window. **19.** The musician was an old gray-headed negro, who had been the itinerant orchestra of the neighborhood for more than half a century. **20.** After he had waited three hours, the general's patience was exhausted, and, as he learned that the Mexicans were busy in preparations for defence, he made immediate dispositions for the assault. — PRESCOTT.

**21.** As I rode along near the coast, I kept a very sharp lookout in the lanes and woods. **22.** Every man desires to live long, but no man would be old. — SWIFT. **23.** If my face had been pale the moment before, it now glowed almost to burning. **24.** The sentinels who paced the ramparts announced that the vanguard of the hostile army was in sight. **25.** Her heart was happy and her courage rose. **26.** There is a report that Clifford is to be secretary. **27.** The season of winter, when, from the shortness of the daylight, labor becomes impossible, is in Zetland the time of revel, feasting, and merriment. **28.** Every log which is carried past us by the current has come from an undiscovered country. **29.** The fair heavens shone over the windy blue seas, and the green island of Ulva lay basking in the sunlight. **30.** The greatest event was, that the Miss Jenkynses had purchased a new carpet for the drawing room. **31.** My grandfather made a bow to the motley assemblage as he entered. **32.** Talk to a man about himself, and he is generally captivated.

**33.** Pen was as elated as if somebody had left him a fortune. **34.** When the morning dawned, the king gazed with admiration at the city, which he hoped soon to add to his dominions. — IRVING. **35.** No one doubts that the sloth and the ant-eater, the kangaroo and the opossum, the tiger and the badger, the tapir and the rhinoceros, are respectively members of the same orders. — HUXLEY. **36.** The traveller, a man of middle age, wrapped in a gray frieze cloak, quickened his pace when he had reached the outskirts of the town, for a gloomy extent of nearly four miles lay between him and his home. **37.** It was a scene on which I had often looked down, but where I had never before beheld a human figure. **38.** He found that he had undertaken a task which was beyond his power. **39.** In the Dutch garden is a fine bronze bust of Napoleon, which Lord Holland put up in 1817, while Napoleon was a prisoner at Saint Helena.

**40.** The girl's was not one of those natures which are most attracted by what is strange and exceptional in human character. **41.** Mrs. Pendennis was sure that he would lead her dear boy into mischief, if Pen went to the same college with him. **42.** I had been some time at sea before I became aware of the fact that hearing plays a perceptible part in gauging the force of the wind. **43.** The Macedonian conqueror, when he was once invited to hear a man that sang like a nightingale, replied with contempt, that he had heard the nightingale herself; and the same treatment must every man expect, whose praise is that he imitates another. —JOHNSON. **44.** Tie a couple of strings across a board and set it in your window, and you have an instrument which no artist's harp can rival. — EMERSON. **45.** I was on the point of asking what part of the country he had chosen for his retreat. **46.** That no man can lawfully promise what he cannot lawfully do is a self-evident proposition. — MACKINTOSH.

**47.** How far the governor contributed towards the expenses of the outfit is not very clear. **48.** The next epoch in the history of Russia was that of Peter the Great, whose genius overcame the obstacles consequent on the remoteness of its situation, and opened to its people the career of European industry, arts, and arms.— ALISON. **49.** As the chase lengthens, the sportsmen drop off, till at last the foremost huntsman is left alone, and his horse, overcome with fatigue, stumbles and dies in a rocky valley. — JEFFREY. **50.** The Lowland knight, though startled, repeats his defiance; and Sir Roderick, respecting his valor, by a signal dismisses his men to their concealment, and assures him anew of his safety. **51.** I stood awe-struck — I cannot tell how long — watching how the live flame-snakes crept and hissed, and leapt and roared, and rushed in long horizontal jets from stack to stack before the howling wind, and fastened their fiery talons on the barn-eaves, and swept over the peaked roofs, and hurled themselves in fiery flakes into the yard beyond. —- KINGSLEY. **52.** When I was at Grand Cairo, I picked up several Oriental manuscripts, which I have still by me. — ADDISON. **53.** Often have I wondered at the temerity of my father, who, in spite of an habitual general respect which we all in common manifested towards him, would venture now and then to stand up against him in some argument touching their youthful days. — LAMB. **54.** By all means begin your folio; even if the doctor does not give you a year, even if he hesitates about a month, make one brave push and see what can be accomplished in a week. — STEVENSON.

# APPENDIX

## LISTS OF VERBS

In the first list, only such verb forms are given as are indisputably correct in accordance with the best prose usage of the present day. The pupil may feel perfectly safe, therefore, in using the forms registered in this list.[1]

A few verbs (marked *) which are seldom or never used in ordinary language are included in this list. These have various irregularities. A few verbs are partly strong and partly weak.

Weak verbs are printed in italics.

For the modal auxiliaries, see page 299.

### I

| PRESENT TENSE | PAST TENSE | PAST PARTICIPLE |
|---|---|---|
| abide | abode | abode |
| am (*subjunc.*, be) | was | been |
| arise | arose | arisen |
| awake | awoke, *awaked* | *awaked* |
| bear | bore | borne, born [2] |
| beat | beat | beaten |
| beget | begot | begotten |
| begin | began | begun |
| behold | beheld | beheld |

---

[1] The omission of a form from the list, then, does not necessarily indicate that it is wrong or even objectionable. There is considerable diversity of usage with regard to the strong verbs, and to state the facts at length would take much space. An attempt to include archaic, poetical, and rare forms in the same list with the usual modern forms is sure to mislead the pupil. Hence the list here presented is confined to forms about whose correctness there can be no difference of opinion. Archaic and poetical tense-forms are treated later (pp. 297-299).

[2] *Born* is used only in the passive sense of " born into the world."

| Present Tense | Past Tense | Past Participle |
|---|---|---|
| *bend* | *bent* | *bent* |
| *bereave* | *bereft, bereaved* | *bereft, bereaved* [1] |
| *beseech* | *besought* | *besought* |
| *bet* | *bet* | *bet* |
| bid (command) | bade | bidden |
| bid (money) | bid | bid |
| bind | bound | bound |
| bite | bit | bitten |
| *bleed* | *bled* | *bled* |
| *bless* (see p. 298) | | |
| blow | blew | blown |
| break | broke | broken |
| *breed* | *bred* | *bred* |
| *bring* | *brought* | *brought* |
| *build* | *built* | *built* |
| *burn* (see p. 298) | | |
| burst | burst | burst |
| *buy* | *bought* | *bought* |
| *cast* | *cast* | *cast* |
| *catch* | *caught* | *caught* |
| chide | chid | chidden |
| choose | chose | chosen |
| *cleave (split) [2] | *cleft, clove* | *cleft, cleaved* (cloven, *adj.*) |
| cling | clung | clung |
| come | came | come |
| *cost* | *cost* | *cost* |
| *creep* | *crept* | *crept* |
| *crow* (see p. 299) | | |
| *curse* (see p. 298) | | |
| cut | cut | cut |
| *dare* (see p. 299) | | |
| *deal* | *dealt* | *dealt* |
| dig | dug | dug |
| do | did | done |
| draw | drew | drawn |

[1] The adjective form is *bereaved:* as, "The bereaved father."
[2] *Cleave,* "to adhere," has *cleaved* in both the past tense and the past participle, and also an archaic past form *clave.*

| PRESENT TENSE | PAST TENSE | PAST PARTICIPLE |
|---|---|---|
| *dream* (see p. 298) | | |
| *dress* (see p. 298) | | |
| drink | drank | drunk (drunken, *adj.*) |
| drive | drove | driven |
| *dwell* | *dwelt* | *dwelt* |
| eat | ate | eaten |
| *engrave* (see p. 299) | | |
| fall | fell | fallen |
| *feed* | *fed* | *fed* |
| *feel* | *felt* | *felt* |
| fight | fought | fought |
| find | found | found |
| *flee* | *fled* | *fled* |
| fling | flung | flung |
| fly | flew | flown |
| forbear | forbore | forborne |
| forget | forgot | forgotten |
| forsake | forsook | forsaken |
| freeze | froze | frozen |
| *freight* (see p. 299) | | |
| get | got | got [1] |
| *gird* (see p. 298) | | |
| give | gave | given |
| go | *went* | gone |
| *grave* (see p. 299) | | |
| grind | ground | ground |
| grow | grew | grown |
| hang | hung, *hanged* [2] | hung, *hanged* [2] |
| *have* | *had* | *had* |
| *hear* | *heard* | *heard* |
| heave | hove, *heaved* [3] | hove, *heaved* [3] |
| *hew* | *hewed* | hewn |

[1] The archaic participle *gotten* is used in the compounds *begotten* and *forgotten*, and as an adjective ("*ill-gotten* gains"). Many good speakers also use it instead of the past participle *got*, but *got* is the accepted modern form.

[2] *Hanged* is used only of execution by hanging.

[3] Usage varies with the context. We say, "The crew *hove* the cargo overboard," but NOT "She *hove* a sigh."

| Present Tense | Past Tense | Past Participle |
|---|---|---|
| hide | hid | hidden |
| *hit* | *hit* | *hit* |
| hold | held | held |
| *hurt* | *hurt* | *hurt* |
| *keep* | *kept* | *kept* |
| *kneel* (see p. 298) | | |
| *knit* (see p. 298) | | |
| know | knew | known |
| *lade* [1] | *laded* | *laded*, laden |
| *lay* | *laid* | *laid* |
| *lead* | *led* | *led* |
| *learn* (see p. 298) | | |
| *leave* | *left* | *left* |
| *lend* | *lent* | *lent* |
| let | let | let |
| lie (recline) [2] | lay | lain |
| *light* | *lighted* or *lit* [3] | *lighted* or *lit* [3] |
| *lose* | *lost* | *lost* |
| *make* | *made* | *made* |
| *mean* | *meant* | *meant* |
| *meet* | *met* | *met* |
| *mow* (see p. 299) | | |
| *pay* | *paid* | *paid* |
| *pen* (shut up) (see p. 298) | | |
| *put* | *put* | *put* |
| *quit* (see p. 298) | | |
| read | rĕad | rĕad |
| *reave | *reft*, *reaved* | *reft*, *reaved* |
| reeve | rove | rove |
| *rend* | *rent* | *rent* |
| *rid* | *rid* | *rid* |
| ride | rode | ridden |

[1] *Load* has *loaded* in both the past tense and the past participle. *Laden* is sometimes used as the past participle of *load*.

[2] *Lie*, "to tell a falsehood," has *lied* in both the past tense and the past participle.

[3] So both *light*, "to kindle," and *light*, "to alight." The verb *alight* has usually *alighted* in both the past tense and the past participle.

| Present Tense | Past Tense | Past Participle |
|---|---|---|
| ring | rang | rung |
| rise | rose | risen |
| *rive | *rived* | riven, *rived* |
| run | ran | run |
| *say* | *said* | *said* |
| see | saw | seen |
| *seek* | *sought* | *sought* |
| *seethe (*transitive*) [1] | sod, *seethed* | *seethed* (sodden, *adj.*) |
| *sell* | *sold* | *sold* |
| *send* | *sent* | *sent* |
| *set* | *set* | *set* |
| *sew* (see p. 299) | | |
| shake | shook | shaken |
| *shape* (see p. 299) | | |
| *shave* | *shaved* | *shaved* (shaven, *adj.*) |
| *shear* (see p. 299) | | |
| *shed* | *shed* | *shed* |
| shine | shone | shone |
| *shoe* | *shod* | *shod* |
| shoot | shot | shot |
| *show* | *showed* | shown |
| *shred* (see p. 298) | | |
| shrink | shrank | shrunk (shrunken, *adj.*) |
| *shrive | shrove, *shrived* | shriven, *shrived* |
| *shut* | *shut* | *shut* |
| sing | sang | sung |
| sink | sank | sunk |
| sit | sat | sat |
| slay | slew | slain |
| *sleep* | *slept* | *slept* |
| slide | slid | slid, slidden |
| sling | slung | slung |
| slink | slunk | slunk |
| *slit* | *slit* | *slit* |
| *smell* (see p. 298) | | |

[1] *Seethe*, intransitive, has usually *seethed* in both the past tense and the past participle. It is in rather common literary use.

| Present Tense | Past Tense | Past Participle |
|---|---|---|
| smite | smote | smitten |
| *sow* | *sowed* | *sowed*, sown |
| speak | spoke | spoken |
| *speed* (see p. 298) | | |
| *spell* (see p. 299) | | |
| *spend* | *spent* | *spent* |
| *spill* (see p. 299) | | |
| spin | spun | spun |
| spit | spit | spit |
| *split* | *split* | *split* |
| *spoil* (see p. 299) | | |
| *spread* | *spread* | *spread* |
| spring | sprang | sprung |
| stand | stood | stood |
| stave | stove, *staved* | stove, *staved* |
| *stay* (see p. 299) | | |
| steal | stole | stolen |
| stick | stuck | stuck |
| sting | stung | stung |
| stink | stunk | stunk |
| *strew* | *strewed* | strewn |
| stride | strode | stridden |
| strike | struck | struck (stricken, *adj.*) [1] |
| string | strung | strung |
| strive | strove | striven |
| swear | swore | sworn |
| *sweat* (see p. 299) | | |
| *sweep* | *swept* | *swept* |
| *swell* | *swelled* | *swelled*, swollen |
| swim | swam | swum |
| swing | swung | swung |
| take | took | taken |
| *teach* | *taught* | *taught* |
| tear | tore | torn |
| *tell* | *told* | *told* |

---

[1] *Stricken* is also used as a participle in a figurative sense. Thus we say, "The community was *stricken* with pestilence," — but "The dog was *struck* with a stick."

| PRESENT TENSE | PAST TENSE | PAST PARTICIPLE |
|---|---|---|
| *think* | *thought* | *thought* |
| thrive | throve, *thrived* | thriven, *thrived* |
| throw | threw | thrown |
| *thrust* | *thrust* | *thrust* |
| tread | trod | trodden |
| wake | woke, *waked* | woke, *waked* |
| *wax* (grow) (see p. 299) | | |
| wear | wore | worn |
| weave | wove | woven |
| *wed* (see p. 299) | | |
| *weep* | *wept* | *wept* |
| *wet* | *wet* | *wet* |
| win | won | won |
| wind | wound | wound |
| wring | wrung | wrung |
| write | wrote | written |

*Bear, break, drive, get* (*beget, forget*), *speak, spin, stink, swear, tear,* have an archaic past tense in *a : bare, brake, drave, gat, spake,* etc.

*Beat, beget* (*forget*), *bite, break, forsake, hide, ride, shake, speak, weave, write,* and some other verbs have archaic forms of the past participle like those of the past tense. The participles in *en,* however, are now the accepted forms. *Chid* and *trod* are common participial forms.

*Begin, drink, ring, shrink, sing, sink, spring, swim,* often have in poetry a *u*-form (*begun, sung,* etc.) in the past tense as well as in the past participle. This form (though good *old* English)[1] should be avoided in modern speech.

*Bend, beseech, bet, build, burst, catch, dwell, rend, split, wet,* have archaic or less usual forms in *ed : bended, beseeched, betted,* etc. *Builded* is common in the proverbial " He *builded* better than he knew." *Bursted* is common as an adjective : " a *bursted* bubble."

*Bid,* " to command," has sometimes *bid* in both the past tense and the past participle ; *bid,* " to offer money," has these forms regularly.

*Blend, leap, lean,* have usually *blended, leaped, leaned ;* but *blent, leapt, leant* are not uncommon.

*Clothe* has commonly *clothed ;* but *clad* is common in literary use, and is regular in the adjectives *well-clad, ill-clad* (for which ordinary speech has substituted *well-dressed, badly* or *poorly dressed*).

---

[1] It is a remnant of the old past plural. In Anglo-Saxon the principal parts of *begin* were: present, *beginne ;* past, *began ;* past plural, *begunnon ;* past participle, *begunnen.*

*Dive* has *dived;* but *dove* (an old form) is common in America.

*Plead* has past tense and past participle *pleaded.* *Plead* (pronounced *plĕd*) is avoided by careful writers and speakers.

*Prove* has past tense and past participle *proved.* The past participle *proven* should be avoided.

*Work* has past tense and past participle *worked.* *Wrought* in the past tense and the past participle is archaic, but is also modern as an adjective (as in *wrought iron*).

Some verbs have rare or archaic weak forms alongside of the strong forms; thus *digged, shined,* past tense and past participle of *dig, shine; showed,* past participle of *show.*

*Ate* and *eaten* are preferred to *eat* (pronounced *ĕt*).

*Quoth,* "said," is an old strong past tense. The compound *bequeath* has *bequeathed* only.

Miscellaneous archaisms are the past tenses *sate* for *sat, trode* for *trod, spat* for *spit;* also *writ* for *wrote* and *written, rid* for *rode* and *ridden, strewed* and *strown* for *strewn.*

## II

The following verbs vary between *ed* and *t (d)* in the past tense and the past participle. In some of them, this variation is a mere difference of spelling. In writing, the *ed* forms are preferred in most cases; in speaking, the *t* forms are very common.

| | |
|---|---|
| bless | blessed, blest [1] |
| burn | burned, burnt [2] |
| curse | cursed, curst [1] |
| dare | dared (*less commonly,* durst) |
| dream | dreamed, dreamt |
| dress | dressed, drest |
| gird | girded, girt [2] |
| kneel | kneeled, knelt [2] |
| knit | knit, knitted [2] |
| learn | learned, learnt [3] |
| pen (shut up) | penned, pent [2] |
| quit | quitted, quit [2] |
| shred | shredded, shred [2] |
| smell | smelled, smelt [2] |
| speed | sped, speeded [2] |

[1] The adjectives are usually pronounced *blessèd, cursèd.* Compare also the adjective *accursèd.*

[2] Both forms are in good use.

[3] Both forms are in good use. The adjective is pronounced *learnèd.*

| | |
|---|---|
| spell | spelled, spelt |
| spill | spilled, spilt [1] |
| spoil | spoiled, spoilt [1] |
| stay | stayed, staid |
| sweat | sweated, sweat [1] |
| wed | wedded ( *p.p. also* wed) [1] |

## III

The following verbs have regular *ed* forms in modern prose, but in poetry and the high style sometimes show archaic forms.

| PRESENT TENSE | PAST TENSE | PAST PARTICIPLE |
|---|---|---|
| crow | crowed, crew | crowed, crown |
| freight | freighted | freighted, fraught ( *figurative* ) |
| grave | graved | graved, graven |
| engrave | engraved | engraved, engraven |
| mow | mowed | mowed, mown |
| sew | sewed | sewed, sewn |
| shape | shaped | shaped, shapen |
| shear | sheared, shore | sheared, shorn |
| wax (grow) | waxed | waxed, waxen |

## IV

The present tense of *may, can, shall,* is an old strong past. Hence the first and third persons singular are alike : — *I may, he may.* The actual past tenses of these verbs are weak forms : — *might, could, should. Must* is the weak past tense of an obsolete *mōt,* and is almost always used as a present tense (§ 292).

*Dare* and *owe* originally belonged to this class. *Owe* has become a regular weak verb, except for the peculiar past tense *ought,* which is used in a present sense (see § 293) ; *dare* has in the third person *dare* or *dares,* and in the past *dared,* more rarely *durst.* The archaic *wot* "know," past *wist,* also belongs to this class. *Will* is inflected like *shall,* having *will* in the first and third singular, *wilt* in the second singular, and *would* in the past.

---

[1] Both forms are in good use.

## CONJUGATION OF THE VERB *TO BE*

### INDICATIVE MOOD

#### PRESENT TENSE

| SINGULAR | PLURAL |
|---|---|
| 1. I am. | We are. |
| 2. Thou art. | You are. |
| 3. He is. | They are. |

#### PAST TENSE

| | |
|---|---|
| 1. I was. | We were. |
| 2. Thou wast (wert). | You were. |
| 3. He was. | They were. |

#### FUTURE TENSE

| | |
|---|---|
| 1. I shall be. | We shall be. |
| 2. Thou wilt be. | You will be. |
| 3. He will be. | They will be. |

#### PERFECT (OR PRESENT PERFECT) TENSE

| | |
|---|---|
| 1. I have been. | We have been. |
| 2. Thou hast been. | You have been. |
| 3. He has been. | They have been. |

#### PLUPERFECT (OR PAST PERFECT) TENSE

| | |
|---|---|
| 1. I had been. | We had been. |
| 2. Thou hadst been. | You had been. |
| 3. He had been. | They had been. |

#### FUTURE PERFECT TENSE

| | |
|---|---|
| 1. I shall have been. | We shall have been. |
| 2. Thou wilt have been | You will have been. |
| 3. He will have been. | They will have been. |

## SUBJUNCTIVE MOOD

### PRESENT TENSE

| SINGULAR | PLURAL |
| --- | --- |
| 1. If I be. | If we be. |
| 2. If thou be. | If you be. |
| 3. If he be. | If they be. |

### PAST TENSE

| | |
| --- | --- |
| 1. If I were. | If we were. |
| 2. If thou wert. | If you were. |
| 3. If he were. | If they were. |

### PERFECT (OR PRESENT PERFECT) TENSE

| | |
| --- | --- |
| 1. If I have been. | If we have been. |
| 2. If thou have been. | If you have been. |
| 3. If he have been. | If they have been. |

### PLUPERFECT (OR PAST PERFECT) TENSE

| | |
| --- | --- |
| 1. If I had been. | If we had been. |
| 2. If thou hadst been. | If you had been. |
| 3. If he had been. | If they had been. |

IMPERATIVE MOOD. *Present. Sing. and Pl.* Be [thou *or* you].
INFINITIVE. *Present,* to be ; *Perfect,* to have been.
PARTICIPLES. *Present,* being ; *Past,* been ; *Perfect,* having been

## CONJUGATION OF THE VERB *TO STRIKE*

### *ACTIVE VOICE*

#### INDICATIVE MOOD

##### PRESENT TENSE

| | |
| --- | --- |
| 1. I strike. | We strike. |
| 2. Thou strikest. | You strike. |
| 3. He strikes. | They strike. |

## Past Tense

| SINGULAR | PLURAL |
|----------|--------|
| 1. I struck. | We struck. |
| 2. Thou struckest. | You struck. |
| 3. He struck. | They struck. |

## Future Tense

| | |
|--|--|
| 1. I shall strike. | We shall strike. |
| 2. Thou wilt strike. | You will strike. |
| 3. He will strike. | They will strike. |

## Perfect (or Present Perfect) Tense

| | |
|--|--|
| 1. I have struck. | We have struck. |
| 2. Thou hast struck. | You have struck. |
| 3. He has struck. | They have struck. |

## Pluperfect (or Past Perfect) Tense

| | |
|--|--|
| 1. I had struck. | We had struck. |
| 2. Thou hadst struck. | You had struck. |
| 3. He had struck. | They had struck. |

## Future Perfect Tense

| | |
|--|--|
| 1. I shall have struck. | We shall have struck. |
| 2. Thou wilt have struck. | You will have struck. |
| 3. He will have struck. | They will have struck |

## SUBJUNCTIVE MOOD

### Present Tense

| | |
|--|--|
| 1. If I strike. | If we strike. |
| 2. If thou strike. | If you strike. |
| 3. If he strike. | If they strike. |

### Past Tense

| | |
|--|--|
| 1. If I struck. | If we struck. |
| 2. If thou struck. | If you struck. |
| 3. If he struck. | If they struck. |

### PERFECT (OR PRESENT PERFECT) TENSE

| SINGULAR | PLURAL |
|---|---|
| **1.** If I have struck. | If we have struck. |
| **2.** If thou have struck. | If you have struck. |
| **3.** If he have struck. | If they have struck. |

### PLUPERFECT (OR PAST PERFECT) TENSE

| | |
|---|---|
| **1.** If I had struck. | If we had struck. |
| **2.** If thou hadst struck. | If you had struck. |
| **3.** If he had struck. | If they had struck. |

IMPERATIVE MOOD. *Present. Sing. and Pl.* Strike [thou *or* you]
INFINITIVE. *Present*, to strike; *Perfect*, to have struck.
PARTICIPLE. *Present*, striking; *Past*, struck; *Perfect*, having struck

## *PASSIVE VOICE*

### INDICATIVE MOOD

#### PRESENT TENSE

| | |
|---|---|
| **1.** I am struck. | We are struck. |
| **2.** Thou art struck. | You are struck. |
| **3.** He is struck. | They are struck. |

#### PAST TENSE

| | |
|---|---|
| **1.** I was struck. | We were struck. |
| **2.** Thou wast (*or* wert) struck. | You were struck. |
| **3.** He was struck. | They were struck. |

#### FUTURE TENSE

| | |
|---|---|
| **1.** I shall be struck. | We shall be struck. |
| **2.** Thou wilt be struck. | You will be struck. |
| **3.** He will be struck. | They will be struck. |

#### PERFECT (OR PRESENT PERFECT) TENSE

| | |
|---|---|
| **1.** I have been struck. | We have been struck. |
| **2.** Thou hast been struck. | You have been struck. |
| **3.** He has been struck. | They have been struck. |

## Pluperfect (or Past Perfect) Tense

| SINGULAR | PLURAL |
|---|---|
| 1. I had been struck. | We had been struck. |
| 2. Thou hadst been struck. | You had been struck. |
| 3. He had been struck. | They had been struck. |

## Future Perfect Tense

| | |
|---|---|
| 1. I shall have been struck. | We shall have been struck. |
| 2. Thou wilt have been struck. | You will have been struck. |
| 3. He will have been struck. | They will have been struck |

## SUBJUNCTIVE MOOD

### Present Tense

| | |
|---|---|
| 1. If I be struck. | If we be struck. |
| 2. If thou be struck. | If you be struck. |
| 3. If he be struck. | If they be struck. |

### Past Tense

| | |
|---|---|
| 1. If I were struck. | If we were struck. |
| 2. If thou wert struck. | If you were struck. |
| 3. If he were struck. | If they were struck. |

### Perfect (or Present Perfect) Tense

| | |
|---|---|
| 1. If I have been struck. | If we have been struck. |
| 2. If thou have been struck. | If you have been struck. |
| 3. If he have been struck. | If they have been struck. |

### Pluperfect (or Past Perfect) Tense

| | |
|---|---|
| 1. If I had been struck. | If we had been struck. |
| 2. If thou hadst been struck. | If you had been struck. |
| 3. If he had been struck. | If they had been struck. |

**Imperative Mood.** *Present.* *Sing. and Pl.* Be [thou *or* you] struck.

**Infinitive.** *Present,* to be struck; *Perfect,* to have been struck.

**Participles.** *Present,* being struck; *Past,* struck; *Perfect,* having been struck.

## USE OF CAPITAL LETTERS

1. Every sentence begins with a capital letter.

2. Every line of poetry begins with a capital letter.

3. The first word of every direct quotation begins with a capital letter.

NOTE. This rule does not apply to quoted fragments of sentences.

4. Every proper noun or abbreviation of a proper noun begins with a capital letter.

5. Most adjectives derived from proper nouns begin with capital letters; as, — *American, Indian, Swedish, Spenserian.*

NOTE. Some adjectives derived from proper nouns have ceased to be closely associated in thought with the nouns from which they come, and therefore begin with small letters. Thus, — voltaic, galvanic, mesmeric, maudlin, stentorian.

6. Every title attached to the name of a person begins with a capital letter.

| | |
|---|---|
| *Mr.* Thomas Smith | C. J. Adams, *M.D.* |
| John Wilson, *Esq.* | *President* Grant |
| *Miss* Allerton | *Professor* Whitney |
| *Dr.* F. E. Wilson | *Sir* Walter Raleigh |

7. In titles of books, etc., the first word, as well as every important word that follows, begins with a capital letter.

8. The interjection *O* and the pronoun *I* are always written in capital letters.

9. Personal pronouns referring to the Deity are often capitalized.

NOTE. Usage varies: the personal pronouns are commonly capitalized when they refer to the Deity, the relatives less frequently. The rule is often disregarded altogether when its observance would result in a multitude of capitals, as in the Bible and in many hymn books and works of theology.

10. Common nouns and adjectives often begin with capital letters when they designate the topics or main points of definitions or similar statements. Such capitals are called *emphatic* (or *topical*) *capitals.*

NOTE. Emphatic (or topical) capitals are analogous to capitals in the titles of books (see Rule 7), but their use is not obligatory. They are especially common in text-books and other elementary manuals.

## RULES OF PUNCTUATION[1]

The common marks of punctuation are the period, the interrogation point, the exclamation point, the comma, the semicolon, the colon, the dash, marks of parenthesis, and quotation marks. The hyphen and the apostrophe may be conveniently treated along with marks of punctuation.

### I

1. The period, the interrogation point, and the exclamation point are used at the end of sentences. Every complete sentence must be followed by one of these three marks.

The end of a declarative or an imperative sentence is marked by a period. But a declarative or an imperative sentence that is likewise exclamatory may be followed by an exclamation point instead of a period.

The end of a direct question is marked by an interrogation point.

An exclamatory sentence in the form of an indirect question is followed by an exclamation point; as, — "How absolute the knave is!"

2. A period is used after an abbreviation.

3. An exclamation point is used after an exclamatory word or phrase.

NOTE. This rule is not absolute. Most interjections take the exclamation point. With other words and with phrases, usage differs; if strong feeling is expressed, the exclamation point is commonly used, but too many such marks deface the page.

### II

The comma is used —

1. After a noun (or a phrase) of direct address (a *vocative nominative*). Thus, —

John, tell me the truth.
Little boy, what is your name?

NOTE. If the noun is exclamatory, an exclamation point may be used instead of a comma.

---

[1] The main rules of punctuation are well fixed and depend on important distinctions in sentence structure and consequently in thought. In detail, however, there is much variety of usage, and care should be taken not to insist on such uniformity in the pupils' practice as is not found in the printed books which they use. If young writers can be induced to indicate the ends of their sentences properly, much has been accomplished.

**2.** Before a direct quotation in a sentence. Thus,—

The cry ran through the ranks, "Are we never to move forward?"

NOTE. When the quotation is long or formal, a colon, or a colon and a dash, may be used instead of a comma, especially with the words *as follows*.

**3.** After a direct quotation when this is the subject or the object of a following verb. Thus,—

"They are coming; the attack will be made on the center," said Lord Fitzroy Somerset.

"I see it," was the cool reply of the duke.

NOTE. If the quotation ends with an interrogation point or an exclamation point, no comma is used.

**4.** To separate words, or groups of words, arranged in a coördinate series, when these are not connected by *and*, *or*, or *nor*.

If the conjunction is used to connect the last two members of the series but omitted with the others, the comma may be used before the conjunction.

I found two saws, an axe, and a hammer.

They were so shy, so subtle, and so swift of foot, that it was difficult to come at them.

It would make the reader pity me to tell what odd, misshapen, ugly things I made.

They groaned, they stirred, they all uprose.

NOTE 1. Commas may be used even when conjunctions are expressed, if the members of the series consist of several words, or if the writer wishes to emphasize their distinctness.

NOTE 2. Clauses in a series are commonly separated by semicolons unless they are short and simple (see pp. 309–310).

**5.** To set off words and phrases out of their regular order. Thus,—

Seated on her accustomed chair, with her usual air of apathy and want of interest in what surrounded her, she seemed now and then mechanically to resume the motion of twirling her spindle. — SCOTT.

**6.** To separate a long subject from the verb of the predicate. Thus,—

To have passed them over in an historical sketch of my literary life and opinions, would have seemed to me like the denial of a debt. — COLERIDGE.

**7.** To set off an appositive noun or an appositive adjective, with its modifiers. Thus,—

I have had the most amusing letter from Hogg, the Ettrick minstrel.

There was an impression upon the public mind, natural enough from the continually augmenting velocity of the mail, but quite erroneous, that an outside seat on this class of carriages was a post of danger. — DE QUINCEY.

NOTE 1. Many participial and other adjective phrases come under this head. Thus, —

The genius, seeing me indulge myself on this melancholy prospect, told me I had dwelt long enough upon it. — ADDISON.

NOTE 2. If a noun and its appositive are so closely connected as to form one idea, no comma is used. Thus, —

My friend Jackson lives in San Francisco.

NOTE 3. An intensive pronoun (*myself*, etc.) is not separated by a comma from the substantive which it emphasizes.

NOTE 4. A series of words or phrases in apposition with a single substantive is sometimes set off, as a whole, by a comma and a dash.

**8.** To set off a subordinate clause, especially one introduced by a descriptive relative. Thus, —

I am going to take a last dinner with a most agreeable family, who have been my only neighbors ever since I have lived at Weston. — COWPER.

NOTE. No comma is used before a restrictive relative. Thus, —

I want to know many things which only you can tell me.
Perhaps I am the only man in England who can boast of such good fortune.

**9.** To set off a phrase containing a nominative absolute. Thus,—

They had some difficulty in passing the ferry at the riverside, the ferryman being afraid of them. — DEFOE.

**10.** To set off *however, nevertheless, moreover*, etc., and introductory phrases like *in the first place, on the one hand*, etc.

**11.** To set off a parenthetical expression. For this purpose commas, dashes, or marks of parenthesis may be used.

When the parenthetical matter is brief or closely related to the rest of the sentence, it is generally set off by commas. Thus, —

I exercised a piece of hypocrisy for which, I hope, you will hold me excused. — THACKERAY.

When it is longer and more independent, it is generally marked off by dashes, or enclosed in marks of parenthesis. The latter are less frequently used at present than formerly.

The connection of the mail with the state and the executive government — a connection obvious, but yet not strictly defined — gave to the whole mail establishment an official grandeur. — DE QUINCEY.

NOTE. Brackets are used to indicate insertions that are not part of the text.

## III

The clauses of a compound sentence may be separated by colons, semicolons, or commas.

1. The colon is used —

    *a.* To show that the second of two clauses repeats the substance of the first in another form, or defines the first as an appositive defines a noun. Thus, —

This was the practice of the Grecian stage. But Terence made an innovation in the Roman: all his plays have double actions. — DRYDEN.

    *b.* To separate two groups of clauses one or both of which contain a semicolon. Thus, —

At that time, news such as we had heard might have been long in penetrating so far into the recesses of the mountains; but now, as you know, the approach is easy, and the communication, in summer time, almost hourly: nor is this strange, for travellers after pleasure are become not less active, and more numerous, than those who formerly left their homes for purposes of gain. — WORDSWORTH.

NOTE. The colon is less used now than formerly. The tendency is to use a semicolon or to begin a new sentence.

2. The semicolon is used when the clauses are of the same general nature and contribute to the same general effect, especially if one or more of them contain commas. Thus, —

The sky was cloudless; the sun shone out bright and warm; the songs of birds, and hum of myriads of summer insects filled the air; and the cottage garden, crowded with every rich and beautiful tint, sparkled in the heavy dew like beds of glittering jewels. — DICKENS.

3. The comma may be used when the clauses are short and simple (see p. 307).

NOTE. The choice between colon, semicolon, and comma is determined in many cases by the writer's feeling of the closer or the looser connection of the ideas expressed by the several clauses, and is to some extent a matter of taste.

## IV

1. In a complex sentence, the dependent clause is generally separated from the main clause by a comma. But when the dependent clause is short and the connection close, the comma may be omitted.

NOTE. A descriptive relative clause is preceded by a comma, a restrictive relative clause is not (see p. 70).

2. The clauses of a series, when in the same dependent construction, are often separated by semicolons to give more emphasis to each. Thus, —

[Mrs. Battle] was none of your lukewarm gamesters, your half and-half players, who have no objection to take a hand if you want one to make up a rubber; who affirm that they have no pleasure in winning; that they like to win one game and lose another; that they can while away an hour very agreeably at a card table, but are indifferent whether they play or no; and will desire an adversary who has slipped a wrong card, to take it up and play another. — LAMB.

## V

1. A direct quotation is enclosed in quotation marks.

NOTE. If the quotation stands by itself and is printed in different type, the marks may be omitted.

2. A quotation within a quotation is usually enclosed in single quotation marks.

3. In a quotation consisting of several paragraphs, quotation marks are put at the beginning of each paragraph and at the end of the last.

NOTE. For the punctuation before a quotation, see p. 307.

4. When a book, poem, or the like, is referred to, the title may be enclosed in quotation marks or italicized.

## VI

1. Sudden changes in thought and feeling or breaks in speech are indicated by dashes. Thus, —

Eh! — what — why — upon my life, and so it is — Charley, my boy, so it 's you, is it? — LEVER.

2. Parenthetical expressions may be set off by dashes (see p. 308).

3. A colon, or colon and dash, may precede an enumeration, a direct quotation, or a statement formally introduced, — especially with *as follows*, *namely*, and the like. Before an enumeration a comma and a dash may be used. Thus, —

There are eight parts of speech: — nouns, pronouns, adjectives, verbs, adverbs, prepositions, conjunctions, and interjections. OR —
There are eight parts of speech, — nouns, pronouns, etc.

4. The dash is sometimes used to strengthen a comma (as in the last paragraph but one).

## VII

**1.** The apostrophe is used —

    *a.* To mark the omission of a letter or letters in contractions

    *b.* As a sign of the possessive or genitive.

    *c.* To indicate the plural of letters, signs, etc.

**2.** The hyphen is used —

    *a.* When the parts of a word are separated in writing.

    *b.* Between the parts of some compound words. (See the dictionary in each case.)

## RULES OF SYNTAX

**1.** The **subject** of a verb is in the **nominative case** (p. 41).

**2.** A substantive standing in the predicate, but describing or defining the subject, agrees with the subject in case and is called a **predicate nominative** (p. 41).

**3.** A substantive used for the purpose of **addressing** a person directly, and not connected with any verb, is called a **vocative**.

A vocative is in the **nominative case,** and is often called a **nominative by direct address** or a **vocative nominative** (p. 42).

**4.** A substantive used as an **exclamation** is called an **exclamatory nominative** or a **nominative of exclamation** (p. 42).

**5.** A substantive, with a participle, may express the cause, time, or circumstances of an action.

This is called the **absolute construction.**

The substantive is in the **nominative case** and is called a **nominative absolute** (p. 144).

**6.** The **possessive case** denotes ownership or possession (p. 43).

**7.** The **object** of a verb or preposition is in the **objective case** (p. 47).

**8.** A substantive that completes the meaning of a transitive verb is called its **direct object,** and is said to be in the **objective case** (p. 48).

**9.** A verb of *asking* sometimes takes **two direct objects,** one denoting the **person** and the other the **thing** (p. 50).

**10.** Verbs of *choosing, calling, naming, making,* and *thinking* may take **two objects** referring to the same person or thing.

The first of these is the **direct object,** and the second, which completes the sense of the predicate, is called a **predicate objective** (pp. 50, 111).

**11.** Some verbs of *giving, telling, refusing,* and the like, may take **two objects,** a **direct object** and an **indirect object.**

The indirect object denotes the person or thing toward whom or toward which is directed the action expressed by the rest of the predicate (p. 50).

**12.** A verb that is regularly intransitive sometimes takes as object a noun whose meaning closely resembles its own.

A noun in this construction is called the **cognate object** of the verb and is in the **objective case** (p. 52).

**13.** A noun, or a group of words consisting of a noun and its modifiers, may be used adverbially. Such a noun is called an **adverbial objective** (p. 53).

**14.** An **appositive** is in the same case as the substantive which it limits (p. 42).

**15.** A pronoun must agree with its antecedent in **gender, number,** and **person** (p. 55).

**16. Relative pronouns** connect dependent clauses with main clauses by referring directly to a substantive in the main clause.

This substantive is the **antecedent** of the relative (p. 66).

A relative pronoun must agree with its antecedent in **gender, number,** and **person.**

The **case** of a relative pronoun has nothing to do with its antecedent, but depends on the construction of its own clause (p. 68).

**17.** A relative pronoun in the objective case is often omitted (p. 69).

**18.** The relative pronoun *what* is equivalent to *that which,* and has a **double construction :** — (1) the construction of the **omitted** or **implied** antecedent *that;* (2) the construction of the **relative** *which* (p. 71).

**19.** The **compound relative pronouns** may include or imply their own antecedents and hence may have a **double construction** (p. 72).

The compound relatives are sometimes used without an antecedent expressed or implied (p. 72).

**20.** An adjective is said to **belong** to the substantive which it describes or limits (pp. 5, 75).

**21.** Adjectives may be classified, according to their position in the sentence, as **attributive, appositive,** and **predicate adjectives** (p. 76).

**1.** An **attributive adjective** is closely attached to its noun and regularly precedes it.

**2.** An **appositive adjective** is added to its noun to explain it, like a noun in apposition.

**3.** A **predicate adjective** completes the meaning of the predicate verb, but describes or limits the subject.

For the use of an adjective as **predicate objective,** see § 488.

**22.** The **comparative degree,** not the superlative, is used in comparing two persons or things.

The **superlative** is used in comparing one person or thing with two or more (p. 88).

**23. Relative adverbs** introduce subordinate clauses and are similar in their use to relative pronouns (p. 86).

**24.** A **verb** must agree with its subject in **number** and **person** (p. 97).

**25.** A **compound subject** with *and* usually takes a verb in the plural number (p. 100).

**26.** A **compound subject** with *or* or *nor* takes a verb in the singular number if the substantives are singular (p. 100).

**27.** Nouns that are **plural in form but singular in sense** commonly take a verb in the singular number (p. 101).

**28. Collective nouns** take sometimes a singular and sometimes a plural verb.

When the persons or things denoted are thought of as **individuals,** the plural should be used. When the collection is regarded as a **unit,** the singular should be used (p. 101).

**29.** A verb is in the **active voice** when it represents the subject as the **doer** of an act (p. 107).

**30.** A verb is in the **passive voice** when it represents the subject as the **receiver** or the **product** of an action (p. 107).

The object of the active verb becomes the subject of the passive, and the subject of the active verb becomes in the passive an adverbial phrase modifying the predicate verb (p. 110).

**31.** When a verb takes both a **direct** and an **indirect object,** one of the two is often retained after the passive, the other becoming the subject (p. 112).

**32.** The **indicative** is the mood of **simple assertion** or **interrogation,** but it is used in other constructions also (p. 115).

**33.** The **imperative** is the mood of **command** or **request** (p. 115).

**34.** The **subject** of an **imperative** is seldom expressed unless it is emphatic.

The subject, when expressed, may precede the imperative: as, — *You go, You read* (p. 117).

**35.** The **subjunctive mood** is used in certain special constructions of **wish, condition,** and the like (pp. 115, 118).

For particulars and examples, see pp. 119–123.

For modal auxiliaries, see pp. 124–132.

**36.** An **infinitive,** with or without a complement or modifiers, may be used as the **subject** of a sentence, as a **predicate nominative,** or as an **appositive** (pp. 134, 135).

**37.** An **infinitive** may be used as the **object** of the prepositions *but, except, about,* (p. 135).

**38.** The **infinitive** may be used as a **nominative of exclamation** (p. 136).

**39.** An **infinitive** may modify a verb by **completing** its meaning, or by expressing the **purpose** of the action (p. 137).

**40.** An **infinitive** may be used as an **adjective modifier** of a **noun** or as an **adverbial modifier** of an **adjective.**

In this use the infinitive is said to **depend** on the word which it modifies (p. 136).

**41.** A kind of **clause,** consisting of a substantive in the objective case followed by an **infinitive,** may be used as the object of certain verbs.

Such clauses are called **infinitive clauses,** and the substantive is said to be the subject of the infinitive.

The **subject** of an **infinitive** is in the objective case.

**Infinitive clauses** are used (1) after verbs of *wishing, commanding, advising,* and the like, and (2) after some verbs of *believing, declaring,* and *perceiving* (p. 138).

An infinitive clause may be the object of the preposition *for.*

An infinitive clause with *for* may be used as a subject, as a predicate nominative, or as the object of a preposition (pp. 138–139).

**42.** The participle is a verb-form which has no subject, but which partakes of the nature of an adjective and expresses action or state in such a way as to describe or limit a substantive (pp. 12, 140).

**43.** A **participle** is said to **belong** to the substantive which it describes or limits (pp. 12, 142).

**44.** A participle should not be used without some substantive to which it may belong (p. 142).

**45.** An **infinitive** or a **participle**, like any other verb-form, may take an **object** if its meaning allows (pp. 134, 143).

**46.** **Infinitives** and **participles**, like other verb-forms, may be **modified** by adverbs, adverbial phrases, or adverbial clauses (pp. 134, 142).

**47.** **Verbal** (or **participial**) **nouns** in *-ing* have the form of present participles, but the construction of nouns (p. 145).

**48.** **Verbal nouns** in *-ing* have certain properties of the verb (p. 146).

1. Verbal nouns in *-ing* may take a **direct** or an **indirect object** if their meaning allows.

2. A verbal noun in *-ing* may take an **adverbial modifier**.

But verbal nouns in *-ing*, like other nouns, may be **modified** by **adjectives**.

**49.** A noun in *-ing* may be used as an **adjective,** or as the adjective element in a **compound noun** (p. 146).

**50.** The substantive which follows a **preposition** is called its **object** and is in the **objective case** (p. 148).

**51.** A **coördinate conjunction** connects words or groups of words that are independent of each other (p. 151).

**52.** A **subordinate conjunction** connects a subordinate clause with the clause on which it depends (p. 151).

**53.** **Interjections** usually have no grammatical connection with the phrases or sentences in which they stand.

Sometimes, however, a substantive is connected with an interjection by means of a preposition (p. 155).

## THE ENGLISH LANGUAGE

English is a member of the great Indo-European Family of languages, which is so called because it includes well-nigh all the languages of Europe and the most important of those found in India. Within this family, English belongs to the Teutonic (or Germanic) Group, which contains also German, Dutch, the Scandinavian tongues (Icelandic, Danish, Norwegian, Swedish), and some others.

English of the oldest period is called either Anglo-Saxon or Old English. This was the speech of certain piratical tribes whose home was in northern Germany, on the eastern and southern shores of the North Sea, but who invaded Britain about A.D. 450, and subdued the Celtic inhabitants of the island in a series of fierce wars. The most considerable of the invading tribes were the Angles and the Saxons. Their dominion was well assured by the beginning of the seventh century, and their language, which they usually called "English" (that is, "the tongue of the Angles"), gradually spread through England and most of Scotland. In Wales, however, the native Britons have maintained their own Celtic speech to the present day; and in the Scottish Highlands, Gaelic — which is akin to Welsh and practically identical with the native language of Ireland — is still extensively used.

At the time of the invasion, the Angles and Saxons were heathen, and the Britons, who had been for four centuries under the sway of the Roman Empire, were Christians, and much more highly civilized than their conquerors. Indeed, they had adopted many features of Roman culture, and Latin was spoken to some extent, at least in the larger towns. By the end of the seventh century, however, the Anglo-Saxons also had embraced Christianity and had made remarkable advances in literature and learning. The language of the Britons exerted but slight influence upon that of the Anglo-Saxons. The Celtic words in English are few in number, and most of them were borrowed in comparatively recent times.

The Norman Conquest (1066) marks a highly significant date in the history of our language. The Normans were a Scandinavian tribe who had been in possession of Normandy (in northern France) for about a hundred and fifty years. They had abandoned their native tongue, and spoke a dialect of French. From 1066 to about the year 1400, two languages were therefore common in England, — English, which was employed by the vast majority of the people, and French, which was the language of the court and the higher orders. French, however, was never a serious rival of English for supremacy in the island. It was the speech of a class, not of the nation, and its use gradually died out, except as an accomplishment. By the time of Chaucer (who was born about 1340 and died in 1400), it was clear that the English tongue was henceforth to be regarded as the only natural language for Englishmen, whether they were of Anglo-Saxon or of Norman origin.

Still, the Norman conquest had a profound influence upon English. It is not true — though often asserted — that the multitude of French words which our language contains were derived from the Norman dialect. Comparatively few of them came into English until after 1300, when Normandy had been lost to the English crown for a hundred years. Since 1300 we have borrowed freely — not from Norman, however, but from Central (or Parisian) French, which had become the standard to which the English descendants of the Normans endeavored to conform. The effect of the Conquest, then, was not to fill English with Norman terms. It was rather to bring England into close social and literary relations with France, and thus to facilitate the adoption of words and constructions from Central French.

Further, since literature was in the middle ages dependent in the main upon private patronage, the existence of a ruling class whose interest was in French, discouraged the maintenance of any national or general standard of English composition. Every English writer had recourse to his local dialect, and one dialect was felt to be as good as another.

By 1350, however, the dialect of London and the vicinity had come, apparently, to be regarded as somewhat more elegant and polished than the others. All that was needed was the appearance of some writer of supreme genius to whom this dialect should be native. Chaucer was such a writer, for he was born in London. To be sure, Chaucer did not "make modern English." None the less, he was a powerful agent in settling the language. Since his time, at all events, the fact of a "standard of literary usage" has been undisputed. Dialects still exist, but they are not regarded as authoritative. Educated speakers and writers of English, the world over, use the language with substantial uniformity.[1]

Meantime, however, the English of the Anglo-Saxons had undergone many changes before Chaucer was born. Most of its inflections had been lost, and still others have been discarded since. Further, there had been extensive borrowing from French and Latin, and this continued throughout the fourteenth century. The habit, once formed, has proved lasting. Our vocabulary has received contributions from many languages, and is still receiving them. Greek may be mentioned in particular as the source of many words, especially in the various departments of science. But French and Latin remain the chief foreign elements in English.

In the following extract from Scott, most of the words printed in Roman type are of Anglo-Saxon origin, whereas the italicized words are derived from Latin or French.

It was not until evening was nearly *closed* that Ivanhoe was *restored* to *consciousness* of his *situation*. He awoke from a broken slumber, under the *confused impressions* which are *naturally attendant* on the *recovery* from a *state* of *insensibility*. He was un*able* for some time to recall *exactly* to *memory* the *circumstances* which had *preceded* his fall in the *lists*, or to make out any *connected chain* of the *events* in which he had been *engaged* upon the yesterday. A *sense* of wounds and *injury*, *joined* to great weakness and *exhaustion*, was mingled with the *recollection* of blows dealt and *received*, of steeds rushing upon each other, overthrowing and overthrown, of shouts and clashing of *arms*, and all the heady *tumult* of a *confused* fight. An *effort* to draw aside the *curtain* of his *couch* was in some *degree* *successful*, although *rendered difficult* by the *pain* of his wound.

English has also adopted a good many Scandinavian words, though they form no such proportion of its vocabulary as French or Latin. Danish and Norwegian pirates began to harry the coast in the eighth century. Permanent settlements followed, as well as wars of conquest, and for about thirty years (1013–1042) a Danish family occupied the English throne. These events explain the Scandinavian element in our language.

[1] It is not meant, of course, that an American or Australian of the present day should exert himself to imitate the speech of a modern Londoner. The point is, that what we now call "English" is, in most respects, the direct descendant of the London dialect of the fourteenth century.

Despite the freedom with which English has adopted words from abroad, it is still essentially a Germanic speech. Its structure is still the native structure. The borrowings have enriched its vocabulary but have had comparatively little effect upon its syntax. The foreign words have been naturalized, and their presence in no wise interferes with the unity and general consistency of the English language. It is a strange error to regard English as a combination of Anglo-Saxon and Norman French. As for the loss or decay of inflection, that is not due to a mixture of dialects. It is a natural tendency which may be seen, for example, in Dutch and Danish, though there was no Norman Conquest in Holland or Denmark. The loss, indeed, is really a gain, for it is progress in the direction of simplicity.

The Anglo-Saxon or Old English Period comes down to about a century, or a century and a half, after the Norman Conquest. The extreme limit may be set at 1200. The period from 1200 to 1500 is usually known as the Middle English Period. From 1500 to the present time may be regarded as the Modern Period, though within these boundaries English has changed enormously in pronunciation and in vocabulary, very largely in syntax, and to some extent in inflection. The almost complete abandonment of the subjunctive in common speech is one of the latest of these changes. This, too, is in the direction of simplicity.

The people of Great Britain have long been famous as travellers, explorers, and colonizers. Their language, once the dialect (or dialects) of a handful of Germanic adventurers, has spread to all parts of the world, so that now it is not merely the language of England, but, to a considerable extent, that of Scotland, Ireland, North America, India, Australasia, and South Africa. In this vast area, numerous varieties of pronunciation and of idiom of course occur, but, on the whole, the uniformity of the language is surprisingly well preserved.

# INDEX